A NARRATIVE OF A REVOLUTIONARY SOLDIER

By JOSEPH PLUMB MARTIN

A Narrative of a Revolutionary Soldier
By Joseph Plumb Martin

Print ISBN 13: 978-1-4209-6104-1
eBook ISBN 13: 978-1-4209-6032-7

This edition copyright © 2018. Digireads.com Publishing.

Cover Image: a detail of "The Nation Makers", c. 1903 (oil on canvas), by Howard Pyle (1853-1911) / American Illustrators Gallery, NYC / www.asapworldwide.com / Bridgeman Images.

Please visit *www.digireads.com*

CONTENTS

A

NARRATIVE

OF SOME OF THE

ADVENTURES, DANGERS AND SUFFERINGS

OF A

REVOLUTIONARY SOLDIER

INTERSPERSED WITH

ANECDOTES OF INCIDENTS THAT OCCURRED WITHIN HIS

OWN OBSERVATION.

By JOSEPH PLUMB MARTIN

"Long sleepless nights in heavy arms I've stood;
"And spent laborious days in dust and blood."
POPE'S HOMER.

DISTRICT OF MAINE—TO WIT:

DISTRICT CLERK'S OFFICE.

BE IT REMEMBERED, That on the eighth day of February, A.D. 1830, and in the fifty-fourth year of the Independence of the United States of America, Mr. James Sullivan Martin, of said District, has deposited in this office, the title of a Book, the right whereof he claims as Proprietor, in the words following, to wit:

"A Narrative of some of the adventures, dangers and sufferings of a Revolutionary Soldier, interspersed with anecdotes of incidents that occurred within his observation. Written by himself.

"'Long sleepless nights in heavy arms I've stood;
"'And spent laborious days in dust and blood.'
Pope's Homer."

In conformity to the act of Congress of the United States, entitled "An Act for the encouragement of learning, by securing the copies of maps, charts and books, to the authors and proprietors of such copies, during the times therein mentioned;" and also, to an act, entitled "An Act supplementary to an act, entitled An Act for the encouragement of learning, by securing the copies of maps, charts, and books, to the authors and proprietors of such copies, during the times therein mentioned; and for extending the benefits thereof to the arts of designing, engraving and etching historical and other prints."
J. MUSSEY, *Clerk of the District of Maine.*
A true copy as of record. Attest,
J. MUSSEY, *Clerk D.C. Maine.*

Preface.

I have somewhere read of a Limner, who, when he had daubed a representation of some animal, was always compelled, for the information of the observer, to write under it what he intended it to represent: as, 'this is a goose,' 'this is a dog,' &c. So, many books, and mine in particular, amongst the rest, would perhaps be quite unintelligible as to the drift of them, unless the reader was informed beforehand what the author intended.

I shall, therefore, by way of preface, inform the reader that my intention is to give a succinct account of some of my adventures, dangers and sufferings during my several campaigns in the revolutionary army. My readers, (who, by the by, will, I hope, none of them be beyond the pale of my own neighbourhood,) must not expect any great transactions to be exhibited to their notice, "No alpine wonders thunder through my tale," but they are here, once for all, requested to bear it in mind, that they are not the achievements of an officer of high grade which they are perusing, but the common transactions of one of the lowest in station in an army, a private soldier.

Should the reader chance to ask himself this question, (and I think it very natural for him to do so,) how could any man of common sense ever spend his precious time in writing such a rhapsody of nonsense?— to satisfy his inquiring mind, I would inform him, that, as the adage says, "every crow thinks her own young the whitest," so every private soldier in an army thinks his particular services as essential to carry on the war he is engaged in, as the services of the most influential general; and why not? what could officers do without such men? Nothing at all. Alexander never could have conquered the world without private soldiers.

But, says the reader, this is low, the author gives us nothing but everyday occurrences; I could tell as good a story myself. Very true, Mr. Reader, every one can tell what he has done in his lifetime, but every one has not been a soldier, and consequently can know but little or nothing of the sufferings and fatigues incident to an army. All know everyday occurrences, but few know the hardships of the "tented field." I wish to have a better opinion of my readers, whoever they may be, than even to think that any of them would wish me to stretch the truth to furnish them with wonders that I never saw, or acts and deeds I never performed. I can give them no more than I have to give, and if they are dissatisfied after all, I must say I am sorry for them and myself too; for them, that they expect more than I can do, and myself, that I am so unlucky as not to have it in my power to please them.

But after all I have said, the real cause of my ever undertaking to rake up circumstances and actions that have so long rested in my own mind, and to spread them upon paper, was this:—my friends, and especially my juvenile friends have often urged me so to do; to oblige such, I undertook it, hoping it might save me often the trouble of verbally relating them.

The critical grammarian may find enough to feed his spleen upon, if he peruses the following pages; but I can inform him beforehand, I do not regard his sneers; if I cannot write grammatically, I can think, talk and feel like other men. Besides, if the common readers can understand it, it is all I desire; and to give them an idea, though but a faint one, of what the army suffered that gained and secured our independence, is all I wish. I never studied grammar an hour in my life, when I ought to have been doing that, I was forced to be studying the rules and articles of war.

As to punctuation, my narrative is in the same predicament as it is in respect to the other parts of grammar. I never learned the rules of punctuation any farther than just to assist in fixing a comma to the British depredations in the State of New-York; a semicolon in New-Jersey; a colon in Pennsylvania, and a final period in Virginia;—a note of interrogation, why we were made to suffer so much in so good and just a cause; and a note of admiration to all the world, that an army voluntarily engaged to serve their country, when starved, and naked, and suffering every thing short of death, (and thousands even that,) should be able to persevere through an eight years war, and come off conquerors at last!

But lest I should make my preface longer than my story, I will here bring it to a close.

ADVENTURES

OF A

REVOLUTIONARY SOLDIER.

Chapter I. Introductory.

Have patience just to hear me out;
And I'll tell you what I've been about.

THE heroes of all Histories, Narratives, Adventures, Novels and Romances, have, or are supposed to have ancestors, or some root from which they sprang. I conclude, then, that it is not altogether inconsistent to suppose that I had parents too. I shall not undertake to trace my pedigree (like the Welsh) some thousand years beyond the creation; but just observe, that my father was the son of a "substantial New England farmer," (as we Yankees say,) in the then Colony, but now State of Connecticut, and county of Windham. When my father arrived at puberty he found his constitution too feeble to endure manual labor, he therefore directed his views to gaining a livelihood by some other means. He, accordingly, fitted himself for, and entered as a student in Yale College, sometime between the years 1750 and '55. My mother was likewise a "farmer's daughter;" her native place was in the county of New-Haven, in the same State. She had a sister, married and settled in the vicinity of the College, who often boarded the students when sick. My father being once in that condition, and being at board at this aunt's, my mother happened to be there on a visit: my father seeing her, it seems, like a great many others in like circumstances, took a fancy to her, followed up his courtship, and very possibly obtained her consent as well as her parents—married her a year and a half before his collegial studies were ended, which, (if known at the time,) would have been cause of his expulsion from College; but it seems it never was known there, and he, of course, escaped a keelhaling.

After my father left College, he studied divinity, had "a call," accepted it, and was settled in the county of Berkshire, in the (now) Commonwealth of Massachusetts, as a gospel minister of the Congregational order; in which county of Berkshire, I, the redoubtable hero of this Narrative, first made my appearance in this crooked, fretful world, upon the twenty-first day of November, in the year 1760. I have been told that the day on which I was born was a thanksgiving day, which day is, generally, celebrated with good cheer. One might have thought it a little ominous being born upon such a day, but I can assure the reader it was no omen of good to me, especially for the seven or eight years I was in the army—nor, indeed ever since.

My grandsire, on my mother's side, having at this time no other daughter but my mother, (my aunt, mentioned above, being dead,) she of course became the darling, for which reason, I suppose, I was his favourite grandson, and received his christian and surnames as my given name.

I lived with my parents until I was upwards of seven years old, when I went to live with this good old grandsire; for good he was, particularly to me. He was wealthy, and I had every thing that was necessary for life, and as many superfluities as was consistent with my age and station. There were none belonging to the family, as constant residents, except the old gentleman, lady and myself. It is true my grandsire kept me pretty busily employed, but he was kind to me in every respect; always gave me a playday when convenient, and was indulgent to me almost to a fault. Ah! I ought not to have left him while he lived; I fouled my own nest most sadly when I did it; but children "are full of notions."

I remember the stir in the country occasioned by the stamp act, but I was so young that I did not understand the meaning of it; I likewise remember the disturbances that followed the repeal of the stamp act, until the destruction of the tea at Boston and elsewhere; I was then thirteen or fourteen years old, and began to understand something of the works going on. I used, about this time, to inquire a deal about the French war, as it was called, which had not been long ended, my grandsire would talk with me about it while working in the fields, perhaps as much to beguile his own time as to gratify my curiosity. I thought then, nothing should induce me to get caught in the toils of an army—"I am well, so I'll keep," was my motto then, and it would have been well for me if I had ever retained it.

Time passed smoothly on with me till the year 1774 arrived, the smell of war began to be pretty strong, but I was determined to have no hand in it, happen when it might; I felt myself to be a real coward. What—venture my carcass where bullets fly! that will never do for me. Stay at home out of harm's way, thought I, it will be as much to your health as credit to do so. But the pinch of the game had not arrived yet; I had seen nothing of war affairs, and consequently was but a poor judge in such matters.

One little circumstance that happened in the autumn of this year, will exhibit my military prowess, at this time, in a high point of view. In the afternoon, one Sabbath day, while the people were assembled at meeting, word was brought that the British (regulars, as the good people then called them) were advancing from Boston, spreading death and desolation in their route in every direction. What was the intent of spreading this rumour, I know not, unless it was to see how the people would stand affected; be it what it would, it caused me a terrible fright. I went out of the house in the dusk of the evening, when I heard the sound of a carriage on the road, in the direction of Boston; I thought they were coming as sure as a gun; I shall be dead or a captive before to-morrow morning; however, I went to bed late in the evening, dreamed of "fire and sword," I suppose; waked in the morning, found myself alive, and the house standing just where it did the evening before.

The winter of this year passed off without any very frightening alarms, and the spring of 1775 arrived. Expectation of some fatal event seemed to fill the minds of most of the considerate people throughout the country. I was ploughing in the field about half a mile from home, about the twenty-first day of April, when all of a sudden the bells fell to ringing, and three guns were repeatedly fired in succession down in the village; what the cause was we could not conjecture. I had some fearful forebodings that something more than the sound of a carriage wheel was in the wind. The regulars are coming in good earnest, thought I. My grandsire sighed, he "smelt the rat." He immediately turned out the team and repaired homeward. I sat off to see what the cause of the commotion was. I found most of the male kind of the people together; soldiers for Boston were in requisition. A dollar deposited upon the drum head was taken up by some one as soon as placed there, and the holder's name taken, and he enrolled, with orders to equip himself as quick as possible. My spirits began to revive at the sight of the money offered; the seeds of courage began to sprout; for, contrary to my knowledge, there was a scattering of them sowed, but they had not as yet germinated; I felt a strong inclination, when I found I had them, to cultivate them. O, thought I, if I were but old enough to put myself forward, I would be the possessor of one dollar, the dangers of war to the contrary notwithstanding; but I durst not put myself up for a soldier for fear of being refused, and that would have quite upset all the courage I had drawn forth.

The men that had engaged "to go to war" went as far as the next town, where they received orders to return, as there was a sufficiency of men already engaged, so that I should have had but a short campaign had I have gone.

This year there were troops raised both for Boston and New-York. Some from the back towns were billeted at my grandsire's; their company and conversation began to warm my courage to such a degree, that I resolved at all events to "go a sogering." Accordingly I used to pump my grandsire, in a roundabout manner, to know how he stood affected respecting it. For a long time he appeared to take but little notice of it. At length, one day, I pushed the matter so hard upon him, he was compelled to give me a direct answer, which was, that he should never give his consent for me to go into the army unless I had the previous consent of my parents. And now I was completely gravelled; my parents were too far off to obtain their consent before it would be too late for the present campaign. What was I to do? why, I must give up the idea, and that was hard; for I was as earnest now to call myself, and be called a soldier, as I had been a year before *not* to be called one. I thought over many things, and formed many plans, but they all fell through, and poor disconsolate I was forced to set down and gnaw my finger nails in silence.

I said but little more about "soldiering," until the troops raised in and near the town in which I resided, came to march off for New-York, then I felt bitterly again; I accompanied them as far as the town line, and it was hard parting with them then. Many of my young associates were with them, my heart and soul went with them, but my mortal part must stay behind. By and by they will come swaggering back, thought I, and tell me of all their exploits, all their "hairbreadth 'scapes," and poor Huff will not have a single sentence to advance. O, that was too much to be borne with by me.

The thoughts of the service still haunted me after the troops were gone, and the town clear of them; but what plan to form to get the consent of all, parents and grandparents, that I might procure thereby to myself, the (to me then) bewitching name of a soldier, I could not devise. Sometimes I thought I would enlist at all hazards, let the consequences be what they would; then again I would think how kind my grandparents were to me, and ever had been, my grandsire in particular: I could not bear to hurt their feelings so much. I did sincerely love my grandsire, my grandma'am I did not love so well, and I feared her less. At length a thought struck my mind: should they affront me grossly, I would make that a plea with my conscience to settle the controversy with. Accordingly, I wished nothing more than to have them, or either of them, give "His Honour" a high affront, that I might thereby form an excuse to engage in the service *without* their consent, leave or approbation.

It happened that in the early part of the autumn of this year, I was gratified in my wishes; for I thought I received provocation enough to justify me in engaging in the army during life; little thinking that I was inflicting the punishment on myself that I fancied I was laying on my grandparents for their (as I thought) wilful obstinacy. And as this affair was one, and the chief cause of my leaving those kind people and their hospitable house, and precipitating myself into an ocean of distress, I will minutely describe the affair.

My grandsire, as I have before observed, often gave me playdays, especially after the spring and fall sowing, when I went where I pleased, a gunning, or fishing, or to whatever recreation took my fancy. "This fall," said the old gentleman to me, one day,—"come, spring to it, and let us get the winter grain in as soon as possible, and you shall have a playday after the work is done." Accordingly, I did do the best I could to forward the business, and I believe I gave him satisfaction, for he repeated his promise to me often. Just before we had done sowing, I told him that all my young associates were going to New-Haven to commencement this season. "Well"—said he, "you shall go too, if you chuse, and you shall have one of the horses, you shall have your choice of them, and I will give you some pocket money." Mighty well, thought I, I hope it will not prove delusive, I shall be happy indeed. Our young club often met in "caucus" to settle the mighty business of going to commencement, formed a thousand and one plans how we should enjoy ourselves—dropped them all successively, and formed as many more, until the time arrived for the consummation of our felicity. My grandsire had a piece of salt marsh about three miles from home, which he had mowed three or four days before the day arrived which was to make me completely happy, at least for a time. Two days previous he sent me to rake up the hay; I buffetted heat and mosquetoes, and got the hay all up; and as that sort of hay is not easily injured by the weather, I thought there was nothing to prevent my promised happiness.

Well, the day arrived; I got up early, did all the little jobs about the place, that my grandsire might have nothing to accuse me of. He had gone out during the morning and did not return till breakfast time. I was waiting with impatience for his coming in, that I might prepare for my excursion,—when, lo, he did come,—much to my sorrow; for the first words I heard, were, 'come, get up the team, I have gotten such a one,' naming a neighbour's boy, somewhat older than myself, 'to go with us and cart home the salt hay.' Had thunder and lightning fallen upon the four corners of the house, it would not have struck me with worse feelings than these words of his did. Shame, grief, spite, revenge, all took immediate possession of me. What could I do; go I must, that was certain, there was no remedy; and go I did, but with a full determination that the old gentleman should know that I had feelings of some sort or other, let him think of me as he would. I, according to his orders, prepared the team, he undertook to act teamster, and I sat off before them for the marsh, alone, that I might indulge myself in my grief, without molestation. The way to the marsh lay about a mile and a half on the highway to the college. I had hardly got into the highway, before I was overtaken by a troop of my young mates, all rigged off for commencement, swaggering like nabobs. The first compliment was, "Hallo, where are you going; we thought you was one of the foremost in the party; your grandsire never intended to let you go, and you was a fool to believe him." I did not believe *them*; my grandsire had never deceived me, in such circumstances before, and I was willing, even then, vexed as I was, to attribute it to forgetfulness or to any thing but wilfulness.—However, I was baulked, no commencement for me; I considered myself as much injured as though it had been done ever so designedly.

I, however, went to the marsh; my grandsire, team and boy arrived soon after me; we put a load of hay upon the cart, and, as it was getting rather late in the day, the old gentleman concluded to go home with the team, and left the other youngster and me to pole the rest of the hay off the marsh to the upland, as it was dangerous going upon the lower part of it, being in many places soft and miry. He told us to go to some of the fences and cut a pair of sassafras poles, those being light, and have the remainder of the hay in readiness by his return.

And now comes the catastrophe of the play. I concluded, now was the time for me to show my spunk; we went up to the upland, where was plenty of fruit; I lay down under an apple tree and fell to eating, the other boy eat too, but still urged me to obey my orders; I was resolved to disobey, let the consequences be what they would. However, he, by his importunity, at length got me down upon the marsh, we poled one cock of hay off the marsh, when we saw the old gentleman coming, full drive, Jehu-like; down he came, when, lo and behold, we had gotten one cock of hay only, in a condition to be taken upon the cart; what was to be done—to go on to the marsh was dangerous in the extreme, to stop then to pole it off would not do, the time would not allow it. O, my grandsire was in a woful passion. I stood aloof. Whose fault was it, he inquired; the blame was quickly laid to my account, and justly too, for I was the only culprit. The old gentleman came at me, hammer and tongs, with his six feet cartwhip. Ah, thought I to myself, good legs, do your duty now, if ever; I houghed the gravel, or rather the marsh, in good earnest. There were twenty people, or more, near us at work; they all suspended their labour to see the race. But I was too light-footed for the old gentleman, and the people on the marsh setting up a laugh, it rather disconcerted him; he, however, chased me about thirty or forty rods when he gave over the pursuit and returned, I ran as much further before I dared to look back; but hearing no sound of footsteps behind me, I at last ventured to look over my shoulder and saw him almost back to his team; I followed him in my turn, but not quite so nimble as I went from him. He endeavoured to spit a little of his spite upon the other youngster, but he stept close up to him, so that he could not use his whip; and then plead his own cause so well that the old gentleman said no more to him.

He then had to venture upon the marsh at all events. I took a rake and raked after the cart, but took especial care to keep out of harm's way, till the hay was all upon the cart; I was then called upon to help bind the load; I complied, but I kept on tiptoe all the time, ready to start in case I saw any symptoms of war; but all passed off—we got off the marsh safe and without any hindrance; and it was well for me, after all, that we met with no disaster.

And here ends my Introductory Chapter. If the reader thinks that some passages in it record incidents not altogether to my credit as a boy, I can tell him, that I thought at the time I did right, and, to tell the truth, I have not materially altered my opinion respecting them since. One thing I am certain of, and that is, reader, if you had been me you would have done just as I did. What reason have you then to cavil?

Chapter II. Campaign of 1776.

At Uncle Joe's I liv'd at ease;
Had cider, and good bread and cheese;
But while I stay'd at Uncle Sam's
I'd nought to eat but—"faith and clams."

DURING the winter of 1775—6, by hearing the conversation and disputes of the good old farmer politicians of the times, I collected pretty correct ideas of the contest between this country and the mother country, (as it was then called.) I thought I was as warm a patriot as the best of them; the war was waged; we had joined issue, and it would not do to "put the hand to the plough and look back." I felt more anxious than ever, if possible, to be called a defender of my country. I had not forgot the commencement affair, that still stuck in my crop; and it would not do for me to forget it, for that affront was to be my passport to the army.

One evening, very early in the spring of this year, I chanced to overhear my grandma'am telling my grandsire that I had threatened to engage on board a man-of-war. I had told her that I would enter on board a privateer then fitting out in our neighbourhood; the good old lady thought it a man-of-war, that and privateer being synonymous terms with her. She said she could not bear the thought of my being on board of a man-of-war; my grandsire told her, that he supposed I was resolved to go into the service in some way or other, and he had rather I would engage in the land service if I must engage in any. This I thought to be a sort of tacit consent for me to go, and I determined to take advantage of it as quick as possible.

Soldiers were at this time enlisting for a year's service; I did not like that, it was too long a time for me at the first trial; I wished only to take a priming before I took upon me the whole coat of paint for a soldier. However, the time soon arrived that gratified all my wishes. In the month of June, this year, orders came out for enlisting men for six months from the twenty-fifth of this month. The troops were stiled new levies, they were to go to New-York; and, notwithstanding I was told that the British army at that place was reinforced by fifteen thousand men, it made no alteration in my mind; I did not care if there had been fifteen times fifteen thousand, I should have gone just as soon as if there had been but fifteen hundred. I never spent a thought about numbers, the Americans were invincible, in my opinion. If any thing affected me, it was a stronger desire to see them.

Well, as I have said, enlisting orders were out; I used frequently to go to the rendezvous, where I saw many of my young associates enlist, had repeated banterings to engage with them, but still, when it came "case in hand," I had my misgivings. If I once undertake, thought I, I must stick to it, there will be no receding. Thoughts like these would, at times, almost overset my resolutions.

But maugre all these "doleful ideas," I one evening went off with a full determination to enlist at all hazards. When I arrived at the place of rendezvous I found a number of young men of my acquaintance there; the old bantering began—come, if you will enlist I will, says one, you have long been talking about it, says another—come, now is the time. "Thinks I to myself," I will not be laughed into it or out of it, at any rate; I will act my own pleasure after all. But what did I come here for to-night? why, to enlist; then enlist I will. So seating myself at the table, enlisting orders were immediately presented to me; I took up the pen, loaded it with the fatal charge, made several mimic imitations of writing my name, but took especial care not to touch the paper with the pen until an unlucky wight who was leaning over my shoulder gave my hand a stroke, which caused the pen to make a woful scratch on the paper. "O, he has enlisted," said he, "he has made his mark, he is fast enough now." Well, thought I, I may as well go through with the business now as not; so I wrote my name fairly upon the indentures. And now I was a *soldier,* in name at least, if not in practice;—but I had now to go home, after performing this, my heroic action. How shall I be received there?—but the report of my adventure had reached there before I did. In the morning when I first saw my grandparents, I felt considerably of the sheepish order. The old gentleman first accosted me with, "Well, you are going a soldiering then, are you?" I had nothing to answer; I would much rather he had not asked me the question. I saw that the circumstance hurt him and the old lady too; but it was too late now to repent. The old gentleman proceeded,—"I suppose you must be fitted out for the expedition, since it is so."—Accordingly, they did "fit me out" in order, with arms and accoutrements, clothing, and cake, and cheese in plenty, not forgetting to put my pocket Bible into my knapsack.—Good old people! they wished me well, soul and body; I sincerely thank them for their kindness and love to me, from the time I first came to live with them to the last parting hour. I hope, nay, I believe, that their spirits now rest in the realms of bliss;—may it be my happy lot to meet them there.

I was now, what I had long wished to be, a soldier; I had obtained my heart's desire; it was now my business to prove myself equal to my profession. Well, to be short, I went, with several others of the company, on board a sloop, bound to New-York; had a pleasant, though protracted passage; passed through the straight called Hellgate, where all who had not before passed it, had to pay a treat, (I had been through it before;) arrived at New-York; marched up into the city, and joined the rest of the regiment that were already there.

And now I had left my good old grandsire's house, as a constant resident, forever, and had to commence exercising my function; I was called out every morning at reveille beating, which was at daybreak, to go to our regimental parade, in Broad-street, and there practice the manual exercise, which was the most that was known in our new levies, if they knew even that. I was brought to an allowance of provisions, which, while we lay in New-York was not bad: if there was any deficiency it could in some measure be supplied by procuring some kind of sauce; but I was a stranger to such living; I began soon to miss grandsire's table and cellar. However, I reconciled myself to my condition as well as I could; it was my own seeking, I had had no compulsion.

Soon after my arrival at New-York, a forty-four gun ship (the Phœnix,) and a small frigate (the Rose, I think) came down the North or Hudson River, (they had been sometime in the river,) and passed the city in fine stile, amidst a cannonade from all our fortifications, in and near the city. I went into what was then called the grand battery, where I had a complete view of the whole affair. Here I first heard the muttering of cannon shot, but they did not disturb my feelings so much as I apprehended they would before I had heard them; I rather thought the sound was musical, or at least grand. I heard enough of them afterwards to form what ideas I pleased of them, whether musical, grand, or doleful, and perhaps I have formed each of those ideas upon different occasions.

I would here, once for all, remark; that as I write altogether from memory, the reader must not expect to have an exact account of dates, I mean of days and weeks; as to years and months I shall not be wide from the mark.

And as I have entitled my book, "The adventures, &c. of a Revolutionary soldier," it is possible the reader may expect to have a minute detail of all my adventures. I have not *promised* any such thing, it was what belonged to me, and what transpired in my line of duty that I proposed to narrate. But when some mischievous incident occurred, I am willing to give a short detail of it. I never wished to do any one an injury, through malice, in my life; nor did I ever do any one an intentional injury while I was in the army, unless it was when sheer necessity drove me to it, and my conscience bears me witness, that innumerable times I have suffered rather than take from any one what belonged of right to them, even to satisfy the cravings of nature. But I cannot say so much in favour of my levity, that would often get the upper hand of me, do what I would; and sometimes it would run riot with me; but still I did not mean to do harm, only recreation, reader, recreation; I wanted often to recreate myself, to keep the blood from stagnating.

The soldiers at New-York had an idea that the enemy, when they took possession of the town, would make a general seizure of all property that could be of use to them as military or commissary stores, hence they imagined that it was no injury to supply themselves when they thought they could do so with impunity, which was the cause of my having any hand in the transaction I am going to relate. Whether the reader will attribute it to levity, necessity or roguery, I am not able to say; perhaps to one or the other of them; it may be, to all.

I was stationed in Stone-street, near the southwest angle of the city; directly opposite to my quarters was a wine cellar, there were in the cellar at this time, several pipes of Madeira wine. By some means the soldiers had "smelt it out." Some of them had, at mid-day, taken the iron grating from a window in the back yard, and one had entered the cellar, and by means of a powder-horn divested of its bottom, had supplied himself, with wine, and was helping his comrades, through the window, with a "delicious draught," when the owner of the wine, having discovered what they were about, very wisely, as it seemed, came into the street and opened an outer door to the cellar in open view of every passenger; the soldiers quickly filled the cellar, when he, to save his property, proposed to sell it, at what he called a cheap rate, I think a dollar a gallon. In one corner of the cellar lay a large pile of oil flasks, holding from half a gallon to a gallon each, they were empty and not very savory neither, as they had lain there till the oil which adhered to the sides and bottoms had become quite rancid. While the owner was drawing for his purchasers on one side of the cellar, behind him on the other side, another set of purchasers were drawing for themselves, filling those flasks. As it appeared to have a brisk sale, especially in the latter case, I concluded I would take a flask amongst the rest, which, I accordingly did, and conveyed it in safety to my room, and went back into the street to see the end. The owner of the wine soon found out what was going forward on his premises, and began remonstrating, but he preached to the wind; finding that he could effect nothing, with them, he went to Gen. Putnam's quarters, which was not more than three or four rods off; the General immediately repaired in person to the field of action; the soldiers getting wind of his approach hurried out into the street, when he, mounting himself upon the doorsteps of my quarters, began "harangueing the multitude," threatening to hang every mother's son of them. Whether he was to be the hangman or not, he did not say; but I took every word he said for gospel, and expected nothing else but to be hanged before the morrow night. I sincerely wished him hanged and out of the way, for fixing himself upon the steps of our door; but he soon ended his discourse, and came down from his rostrum, and the soldiers dispersed, no doubt much edified. I got home as soon as the General had left the coast clear, took a draught of the wine, and then flung the flask and the remainder of the wine out of my window, from the third story, into the water cistern in the back yard, where it remains to this day for aught I know. However, I might have kept it, if I had not been in too much haste to free myself from being hanged by General Putnam, or by his order. I never heard any thing further about the wine or being hanged about it; he doubtless forgot it.

I remained in New-York two or three months, in which time several things occurred, but so trifling that I shall not mention them; when, sometime in the latter part of the month of August, I was ordered upon a fatigue party; we had scarcely reached the grand parade, when I saw our sergeant-major directing his course up Broadway, towards us, in rather an unusual step for him; he soon arrived and informed us, and then the commanding officer of the party, that he had orders to take off all belonging to our regiment and march us to our quarters, as the regiment was ordered to Long-Island, the British having landed in force there. Although this was not unexpected to me, yet it gave me rather a disagreeable feeling, as I was pretty well assured I should have to snuff a little gunpowder. However, I kept my cogitations to myself, went to my quarters, packed up my clothes, and got myself in readiness for the expedition as soon as possible. I then went to the top of the house where I had a full view of that part of the Island; I distinctly saw the smoke of the field-artillery, but the distance and the unfavourableness of the wind prevented my hearing their report, at least but faintly. The horrors of battle then presented themselves to my mind in all their hideousness; I must come to it now, thought I,—well, I will endeavour to do my duty as well as I am able and leave the event with Providence. We were soon ordered to our regimental parade, from which, as soon as the regiment was formed, we were marched off for the ferry. At the lower end of the street were placed several casks of sea-bread, made, I believe, of canel and peas-meal, nearly hard enough for musket flints; the casks were unheaded and each man was allowed to take as many as he could, as he marched by. As my good luck would have it, there was a momentary halt made; I improved the opportunity thus offered me, as every good soldier should upon all important occasions, to get as many of the biscuit as I possibly could; no one said any thing to me, and I filled my bosom, and took as many as I could hold in my hand, a dozen or more in all, and when we arrived at the ferry-stairs I stowed them away in my knapsack. We quickly embarked on board the boats; as each boat started, three cheers were given by those on board, which was returned by the numerous spectators who thronged the wharves; they all wished us good luck, apparently; although it was with most of them, perhaps, nothing more than ceremony. We soon landed at

Brooklyn, upon the Island, marched up the ascent from the ferry, to the plain. We now began to meet the wounded men, another sight I was unacquainted with, some with broken arms, some with broken legs, and some with broken heads. The sight of these a little daunted me, and made me think of home, but the sight and thought vanished together. We marched a short distance, when we halted to refresh ourselves. Whether we had any other victuals besides the hard bread I do not remember, but I remember my gnawing at them; they were hard enough to break the teeth of a rat. One of the soldiers complaining of thirst to his officer; look at that man, said he, pointing to me, he is not thirsty, I will warrant it. I felt a little elevated to be stiled a man. While resting here, which was not more than twenty minutes or half an hour, the Americans and British were warmly engaged within sight of us. What were the feelings of most or all the young soldiers at this time, I know not, but I know what were mine;—but let mine or theirs be what they might, I saw a Lieutenant who appeared to have feelings not very enviable; whether he was actuated by fear or the canteen I cannot determine now; I thought it fear at the time; for he ran round among the men of his company, snivelling and blubbering, praying each one if he had aught against him, or if *he* had injured any one that they would forgive him, declaring at the same time that he, from his heart, forgave them if they had offended him, and I gave him full credit for his assertion; for had he been at the gallows with a halter about his neck, he could not have shown more fear or penitence. A fine soldier you are, I thought, a fine officer, an exemplary man for young soldiers! I would have then suffered any thing short of death rather than have made such an exhibition of myself; but, as the poet says,

> "Fear does things so like a witch,
> "'Tis hard to distinguish which is which."

The officers of the new levies wore cockades of different colours to distinguish them from the standing forces, as they were called; the field officers wore red, the captains white, and the subaltern officers green. While we were resting here our Lieutenant-Colonel and Major, (our Colonel not being with us,) took their cockades from their hats; being asked the reason, the Lieutenant-Colonel replied, that he was willing to risk his life in the cause of his country, but was unwilling to stand a particular mark for the enemy to fire at. He was a fine officer and a brave soldier.

We were soon called upon to fall in and proceed. We had not gone far, about half a mile, when I heard one in the rear ask another where his musket was; I looked round and saw one of the soldiers stemming off without his gun, having left it where we last halted; he was inspecting his side as if undetermined whether he had it or not, he then fell out of the ranks to go in search of it: one of the company, who had brought it on (wishing to see how far he would go before he missed it) gave it to him. The reader will naturally enough conclude that he was a brave soldier. Well, he was a brave fellow for all this accident, and received two severe wounds, by musket balls, while fearlessly fighting for his country at the battle of White Plains. So true is the proverb, "A singed cat may make a good mouser." Stranger things may happen.

We overtook a small party of the artillery here, dragging a heavy twelve pounder upon a field carriage, sinking half way to the naves in the sandy soil. They plead hard for some of us to assist them to get on their piece; our officers, however, paid no attention to their entreaties, but pressed forward towards a creek, where a large party of Americans and British were engaged. By the time we arrived, the enemy had driven our men into the creek, or rather mill-pond, (the tide being up,) where such as could swim got across; those that could not swim, and could not procure any thing to buoy them up, sunk. The British having several fieldpieces stationed by a brick house, were pouring the cannister and grape upon the Americans like a shower of hail; they would doubtless have done them much more damage than they did, but for the twelve pounder mentioned above; the men having gotten it within sufficient distance to reach them, and opening a fire upon them, soon obliged them to shift their quarters. There was in this action a regiment of Maryland troops, (volunteers,) all young gentlemen. When they came out of the water and mud to us, looking like water rats, it was a truly pitiful sight. Many of them were killed in the pond, and more were drowned. Some of us went into the water after the fall of the tide, and took out a number of corpses and a great many arms that were sunk in the pond and creek.

Our regiment lay on the ground we then occupied the following night; the next day in the afternoon, we had a considerable tight scratch with about an equal number of the British, which began rather unexpectedly, and a little whimsically. A few of our men, (I mean of our regiment,) went over the creek upon business that usually employed us, that is, in search of something to eat. There was a field of indian corn at a short distance from the creek, with several cocks of hay about half way from the creek to the cornfield; the men purposed to get some of the corn, or any thing else that was eatable. When they got up with the haycocks, they were fired upon by about an equal number of the British, from the cornfield; our people took to the hay, and the others to the fence, where they exchanged a number of shots at each other, neither side inclining to give back. A number, say forty or fifty more of our men, went over and drove the British from the fence; they were by this time reinforced in their turn, and drove us back. The two parties kept thus alternately reinforcing until we had the most of our regiment in the action. After the officers came to command, the English were soon routed from the place, but we dare not follow them for fear of falling into some snare, as the whole British army was in the vicinity of us; I do not recollect that we had any one killed outright, but we had several severely wounded, and some, I believe, mortally.

Our regiment was alone, no other troops being near where we were lying; we were upon a rising ground, covered with a young growth of trees; we felled a fence of trees around us to prevent the approach of the enemies' horse. We lay there a day longer, in the latter part of the afternoon there fell a very heavy shower of rain which wet us all to the skin, and much damaged our ammunition; about sunset, when the shower had passed over, we were ordered to parade and discharge our pieces, we attempted to fire by platoons for improvement, but we made blundering work of it; it was more like a running fire, than firing by divisions: however, we got our muskets as empty as our stomachs, and with half the trouble, nor was it half the trouble to have reloaded them, for we had wherewithal to do that, but not so with our stomachs.

Just at dusk, I, with one or two others of our company, went off to a barn, about half a mile distant, with intent to get some straw to lodge upon, the ground and leaves being drenched in water, and we as wet as they; it was quite dark in the barn, and while I was fumbling about the floor some one called to me from the top of the mow, inquiring where I was from; I told him. He asked me if we had not had an engagement there, (having heard us discharging our guns,) I told him we had and a severe one too;—he asked if many were killed;—I told him that I saw none killed, nor any very badly wounded. I then heard several others, as it appeared, speaking on the mow. Poor fellows, they had better have been at their posts, than skulking in a barn on account of a little wet, for I have not the least doubt but that the British had possession of their mortal parts before the noon of the next day.

I could not find any straw, but I found some wheat in the sheaf, standing by the side of the floor; I took a sheaf or two and returned as fast as I could to the regiment. When I arrived the men were all paraded to march off the ground; I left my wheat, seized my musket and fell into the ranks. We were strictly enjoined not to speak, or even cough, while on the march. All orders were given from officer to officer, and communicated to the men in whispers. What such secrecy could mean we could not divine. We marched off in the same way that we had come on to the island, forming various conjectures among ourselves as to our destination. Some were of opinion that we were to endeavour to get on the flank, or in the rear of the enemy. Others, that we were going up the East river, to attack them in that quarter; but none, it seems, knew the right of the matter. We marched on, however, until we arrived at the ferry, where we immediately embarked on board the batteaux, and were conveyed safely to New-York, where we were landed about three o'clock in the morning, nothing against our inclinations.

The next day the British showed themselves to be in possession of our works upon the island, by firing upon some of our boats, passing to and from Governor's Island. Our regiment was employed, during this day, in throwing up a sort of breastwork, at their alarm post upon the wharves, (facing the enemy,) composed of spars and logs, and filling the space between with the materials of which the wharves were composed,—old broken junk bottles, flint stones, &c. which, had a cannon ball passed through, would have chanced to kill five men where the ball would one. But the enemy did not see fit to molest us.

We staid several days longer in the city, when one morning we discovered that a small frigate had advanced up, and was lying above Governor's Island, close under the Long-Island shore; several other ships had come up, and were lying just below the town. They seemed to portend evil. In the evening, just at dark, our regiment was ordered to march to Turtle Bay, a place about four miles distant, on the East river, where were a large warehouse or two, called (then) the King's stores, built for the storing of marine stores belonging to the government, before the war. There was at this time about twenty-five hundred barrels of flour in those storehouses, and it was conjectured that the design of the forementioned frigate, or rather the officers and crew of her, was to seize on this flour; we were, therefore ordered to secure it, before the British should have an opportunity to lay their unhallowed hands upon it. We arrived at the place about midnight, and by sunrise, or a little after, had secured the whole of it, by rolling it up a steep bank, and piling it behind a ledge of rocks. While we were employed in doing this, some other troops were constructing a small battery on a point of land opposite the frigate, (she having arrived during the night, and anchored just below us, not being able to get quite up, by the failure of the wind;) and as soon as we had finished our work at the flour, the battery opened upon her with two long twelve pounders, which so galled her ribs that her situation began to grow rather uneasy to her. She never returned a shot at the battery, but got under weigh as quick as possible and ran by us, (there being then a little wind.) We all stood gazing at her, as she passed, when she sent us a nine pound shot, (perhaps the best she had to send us,) which passed through amongst us without injuring any one: she ran a little way up the river and came to anchor again.

We continued here some days to guard the flour. We were forbidden by our officers to use any of it, except our daily allowance; we used, however, to purloin some of it to eat and exchange with the inhabitants for milk, sauce, and such small matters as we could get for it, of them. While we lay here I saw a piece of American workmanship that was (as I thought) rather remarkable. Going one evening upon a piquet guard, in a subaltern officer's command, a mile or two farther up the river, we had to march through the inclosures close upon the bank of the river. There was a small party of British upon an island in the river, known, generally, by a queer name, given it upon as queer an occasion, which I shall not stop now to unfold. These British soldiers seemed to be very busy in chasing some scattering sheep, that happened to be so unlucky as to fall in their way. One of the soldiers, however, thinking, perhaps, he could do more mischief by killing some of us, had posted himself on a point of rocks, at the southern extremity of the Island, and kept firing at us as we passed along the bank. Several of his shots passed between our files, but we took little notice of him, thinking he was so far off that he could do us but little hurt, and that we could do him none at all, until one of the guard asked the officer if he might discharge his piece at him; as it was charged and would not hinder us long, the officer gave his consent. He rested his old six feet barrel across a fence and sent an express to him. The man dropped, but as we then thought it was only to amuse us, we took no further notice of it but passed on. In the morning, upon our return, we saw the brick coloured coat still lying in the same position we had left it in the evening before: it was a long distance to hit a single man with a musket, it was certainly over half a mile.

The other evening, while lying here, we heard a heavy cannonade at the city; and before dark saw four of the enemy's ships that had passed the town, and were coming up the East river; they anchored just below us. These ships were the Phœnix, of forty-four guns; the Roebuck, of forty-four; the Rose, of thirty-two; and another, the name of which I have forgotten. Half of our regiment was sent off under the command of our Major, to man something that were called "lines," although they were nothing more than a ditch dug along on the bank of the river, with the dirt thrown out towards the water. They staid in these lines during the night, and returned to the camp in the morning unmolested.

The other half of the regiment went the next night, under the command of the Lieut. Colonel, upon the like errand. We arrived at the lines about dark, and were ordered to leave our packs in a copse wood, under a guard, and go into the lines without them; what was the cause of this piece of *wise* policy I never knew; but I knew the effects of it, which was, that I never saw my knapsack from that day to this; nor did any of the rest of our party, unless they came across them by accident in our retreat. We "manned the lines," and lay quite as unmolested during the whole night, as Samson did the half of his in the city of Gaza, and upon about as foolish a business, though there was some difference in our getting away; we did not go off in so much triumph quite as he did. We had a chain of sentinels quite up the river, for four or five miles in length. At an interval of every half hour they passed the watchword to each other—"all is well." I heard the British on board their shipping answer, "We will alter your tune before to-morrow night;"—and they were as good as their word for once.

It was quite a dark night, and at daybreak, the first thing that "saluted our eyes," was all the four ships at anchor, with springs upon their cables, and within musket shot of us. The Phœnix lying a little quartering, and her stern towards me, I could read her name as distinctly as though I had been directly under her stern. What is the meaning of all this, thought I, what is coming forward now?—They appeared to be very busy on shipboard, but we lay still and showed our good breeding by not interfering with them, as they were strangers, and we knew not but they were bashful withal. As soon as it was fairly light, we saw their boats coming out of a creek or cove, on the Long-Island side of the water, filled with British soldiers. When they came to the edge of the tide, they formed their boats in line. They continued to augment their forces from the Island until they appeared like a large clover field in full bloom. And now was coming on the famous Kipp's Bay affair, which has been criticised so much by the Historians of the Revolution. I was there, and will give a true statement of all that *I* saw during that day.

It was on a Sabbath morning, the day in which the British were always employed about their deviltry, if possible; because, they said, they had the prayers of the church on that day. We lay very quiet in our ditch, waiting their motions, till the sun was an hour or two high; we heard a cannonade at the city, but our attention was drawn toward our own guests. But they being a little dilatory in their operations, I stepped into an old warehouse which stood close by me, with the door open, inviting me in, and sat down upon a stool; the floor was strewed with papers which had in some former period been used in the concerns of the house, but were then lying in "woful confusion." I was very demurely perusing these papers, when, all of a sudden, there came such a peal of thunder from the British shipping that I thought my head would go with the sound. I made a frog's leap for the ditch, and lay as still as I possibly could, and began to consider which part of my carcass was to go first. The British played their parts well; indeed, they had nothing to hinder them. We kept the lines till they were almost levelled upon us, when our officers, seeing we could make no resistance, and no orders coming from any superior officer, and that we must soon be entirely exposed to the rake of their guns, gave the order to leave the lines. In retreating, we had to cross a level clear spot of ground, forty or fifty rods wide, exposed to the whole of the enemy's fire; and they gave it to us in prime order; the grape shot and langrage flew merrily, which served to quicken our motions. When I had gotten a little out of the reach of their combustibles, I found myself in company with one who was a neighbour of mine when at home, and one other man belonging to our regiment; where the rest of them were I knew not. We went into a house by the highway, in which were two women and some small children, all crying most bitterly; we asked the women if they had any spirits in the house; they placed a case bottle of rum upon the table, and bid us help ourselves. We each of us drank a glass, and bidding them good bye, betook ourselves to the highway again. We had not gone far before we saw a party of men, apparently hurrying on in the same direction with ourselves; we endeavoured hard to overtake them, but on approaching them we found that they were not of our way of thinking; they were Hessians. We immediately altered our course, and took the main road leading to King's bridge. We had not long been on this road before we saw another party, just ahead of us, whom we knew to be Americans; just as we overtook these, they were fired upon by a party of British from a cornfield, and all was immediately in confusion again. I believe the enemies' party was small; but our people were all militia, and the demons of fear and disorder seemed to take full possession of all and every thing on that day. When I came to the spot where the militia were fired upon, the ground was literally covered with arms, knapsacks, staves, coats, hats and old oil flasks, perhaps some of those from the Madeira wine cellar, in New-York; all I picked up of the plunder, was a blocktin syringe, which afterwards helped to procure me a thanksgiving dinner. Myself and the man whom I mentioned as belonging to our company, were all who were in company at this time, the other man having gone on with those who were fired upon; they did not tarry to let the grass grow much under their feet. We had to advance slowly, for my comrade having been sometime unwell, was now so overcome by heat, hunger and fatigue that he became suddenly and violently sick. I took his musket and endeavoured to encourage him on. He was, as I before observed, a nigh neighbour of mine when at home, and I was loath to leave him behind, although I was anxious to find the main part of the regiment, if possible, before night—for I thought that that part of it which was not in the lines was in a body somewhere. We soon came in sight of a large party of Americans, ahead of us, who appeared to have come into this road by some other rout; we were within sight of them when they were fired upon by another party of the enemy; they returned but a very few shots and then scampered off as fast as their legs would carry them. When we came to the ground they had occupied, the same display of lumber presented itself as at the other place. We here found a wounded man and some of his comrades endeavouring to get him off. I stopped to assist them in constructing a sort of litter to lay him upon, when my sick companion growing impatient, moved on, and as soon as we had placed the wounded man upon the litter I followed him. While I was here one or two of our regiment came up and we went on together;—we had proceeded but a short distance, however, before we found our retreat cut off by a party of the enemy, stretched across the Island. I immediately quitted the road and went into the fields, where there happened to be a small spot of boggy land, covered with low bushes and weeds; into these I ran, and squatting down, concealed myself from their sight. Several of the British came so near to me that I could see the buttons on their clothes. They, however, soon withdrew and left the coast clear for me again. I then came out of my covert and went on; but what had become of my sick comrade, or the rest of my companions, I knew not. I still kept the sick man's musket; I was unwilling to leave it, for it was his own property, and I knew he valued it highly, and I had a great esteem for him. I had, indeed, enough to do to take care of my own concerns; it was exceeding hot weather, and I was faint, having slept but very little the preceding night, nor had I eaten a mouthful of victuals for more than twenty-four hours. I waddled on as well and as fast as I could, and soon came up with a number of men at a small brook, where they had stopped to drink and rest themselves a few moments. Just as I arrived, a man had lain down to drink at the brook, and as he did not rise very soon, one of the company observed, that he would kill himself with drinking; upon which, another, touching him without his appearing to notice it, said he had already killed himself, which was the case. Leaving them, I went on again, and directly came to a foul place in the road, where the soldiers had taken down the fence to pass into the fields. I passed across the corner of one field and through a gap in a cross fence into another; here I found a number of men resting under the trees and bushes in the fences. Almost the first I saw, after passing the gap in the fence, was my sick friend. I was exceeding glad to find him, for I had but little hope of ever seeing him again; he was sitting near the fence with his head between his knees. I tapped him upon the shoulder and asked him to get up and go on with me; no, said he, (at the same time regarding me with a most pitiful look,) I must die here. I endeavoured to argue the case with him, but all to no purpose,—he insisted upon dying there. I told him he should not die there nor any where else that day, if I could help it; and at length, with more persuasion and some force, I succeeded in getting him upon his feet again, and to moving on. There happened just at this instant a considerable shower of rain, which wet us all to the skin, being very thinly clad; we, however, continued to move forward, although but slowly. After proceeding about half a mile we came to a place where our people had begun to make a stand. A number, say two or three hundred, had collected here, having been stopped by the artillery officers; they had two or three fieldpieces fixed and fitted for action, in case the British came on, which was momentarily expected. I and my comrades (for I had found another of our company when I found my sick man,) were stopped here, a sentinel being placed in the road to prevent our going any further. I felt very much chagrined to be thus hindered from proceeding, as I felt confident that our regiment, or some considerable part of it, was not far ahead, unless they had been more unlucky than I had. I remonstrated with the officer who detained us. I told him that our regiment was just ahead; he asked me how I knew that—I could not tell him—but I told him I had a sick man with me who was wet and would die if exposed all night to the damp cold air, hoping by this to move his compassion; but it would not do, he was inexorable. I shall not soon forget the answer he gave me when I made the last mentioned observation respecting the sick man,—"Well," said he, "if he dies the country will be rid of one who can do it no good." Pretty fellow! thought I, a very compassionate gentleman! When a man has got his bane in his country's cause, let him die like an old horse or dog, because he can do no more!—The *only wish* I would wish such men, would be, to let them have exactly the same treatment which they would give to others.—I saw but little chance of escaping from this very humane gentleman by fair means, so I told my two comrades to stick by me and keep together, and we would get from them by some means or other during the evening. It was now almost sundown and the air quite chilly after the shower, and we were as wet as water could make us. I was really afraid my sick man would die in earnest. I had not staid there long, after this entertaining dialogue with my obliging friend, the officer, waiting for an opportunity to escape, before one offered. There came to the sentinel, I suppose, an old acquaintance of his, with a canteen containing some sort of spirits; after drinking himself, he gave it to the sentinel, who took a large pull upon it;—they then fell into conversation together, but soon taking a hare from the same hound, it put them into quite "a talkative mood;" I kept my eyes upon them, and when I thought I saw a chance of getting from them, I gave my companions a wink, and we passed by the sentinel without his noticing us at all. A walk of a very few rods concealed us from his view, by a turn in the road and some bushes, and thus we escaped from prison, for we thought we were hardly dealt by, to be confined by those whom we took to be our friends, after having laboured so hard to escape being made prisoners by the common enemy.

We went on a little distance, when we overtook another man belonging to our company. He had just been refreshing himself with some bread and dry salt fish, and was putting "the fragments" into his knapsack. I longed for a bite, but I felt too bashful to ask him, and he was too thoughtless or stingy to offer it. We still proceeded, but had not gone far, when we came up with the regiment, resting themselves on the "cold ground," after the fatigues of the day. Our company all *appeared* to rejoice to see us, thinking we were killed or prisoners. I was *sincerely* glad to see them; for I was once more among friends, or at least acquaintances. Several of the regiment were missing, among whom was our Major, he was a fine man, and his loss was much regretted by the men of the regiment. We were the last who came up, all the others who were missing, were either killed or taken prisoners.

And here ends the "Kipp's Bay" affair, which caused at the time, and has since caused much "inkshed." Anecdotes, jests, imprecations and sarcasms, have been multiplied; and even the grave writers of the revolution have said and written more about it than it deserved. I could make some observations, but it is beyond my province.

One anecdote which I have seen more than once in print, I will notice. A certain man, or the friends of a certain man, have said, that this certain man was sitting by the highway side, when the Commander-in-chief passed by, and asked why he sat there. His answer, as he or they say, was, "That he had rather be killed or taken by the enemy, than trodden to death by cowards."—A brave man he! I doubt whether there was such another there that day, and I much doubt whether he himself was there, under such circumstances as he, or his friends relate; every man that I saw was endeavouring by all sober means to escape from death or captivity, which, at that period of the war was almost certain death. The men were confused, being without officers to command them;—I do not recollect of seeing a commissioned officer from the time I left the lines on the banks of the East river, in the morning, until I met with the *gentlemanly* one in the evening. How could the men fight without officers? The man who represented himself as being so valiant, was a bragadocia, and I never yet met with one of that class who was not at heart a sheer coward.

We lay that night upon the ground, which the regiment occupied when I came up with it. The next day, in the forenoon, the enemy, as we expected, followed us "hard up," and were advancing through a level field; our rangers and some few other light troops, under the command of Colonel Knowlton, of Connecticut, and Major Leitch of (I believe) Virginia, were in waiting for them. Seeing them advancing, the rangers, &c. concealed themselves in a deep gully overgrown with bushes; upon the western verge of this defile was a post and rail fence, and over that the forementioned field. Our people let the enemy advance until they arrived at the fence, when they arose and poured in a volley upon them. How many of the enemy were killed and wounded could not be known, as the British were always as careful as Indians to conceal their losses. There were, doubtless, some killed, as I myself counted nineteen ball-holes through a single rail of the fence at which the enemy were standing when the action began. The British gave back and our people advanced into the field. The action soon became warm. Colonel Knowlton, a brave man, and commander of the detachment, fell in the early part of the engagement. It was said, by those who saw it, that he lost his valuable life by unadvisedly exposing himself singly to the enemy. In my boyhood I had been acquainted with him; he was a brave man and an excellent citizen. Major Leitch fell soon after, and the troops, who were then engaged, were left with no higher commanders than their captains, but they still kept the enemy retreating.

Our regiment was now ordered into the field, and we arrived on the ground just as the retreating enemy were entering a thick wood, a circumstance as disagreeable to them as it was agreeable to us at that period of the war. We soon came to action with them. The troops engaged, being reinforced by our regiment, kept them still retreating, until they found shelter under the cannon of some of their shipping, lying in the North river. We remained on the battle ground till nearly sunset, expecting the enemy to attack us again, but they showed no such inclination that day. The men were very much fatigued and faint, having had nothing to eat for forty-eight hours,—at least the greater part were in this condition, and I among the rest. While standing on the field, after the action had ceased, one of the men near the Lieut. Colonel, complained of being hungry; the Colonel, putting his hand into his coat pocket, took out a piece of an ear of Indian corn, burnt as black as a coal, "Here," said he to the man complaining, "eat this and learn to be a soldier."

We now returned to camp, if camp it was;—our tent held the whole regiment and might have held ten millions more. When we arrived on the ground we had occupied previous to going into action, we found that our invalids, consisting of the sick, the lame, and the lazy, had obtained some fresh beef;—where the commissaries found the beef or the men found the commissaries in this time of confusion, I know not, nor did I stop to ask. They were broiling the beef on small sticks, in Indian stile, round blazing fires, made of dry chestnut rails. The meat, when cooked, was as black as a coal on the outside, and as raw on the inside as if it had not been near the fire. "I asked no questions, for conscience's sake," but fell to and helped myself to a feast of this raw beef, without bread or salt.

We had eight or ten of our regiment killed in the action, and a number wounded, but none of them belonged to our company. Our Lieut. Colonel was hit by a grape-shot, which went through his coat, westcoat and shirt, to the skin on his shoulder, without doing any other damage than cutting up his epaulette.

A circumstance occurred on the evening after this action, which, although trifling in its nature, excited in me feelings which I shall never forget. When we came off the field we brought away a man who had been shot dead upon the spot; and after we had refreshed ourselves we proceeded to bury him. Having provided a grave, which was near a gentleman's country seat, (at that time occupied by the Commander-in-chief,) we proceeded, just in the dusk of evening, to commit the poor man, then far from friends and relatives, to the bosom of his mother earth. Just as we had laid him in the grave, in as decent a posture as existing circumstances would admit, there came from the house, towards the grave, two young ladies, who appeared to be sisters;—as they approached the grave, the soldiers immediately made way for them, with those feelings of respect which beauty and modesty combined seldom fail to produce, more especially when, as in this instance, accompanied by piety. Upon arriving at the head of the grave, they stopped, and, with their arms around each other's neck, stooped forward and looked into it, and with a sweet pensiveness of countenance which might have warmed the heart of a misoganist, asked if we were going to put the earth upon his naked face; being answered in the affirmative, one of them took a fine white gauze handkerchief from her neck and desired that it might be spread upon his face, tears, at the same time, flowing down their cheeks. After the grave was filled up they retired to the house in the same manner they came. Although the dead soldier had no acquaintance present, (for there were none at his burial who knew him,) yet he had mourners, and females too. Worthy young ladies! You, and such as you, are deserving the regard of the greatest of men. What sisters, what wives, what mothers and what neighbours would you make!—Such a sight as those ladies afforded at that time, and on that occasion, was worthy, and doubtless received the attention of angels.

Another affair which transpired during and after the abovementioned engagement, deserves to be recorded by me, as no one else has, to my knowledge, ever mentioned it. A sergeant belonging to the Connecticut forces, being sent by his officers in the heat of the action, to procure ammunition, was met by a superior officer, an Aid-de-camp to some General officer, (I believe,) who accused him of deserting his post in time of action. He remonstrated with the officer, and informed him of the absolute necessity there was of his obeying the orders of his own officers; that the failure of his procuring a supply of ammunition might endanger the success of the day; but all to no purpose, the officer would not allow himself to believe him, but drew his sword and threatened to take his life on the spot if he did not immediately return to his corps. The sergeant, fired with just indignation at hearing and seeing his life threatened, cocked his musket and stood in his own defence. He was, however, taken, confined and tried for mutiny and condemned to be shot. The sentence of the court-martial was approved by the Commander-in-chief, and the day for his execution set; when it arrived, an embankment was thrown up, to prevent the shot fired at him from doing other damage, and all things requisite on such occasions were in readiness; the Connecticut troops were then drawn out and formed in a square, and the prisoner brought forth; after being blindfolded and pinioned, he knelt upon the ground. The corporal with his six executioners were then brought up before him, ready, at the fatal word of command, to send a brave soldier into the eternal world, because he persisted in doing his duty and obeying the lawful and urgent orders of his superior officers, the failure of which might, for aught the officer who stopped him knew, have caused the loss of hundreds of lives. But the sergeant was reprieved, and I believe it was well that he was, for his blood would not have been the only blood that would have been spilt;—the troops were greatly exasperated, and they showed what their feelings were by their lively and repeated cheerings after the reprieve, but more so by their secret and open threats before it. The reprieve was read by one of the Chaplains of the army, after a long harangue to the soldiers, setting forth the enormity of the crime charged upon the prisoner, repeatedly using this sentence, "crimes for which men ought to die,"—which did much to further the resentment of the troops already raised to a high pitch. But, as I said before, it was well that it ended as it did, both on account of the honour of the soldiers and the safety of some others. I was informed that this same sergeant was honoured, the year following, by those who better knew his merits, with a captain's commission.

We remained here till sometime in the month of October, without any thing very material transpiring, excepting starvation, and *that* had by this time become quite a secondary matter; hard duty and nakedness were considered the prime evils, for the reader will recollect that we lost all our clothing in the Kipp's Bay affair. The British were quite indulgent to us, not having interrupted our happiness since the check they received in the action before mentioned, but left us at our leisure to see that they did not get amongst us before we were apprised of their approach, and that, in all its bearings, was enough. It now began to be cool weather, especially the nights. To have to lie, as I did, almost every other night, (for our duty required it,) on the cold and often wet ground, without a blanket, and with nothing but thin summer clothing, was tedious. I have often, while upon guard, lain on one side until the upper side smarted with cold, then turned that side down to the place warmed by my body, and let the other take its turn at smarting, while the one on the ground warmed; thus alternately turning for four or six hours, till called upon to go on sentry, as the soldiers term it; and when relieved from a tour of two long hours at that business, and returned to the guard again, have had to go through the operation of freezing and thawing for four or six hours more;—in the morning, the ground as white as snow, with hoar frost. Or, perhaps it would rain all night like a flood; all that could be done in that case, was, to lie down, (if one could lie down,) take our musket in our arms and place the lock between our thighs, "and weather it out."

A simple affair happened while I was upon guard at a time, while we were here, which made considerable disturbance amongst the guard and caused me some extra hours of fatigue at the time;—as I was the cause of it at first, I will relate it. The guard consisted of nearly two hundred men, commanded by a field-officer;—we kept a long chain of sentinels, placed almost within speaking distance of each other, and, being in close neighbourhood with the enemy, we were necessitated to be pretty alert. I was upon my post, as sentinel, about the middle of the night; thinking we had overgone the time in which we ought to have been relieved, I stepped a little off my post towards one of the next sentries, it being quite dark, and asked him in a low voice how long he had been on sentry; he started as if attacked by the enemy, and roared out, "who comes there?" I saw I had alarmed him, and stole back to my post as quick as possible. He still kept up his cry, 'Who comes there?' and receiving no answer, he discharged his piece, which alarmed the whole guard, who immediately formed and prepared for action, and sent off a non-commissioned officer and file of men to ascertain the cause of alarm. They came first to the man who had fired, and asked him what was the matter; he said that some one had made an abrupt advance upon his premises and demanded, "How comes you on, sentry?" They next came to me, inquiring what I had seen;—I told them that I had not seen or heard any thing to alarm me but what the other sentinel had caused. The men returned to the guard, and we were soon relieved, which was all I that wanted. Upon our return to the guard, I found, as was to be expected, that the alarm was the subject of general conversation among them. They were confident that a spy or something worse had been amongst us, and consequently greater vigilance was necessary. We were accordingly kept the rest of the night under arms, and I cursed my indiscretion for causing the disturbance, as I could get no more rest during the night. I could have set all to rights by speaking a word, but it would not do for me to betray my own secret. But it was diverting to me to see how much the story gained by being carried about,—both among the guard, and after its arrival in the camp.

I had been one night upon a piquet guard,—that is, a guard only for the night. Having been dismissed early in the morning, I was returning through a by-road to my quarters;—this road led from the main road to the shore of the North river; I was alone, the rest of the guard having, for some cause which I have now forgotten, passed on, and were out of sight. I saw Gen. Putnam on horseback and alone, coming up the road in my rear. In my front, and nearer to me than I was to the General, was a high fence and a set of high and very heavy bars, composed of pretty large poles or young trees. I had only just to go through the bars and cross another fence on my left, and I should be in the deep gully and at the very spot where the late action began;—this was the way I was actually to go to reach the camp. The General seeing me near the bars, bawled out, "Soldier, let down those bars." I was then *at* the bars, but seeing that the General was some distance off, I took down one bar, and slipped through, leaving him to let down the bars himself. He was apparently in a dreadful passion; drawing a pistol from his holsters, he came after me to the bars, with his usual exclamation,—"curse ye!"—

but I was where he could not see me, although I could see him, and hear him too;—I was safe, and perhaps it was well for me that I was; for I verily believe the old fellow would have shot me, or endeavoured to have done it, if he could have got within reach of me. Thus was my life twice threatened by him, here, and at the wine-cellar in New-York; but I was not much afraid of his putting either of his threats into execution.

Sometime in October, the British landed at Frogg's neck, or point, and by their motions seemed to threaten to cut off our retreat to York-Island. We were thereupon ordered to leave the Island. We crossed King's bridge and directed our course toward the White Plains. We saw parties of the enemy foraging in the country, but they were generally too alert for us. We encamped on the heights called Valentine's hill, where we continued some days, keeping up the old system of starving. A sheep's head which I begged of the butchers, who were killing some for the "gentleman officers," was all the provisions I had for two or three days.

While lying here, I one day rambled into the woods and fields, in order, if possible, to procure something to satisfy the cravings of nature. I found and ate a considerable quantity of chestnuts, which are, as Bloomfield says of his acorns, "Hot thirsty food," which was, I suppose, the cause of our Doctor's blunder, as I shall relate directly. I returned to camp just at sunset, and met our orderly sergeant, who immediately warned me to prepare for a two day's command.—What is termed going on command, is what is generally called going on a scouting party, or something similar.—I told the sergeant I was sick and could not go; he said I must go to the Doctor, and if he said I was unfit for duty, he must excuse me. I saw our Surgeon's mate close by, endeavouring to cook his supper, blowing the fire and scratching his eyes. We both stepped up to him, and he felt my pulse, at the same time very demurely shutting his eyes, while I was laughing in his face. After a minute's consultation with his medical talisman, he very gravely told the sergeant, that I was unfit for duty, having a high fever upon me. I was as well as he was; all the medicine I needed was a bellyful of victuals. The sergeant turned to go off for another man, when I told him that I would go, for I meant to go; I only felt a little cross, and did not know how, just then, to vent my spleen in any other way. I had much rather go on such an expedition than stay in camp; as I stood some chance while in the country to get something to eat. But I admired the Doctor's skill; although, perhaps not more extraordinary than that of many others of the "faculty."

We marched from Valentine's hill for the White Plains, in the night. There were but three of our men present. We had our cooking utensils, (at that time the most useless things in the army,) to carry in our hands. They were made of cast iron and consequently heavy. I was so beat out before morning, with hunger and fatigue, that I could hardly move one foot before the other. I told my messmates that I *could not* carry our kettle any further; they said they *would* not carry it any further; of what use was it? they had nothing to cook and did not want any thing to cook with. We were sitting down on the ascent of a hill when this discourse happened. We got up to proceed, when I took up the kettle, which held nearly a common pail full, I could not carry it; my arms were almost dislocated; I sat it down in the road, and one of the others gave it a shove with his foot, and it rolled down against the fence, and that was the last I ever saw of it. When we got through the night's march we found our mess was not the only one that was rid of their iron bondage.

We arrived at the White Plains just at dawn of day, tired and faint—encamped on the plains a few days and then removed to the hills in the rear of the plains. Nothing remarkable transpired, while lying here, for some time. One day, after roll-call, one of my messmates with me, sat off upon a little jaunt into the country to get some sauce of some kind or other. We soon came to a field of English turnips; but the owner was there, and we could not get any of them without paying for them in some way or other. We soon agreed with the man to pull and cut off the tops of the turnips at the halves, until we got as many as we needed. After the good man had sat us to work, and chatted with us a few minutes, he went off and left us. After he was gone, and we had pulled and cut as many as we wanted, we packed them up and decamped, leaving the owner of the turnips to pull his share himself.

When we arrived at the camp, the troops were all parading. Upon inquiry, we found that the British were advancing upon us. We flung our turnip plunder into the tent—packed up our things, which was easily done, for we had but a trifle to pack, and fell into the ranks. Before we were ready to march, the battle had begun. Our regiment then marched off, crossed a considerable stream of water which crosses the plain, and formed behind a stone wall in company with several other regiments, and waited the approach of the enemy. They were not far distant; at least, that part of them with which we were quickly after engaged. They were constructing a sort of bridge to convey their artillery, &c. across the before mentioned stream. They however soon made their appearance in our neighbourhood. There was in our front, about ten rods distant, an orchard of apple trees. The ground on which the orchard stood was lower than the ground that we occupied, but was level from our post to the verge of the orchard, when it fell off so abruptly that we could not see the lower parts of the trees. A party of Hessian troops, and some English, soon took possession of this ground: they would advance so far as just to show themselves above the rising ground, fire, and fall back and reload their muskets. Our chance upon them was, as soon as they showed themselves above the level ground, or when they fired, to aim at the flashes of their guns—their position was as advantagious to them as a breastwork. We were engaged in this manner for some time, when finding ourselves flanked and in danger of being surrounded, we were compelled to make a hasty retreat from the stone wall. We lost, comparatively speaking, very few at the fence: but when forced to retreat, we lost, in killed and wounded, a considerable number. One man who belonged to our company, when we marched from the parade, said, "Now I am going out to the field to be killed;" and he said more than once afterwards, that he should be killed; and he was—he was shot dead on the field. I never saw a man so prepossessed with the idea of any mishap as he was. We fell back a little distance and made a stand: detached parties engaging in almost every direction. We did not come in contact with the enemy again that day, and just at night we fell back to our encampment. In the course of the afternoon the British took possession of a hill on the right of our encampment, which had in the early part of the day been occupied by some of the New-York troops. This hill overlooked the one upon which we were, and was not more than half or three fourths of a mile distant. The enemy had several pieces of field artillery upon this hill, and, as might be expected, entertained us with their music all the evening. We entrenched ourselves where we now lay, expecting another attack. But the British were very civil, and indeed they generally were, after they had received a check from Brother Jonathan, for any of their rude actions; they seldom repeated them, at least, not till the affair that caused the reprimand, had ceased in some measure to be remembered.

During the night we remained in our new made trenches, the ground of which was in many parts springy; in that part where I happened to be stationed, the water, before morning, was nearly over shoes, which caused many of us to take violent colds, by being exposed upon the wet ground after a profuse perspiration. I was one who felt the effects of it, and was the next day sent back to the baggage to get well again, if I could, for it was left to my own exertions to do it, and no other assistance was afforded me. I was not alone in misery; there were a number in the same circumstances. When I arrived at the baggage, which was not more than a mile or two, I had the canopy of heaven for my hospital, and the ground for my hammock. I found a spot where the dry leaves had collected between the knolls; I made up a bed of these, and nestled in it, having no other friend present but the sun to smile upon me. I had nothing to eat or drink, not even water, and was unable to go after any myself, for I was sick indeed. In the evening, one of my messmates found me out, and soon after brought me some boiled hog's flesh (it was not pork) and turnips, without either bread or salt. I could not eat it, but I felt obliged to him notwithstanding; he did all he could do—he gave me the best he had to give, and had to steal that, poor fellow;—necessity drove him to do it to satisfy the cravings of his own hunger, as well as to assist a fellow sufferer.

The British, soon after this, left the White Plains, and passed the Hudson, into New-Jersey. We, likewise, fell back to New-Castle and Wright's mills. Here a number of our sick were sent off to Norwalk, in Connecticut, to recruit. I was sent with them as a nurse. We were billetted among the inhabitants. I had, in my ward, seven or eight *sick soldiers*, who were (at least, soon after their arrival there,) as well in health as I was: all they wanted was a cook and something for a cook to exercise his functions upon. The inhabitants here were almost entirely what were in those days termed tories. An old lady, of whom I often procured milk, used always, when I went to her house, to give me a lecture on my opposition to our good king George. She had always said, (she told me,) that the regulars would make us fly like pigeons. My patients would not use any of the milk I had of her, for fear, as they said, of poison;—I told them I was not afraid of her poisoning the milk, she had not wit enough to think of such a thing, nor resolution enough to do it if she did think of it.

The man of the house where I was quartered had a smart looking negro man, a great politician; I chanced one day to go into the barn where he was threshing. He quickly began to upbraid me with my opposition to the British. The king of England was a very powerful prince, he said,—a very powerful prince; and it was a great pitty that the colonists had fallen out with him; but as we had, we must abide by the consequences. I had no inclination to waste the shafts of my rhetoric upon a negro slave. I concluded he had heard his betters say so. As the old cock crows so crows the young one; and I thought, as the white cock crows so crows the black one. He ran away from his master, before I left there, and went to Long-Island to assist king George; but it seems the king of terrors was more potent than king George, for his master had certain intelligence that poor Cuff was laid flat on his back.

This man had likewise a negress who (as he was a widower) kept his house. She was as great a doctress as Cuff was a politician, and she wished to be a surgeon. There was an annual thanksgiving while we were here. The *sick* men of my ward had procured a fine roasting pig, and the old negro woman having seen the syringe that I picked up in the retreat from Kipp's bay, fell violently in love with it, and offered me a number of pies, of one sort or other for it. Of the pig and the pies we made an excellent thanksgiving dinner, the best meal I had eaten since I left my grandsire's table.

Our surgeon came amongst us soon after this, and packed us all off to camp, save two or three, who were discharged. I arrived at camp with the rest, where we remained, moving from place to place as occasion required, undergoing hunger, cold and fatigue, until the twenty-fifth day of December, 1776, when I was discharged, (my term of service having expired,) at Philip's manor, in the State of New-York, near Hudson's river.

Here ends my first campaign. I had learned something of a soldier's life; enough, I thought, to keep me at home for the future. Indeed, I was then fully determined to rest easy with the knowledge I had acquired in the affairs of the army. But the reader will find, if he has patience to follow me a little longer in my details, that the ease of a winter spent at home, caused me to alter my mind. I had several *kind* invitations to enlist into the standing army, then about to be raised, especially a very pressing one to engage in a regiment of horse, but I concluded to try a short journey on foot first. Accordingly, I sat off for my good old grandsire's, where I arrived, I think, on the twenty-seventh, two days after my discharge, and found my friends all alive and well; they appeared to be glad to see me, and I am sure I was *really* glad to see them.

Chapter III. Campaign of *1777.*

When troubles fall within your dish,
And things don't tally with your wish:
It's just as well to laugh as cry—
To sing and joke, as moan and sigh;—
For a pound of sorrow never yet
Cancel'd a single ounce of debt.

THE spring of 1777 arrived; I had got recruited during the winter, and begun to think again about the army. In the month of April, as the weather warmed, the young men began to enlist. Orders were out for enlisting men for three years, or during the war. The general opinion of the people was, that the war would not continue three years longer; what reasons they had for making such conjectures I cannot imagine, but so it was;—perhaps it was their wish that it *might* be so, induced them to think that it *would* be so.

One of my mates, and my most familiar associate, who had been out ever since the war commenced, and who had been with me the last campaign, had enlisted for the term of the war, in the capacity of sergeant. He had enlisting orders, and was, every time he saw me, which was often, harrassing me with temptations to engage in the service again. At length he so far overcame my resolution as to get me into the scrape again, although it was, at this time, against my inclination, for I had not fully determined with myself, that if I did engage again, into what corps I should enter. But I would here just inform the reader, that that little insignificant monosyllable—No—was the hardest word in the language for me to pronounce, especially when solicited to do a thing which was in the least degree indifferent to me;—I could say Yes, with half the trouble. But I had enlisted. However, when I was alone, and had time to reflect, I began sorely to repent. The next day I met the sergeant and told him that I repented my bargain; he endeavoured to persuade me to stick to it, but I could then say—No.—He told me that he would speak to his Captain about the matter, and as I had taken no bounty money, he thought that he would dismiss me. Accordingly, he told the Captain of my unwillingness to be held, and he let me run at large once more; I then determined to wait my own time before I engaged again.

The inhabitants of the town were about this time put into what were called squads, according to their rateable property. Of some of the most opulent, one formed a squad,—of others, two or three, and of the lower sort of the people, several formed a squad. Each of these squads were to furnish a man for the army, either by hiring or by sending one of their own number.

I had an elbow relation, a sort of (as the Irishman said) cousin-in-law, who had been in the army the two preceding campaigns, and now had a Lieutenant's commission in the standing army. He was continually urging my grandparents to give their consent for me to go with him. He told the old gentleman a power of fine stories, and made him promises, respecting his behaviour to me, which he never intended to perform, until he obtained my grandsire's consent, and at length, after much persuasion, my consent likewise.

One of the above-mentioned squads, wanting to procure a man, the Lieutenant told them that he thought they might persuade me to go for them, and they accordly attacked me, front, rear and flank. I thought, as I must go, I might as well endeavour to get as much for my skin as I could;—accordingly, I told them that I would go for them, and fixed upon a day when I would meet them and clinch the bargain. The day, which was a muster-day of the militia of the town, arrived;—I went to the parade, where all was liveliness, as it generally is upon such occasions; but poor *I* felt miserably; my execution-day was come. I kept wandering about till the afternoon, among the crowd, when I saw the Lieutenant, who went with me into a house where the men of the squad were, and there I put my name to enlisting indentures for the last time. And now I was hampered again. The men gave me what they agreed to, I forget the sum, perhaps enough to keep the blood circulating during the short space of time which I tarried at home after I had enlisted. They were now freed from any further trouble, at least for the present, and I had become the scape-goat for them.

Well, I was again a soldier!—I staid at home a few days, which I endeavoured to make as agreeable as possible, well knowing that the army would bring trouble enough to counterbalance all the happiness I could procure for myself in the short time I had to tarry at home.

Just at this time the British landed in Connecticut, and marched twenty miles into the country, where they burnt the town of Danbury with all the public stores it contained, which were considerable, among which was all the clothing of our regiment. The militia were generally turned out and sent to settle the account with them; the newly enlisted soldiers went with the militia; the enemy had, however, executed his commission, and made considerable progress on his return before we came up. We had some pretty severe scratches with them; killed some, wounded some, and took some prisoners; the remainder reached their shipping, embarked, and cleared out for New-York, where they arrived soon after, (I suppose,) much gratified with the mischief they had done. We likewise returned home, with the loss of three men belonging to the town, one of whom was an enlisted soldier. Major-General David Wooster, of New-Haven, an old and experienced officer, likewise fell in this expedition; Gen. Arnold had a very close rub, but escaped.

Soon after the above transaction, we had orders to join our regiment, (or rather, to begin to assemble the regiment,) at Newtown, the residence of our Colonel. We accordingly marched and arrived there. Here we drew our arms and equipments. Uncle Sam was always careful to supply us with these articles, even if he could not give us any thing to eat, drink or wear. We staid but a short time here, but went on to Danbury, where I had an ample opportunity to see the devastation caused there by the British. The town had been laid in ashes, a number of the inhabitants murdered and cast into their burning houses, because they presumed to defend their persons and property, or to be avenged on a cruel, vindictive invading enemy. I saw the inhabitants, after the fire was out, endeavouring to find the burnt bones of their relatives amongst the rubbish of their demolished houses. The streets, in many places, were literally flooded by the fat which ran from the piles of barrels of pork burnt by the enemy.—They fully executed their design.

We staid here but a short time, and then marched to Peekskill, on the Hudson river, and encamped in the edge of the Highlands, at a place called Old Orchard; here we were tormented by the whip-poor-wills. A potent enemy! says the reader. Well, a potent enemy they were,— particularly to our rest at night;—they would begin their imposing music in the twilight and continue it till ten or eleven o'clock, and commence again before the dawn, when they would be in a continual roar. No man, unless he were stupified, could get a wink of sleep during the serenade, which, in the short nights in the month of May, was almost the whole of the night.

I was one day, while lying here, upon what was called a camp guard;—we kept a considerable chain of sentinels. In the night there came, what in military phrase is called the visiting rounds, which is, an officer attended by a small escort, to inspect the condition of the guards, and see that they do their duty. The officer, at the time I mention, was a field officer, a young man; he went to the extreme end of the line of sentinels and began his examination;—one sentry, he found, who had stowed himself away snugly in an old papermill; another had left his post to procure a draught of milk from the cows in a farmer's yard, and others were found, here and there, neglecting their duty. He brought off all the delinquents to deliver them up to the *righteous* sentence of a court-martial. In his progress he came to me, I being at the time on sentry too. I hailed him and demanded of him the countersign, which he regularly gave me and passed on. I did not expect to hear any thing further about it, as I concluded that I had done my duty to perfection. In the morning, before guard relieving, I happened to be posted at the Colonel's marque-door, when the above-mentioned officer came into the tent, and was telling some of our officers the consequences of his last night's expedition. I listened attentively to his recital. "At last," said he, "I came to a sentinel who challenged me like a man; I thought I had found a soldier after detecting so many scoundrels; but what think ye!—as soon as I had given him the countersign, the puppy shouldered his piece, and had I been an enemy I could have knocked his brains out." At the first part of his recital, I grew a foot, in my own estimation, in a minute, and I shrunk as much, and as fast, at the latter part of it. I was confident he did not know me, and I as well knew it was me he had reference to. Aha! thought I, this admonition shall not lose its effect upon me; nor did it so long as I remained in the army.

I was soon after this transaction, ordered off, in company with about four hundred others of the Connecticut forces, to a set of old barracks, a mile or two distant in the Highlands, to be innoculated with the small pox. We arrived at and cleaned out the barracks, and after two or three days received the infection, which was on the last day of May. We had a guard of Massachusetts troops to attend us. Our hospital stores were deposited in a farmer's barn in the vicinity of our quarters. One day, about noon, the farmer's house took fire and was totally consumed, with every article of household stuff it contained, although there were five hundred men within fifty rods of it, and many of them within five, when the fire was discovered, which was not till the roof had fallen in. Our officers would not let any of the inoculated men go near the fire, and the guard had enough to do to save the barn, the fire frequently catching in the yard and on the roof, which was covered with thatch or straw. I was so near to the house, however, that I saw a cat come out from the cellar window, after the house had apparently fallen into the cellar; she was all in flames when she emerged from her premises and directed her course for the barn, but her nimble gait had so fanned her carcass before she reached the place of her destination that she caused no damage at all.

I had the small pox favorably as did the rest, generally; we lost none; but it was more by good luck, or rather a kind Providence interfering, than by my good conduct that I escaped with life. There was a considerable large rivulet which ran directly in front of the barracks; in this rivulet were many deep places and plenty of a species of fish called suckers. One of my room-mates, with myself, went off one day, the very day on which the pock began to turn upon me, we went up the brook until we were out of sight of the people at the barracks, when we undressed ourselves and went into the water, where it was often to our shoulders, to catch suckers by means of a fish-hook fastened to the end of a rod;—we continued at this business three or four hours, and when we came out of the water the pustules of the small pox were well cleansed. We then returned to the barracks, and I, feeling a pretty sharp appetite after my expedition, went to the side of the brook where the nurses had been cooking and eating their dinners; I found a kettle standing there half full of stewed peas, and, if I remember rightly, a small piece of pork with them. I knew the kettle belonged to the nurses in our room, and therefore conceived myself the better entitled to its contents; accordingly I fell to and helped myself. I believe I should have killed myself in good earnest, had not the owners come and caught me at it, and broke up my feast. It had like to have done the job for me as it was; I had a sorry night of it, and had I not got rid of my freight, I know not what would have been the final consequences of my indiscretion.

I left the hospital on the sixteenth day after I was inoculated, and soon after joined the regiment, when I was attacked with a severe turn of the dysentery, and immediately after recovering from that, I broke out all over with boils; good old Job could scarcely have been worse handled by them than I was;—I had eleven at one time upon my arm, each as big as half a hen's egg, and the rest of my carcass was much in the same condition. I attributed it to my not having been properly physicked after the small pox; in consequence of our hospital stores being in about the same state as the commissary's.

In the latter part of the month of June, or the beginning of July, I was ordered off in a detachment of about a hundred men, under the command of a Captain, to the lines near King's bridge, to join two regiments of New-York troops which belonged to our brigade. Upon the march (which was very fatiguing, it being exceeding hot weather) we halted to rest. I went into a house, hoping to get something to eat, of which I, as usual, stood in much need. The woman of the house had just been churning; I asked her for a drink of buttermilk; she told me to drink as much as I pleased. I drank as much as I could swallow and went out, but soon after returned and drank again; and as we staid here some hours, I improved the time by helping myself to the buttermilk. I could never before relish buttermilk, but extreme hunger at this time gave it a new relish. So true is the observation of the wise man, "A full belly loatheth a honeycomb: but to the hungry soul every bitter thing is sweet." While I was in this house I went into the kitchen where I saw a simple incident which excited my risibility, maugre my fatigue. There was a large pot hanging over a considerable fire, but more smoke; the pot contained, to appearance, a large hock of fresh beef, the water in the pot had ebbed considerably and the meat made its appearance some way above it; upon the top of the meat, surrounded by fire and smoke, sat the old house-cat wreathing her head one way and the other, and twisting the beef into her face as fast as possible, winking and blinking in the steam and smoke like a toad in a shower. I left her at her occupation and went out.

We arrived upon the lines and joined the other corps which was already there. No one who has never been upon such duty as those advanced parties have to perform, can form any adequate idea of the trouble, fatigue and dangers which they have to encounter. Their whole time is spent in marches, (especially night marches,) watching, starving, and, in cold weather, freezing and sickness. If they get any chance to rest, it must be in the woods or fields, under the side of a fence, in an orchard or in any other place but a comfortable one;—lying down on the cold and often wet ground, and, perhaps, before the eyes can be closed with a moment's sleep, alarmed and compelled to stand under arms an hour or two, or to receive an attack from the enemy; and when permitted again to endeavour to rest, called upon immediately to remove some four or five miles to seek some other place, to go through the same manœuvring as before; for it was dangerous to remain any length of time in one place for fear of being informed of by some tory inhabitant, (for there were a plenty of this sort of savage beast during the revolutionary war,) and ten thousand other causes to harrass, fatigue and perplex, which time and room will not permit me to enumerate.

We were once on one of those night marches, advancing toward the enemy and not far from them, when, towards the latter part of the night, there came on a heavy thunder shower; we were ordered into some barns near by, the officers, as usual, ordering themselves into the houses. I thought I might get a nap if it did storm, but hardly had I sunk into a slumber when we were informed that we were discovered by the enemy, and that two or three thousand Hessians were advancing upon, and very near us. We were immediately hurried out, the shower then being at its height, and the night as dark as Egypt, except when it lightened, which, when passed, only served to render it, if possible, still darker; we were then marched across fields and fences, pastures and brooks, swamps and ravines, a distance of two or three miles, and stationed upon a hill, or rather a ledge of rocks, which was as completely fortified by nature with a breastwork of rocks as it could have been by art. Here we waited for Mynheer till the sun was two hours high, but no one coming to visit us, we marched off, and left the enemy to do the same, if they had not already done it.

We remained on this hard and fatiguing duty about six weeks, during which time many things transpired incidental to a military life, but which would be of little interest to the reader, and tedious for me to relate.

We marched to Peekskill and rejoined our regiments sometime in the fore part of the month of August. A short time after my arrival at Peekskill, I was sent off to King's ferry (about five miles below) to take some batteaux that were there and carry them to fort Montgomery, in the edge of the Highlands. While upon this tour of duty, an accident happened to me which caused me much trouble and pain. After we had arrived at the fort with the boats, we tarried an hour or two to rest ourselves, after which we were ordered to take a couple of the boats and return again to King's ferry. Wishing to be the first in the boat, I ran down the wharf, and jumped into it. There happened to be the butt part of an oar lying on the bottom of the boat, and my right foot, on which the whole weight of my body bore, alighted, in my leap, directly upon it, lengthwise; it rolled over and turned my foot almost up to my ankle,—so much so, that my foot lay nearly in a right angle with my leg. I had then to go to the ferry, where I was landed, and having no acquaintance with any of the party, most of whom were New-Yorkers, and consequently, at that time, no great friends to the Yankees, I was obliged to hop on one foot all the way, (upwards of five miles,) not being able in the whole distance to procure a stick to assist me, although I often hobbled to the fences on each side of the road in hopes to obtain one. It was dark when I was landed at the ferry, and it was quite late before I arrived at the camp; some of my messmates went immediately for the Surgeon, but he was at a game of backgammon and could not attend to minor affairs; however, in about an hour he arrived, bathed my foot, which was swelled like a bladder, fumbled about it for sometime, when he gave it a wrench, which made me, like the old woman's dying cat, "merely yawl out." The next day as I was sitting under the shade before my tent, my foot lying upon a bench, swelled like a puff-ball, my Captain passed by and must needs have a peep at it; I indulged his curiosity, upon which he said it was not set right, and taking hold of it, he gave it a twist, which put it nearly in the same condition it was at first. I had then to send for Mr. Surgeon again, but he was not to be found. There was a corporal in our company who professed to act the surgeon in such cases, and he happening at the time to be present, undertook the job and accomplished it, but it was attended with more difficulty than at the first time, and with more pain to me. It was a long time before it got well and strong again, indeed it never has been entirely so well as it was before the accident happened.

I was not long confined by it, however, but was soon able to perform my duty in the army again.

Our troops, not long after this, marched to join the main army in Pennsylvania; the heavy baggage was left to come on after them, and I, being an invalid, was left as one of the guard to conduct it. The baggage soon followed the troops, and I underwent not a little trouble on the march in consequence of my lame foot. When I joined the regiment the baggage was immediately sent back to Bethlehem, nearly fifty miles in the country, and I was again sent with it as a guard. It was much against my inclination to go on this business, for I had for sometime past been under the command of other officers than my own, and now I must continue longer under them. Soldiers always like to be under the command of their own officers; they are generally bad enough, but strangers are worse. I was obliged to obey my officers' orders and go on this duty, but when I was away they could not hinder me from coming back again. I was resolved not to stay at Bethlehem, and as soon as we arrived there I contrived to get the permission of the officers of the guard to return to camp again immediately. I arrived at camp the second day after leaving the baggage. My officers inquired of me why I had returned?—if I was able to do hard duty, they said they were glad that I had joined the company again; if not, they were sorry. I endeavoured to appear to be as well as possible, for I had no notion of being sent away from my officers and old messmates again, if I could avoid it.

When I arrived at camp it was just dark, the troops were all preparing for a march; their provisions (what they had) were all cooked, and their arms and ammunition strictly inspected and all deficiencies supplied. Early in the evening we marched in the direction of Philadelphia; we naturally concluded there was something serious in the wind. We marched slowly all night; in the morning there was a low vapour lying on the land which made it very difficult to distinguish objects at any considerable distance. About daybreak our advanced guard and the British outposts came in contact. The curs began to bark first and then the bull-dogs. Our brigade moved off to the right into the fields. We saw a body of the enemy drawn up behind a rail fence on our right flank; we immediately formed in line and advanced upon them,—our orders were, not to fire till we could see the buttons upon their clothes; but they were so coy that they would not give us an opportunity to be so curious, for they hid their clothes in fire and smoke before we had either time or leisure to examine their buttons. They soon fell back and we advanced, when the action became general. The enemy were driven quite through their camp. They left their kettles, in which they were cooking their breakfasts, on the fires, and some of their garments were lying on the ground, which the owners had not time to put on. Affairs went on well for sometime; the enemy were retreating before us, until the first division that was engaged had expended their ammunition; some of the men unadvisedly calling out that their ammunition was spent, the enemy were so near that they overheard them, when they first made a stand and then returned upon our people, who, for want of ammunition and reinforcements, were obliged in their turn to retreat, which ultimately resulted in the route of the whole army.

There were several other circumstances which contributed to the defeat of our army on that day, but as I am narrating my own adventures, and not a history of the war, I shall omit to mention them. Those who wish to know more, may consult any or all the authors who have given the history of the revolutionary war.

I had now to travel the rest of the day, after marching all the day and night before and fighting all the morning. I had eaten nothing since the noon of the preceding day, nor did I eat a morsel till the forenoon of the next day, and I needed rest as much as victuals. I could have procured that if I had had time to seek it, but victuals was not to be found. I was tormented with thirst all the morning, (fighting being warm work,) but after the retreat commenced I found ample means to satisfy my thirst. "I could drink at the brook," but I could not "bite at the bank."

There was one thing in such cases as I have just mentioned, (I mean, in retreating from an enemy,) that always galled my feelings, and that was, whenever I was forced to a quick retreat to be obliged to run till I was worried down. The Yankees are generally very nimble of foot and in those cases are very apt to practice what they have the ability of performing. Some of our men at this time seemed to think that they could never run fast or far enough. I never wanted to run, if I was forced to run, further than to be beyond the reach of the enemy's shot, after which I had no more fear of their overtaking me than I should have of an army of lobsters doing it, unless it were their horsemen, and they *dared* not do it.

After the army had collected again and recovered from their panic, we were kept marching and countermarching, starving and freezing,— nothing else happening, although that was enough, until we encamped at a place called the White Marsh, about twelve miles to the northward of Philadelphia; while we lay here there was a spell of soft still weather, there not being wind enough for several days to dispel the smoke caused by the fires in camp. My eyes were so affected by it that I was not able to open them for hours together; the ground, which was soft and loamy, was converted into mortar, and so dirty was it, that any hogsty was preferable to our tents to sleep in; and to cap the climax of our misery, we had nothing to eat, nor scarcely any thing to wear. Being pinched with hunger, I one day strolled to a place, where sometime before, some cattle had been slaughtered; here I had the good luck, (or rather bad luck, as it turned out in the end,) to find an ox's milt, which had escaped the hogs and dogs. With this prize I steered off to my tent, threw it upon the fire and broiled it, and then sat down to eat it, without either bread or salt. I had not had it long in my stomach before it began to make strong remonstrances and to manifest a great inclination to be set at liberty again. I was very willing to listen to its requests, and with eyes overflowing with tears, at parting with what I had thought to be a friend, I gave it a discharge. But the very thoughts of it, would for sometime after, almost make me think that I had another milt in my stomach.

About this time information was received at headquarters that a considerable body of British troops were advanced and encamped on the western side of the river Schuylkill, near the lower bridge, two or three miles from Philadelphia. Forces were immediately put in requisition to rout them from thence. Our brigade was ordered off, with some detachments from other parts of the army. We marched from camp just before night, as light troops, light in every thing, especially in eatables. We marched to a place called Barren Hill, about twelve or fifteen miles from the city. From here, about ten o'clock in the evening, we forded the Schuylkill where the river (including a bare gravelly island, or flat, which we crossed) was about forty rods wide, as near as I could judge, and the water about to the waist. It was quite a cool night, in the month of October; the water which spattered on to our clothes, froze as we passed the river. Many of the young and small soldiers fell while in the water, and were completely drenched; we, however, got over and marched two or three miles on a dreary road, (for that part of the country,) surrounded by high hills and thick woods. All of a sudden we were ordered to halt; we were, to appearance, in an unfrequented road, cold and wet to our middles, and half starved: we were sorry to be stopped from travelling, as exercise kept us warm in some degree. We endeavoured to kindle fires, but were ordered by the officers immediately to extinguish them, which was done by all except one, which having been kindled in a hollow tree could not be put out. I got so near to this that I could just see it between the men's legs, which was all the benefit that I derived from it.

We lay here freezing, about two hours, and then were ordered to fall in and march back again. About an hour before day we dashed through the river again, at the same place at which we had crossed the preceding evening, and I can assure the reader, that neither the water nor weather had become one degree warmer than it was then.

We went on to Barren hill again, where we lay all the day, waiting, as it appeared, for reinforcements, which arrived and joined us towards night. We drew a day's ration of beef and flour,—what was called a pound of each; the flour, perhaps, was not far from its nominal weight, but the beef was, as it always was in such cases, and indeed in all others in the army, not more than three fourths of a pound, and that, at the best, half bone. And how was it cooked?—Why, as it usually was when we had no cooking utensils with us,—that is, the flour was laid upon a flat rock and mixed up with cold water, then daubed upon a flat stone and scorched on one side, while the beef was broiling on a stick in the fire. This was the common way of cookery when on marches, and we could get any thing to cook, and this was the mode at the time mentioned. After I had satisfied my hunger, I lay down upon the ground and slept till within about half an hour of sunset. When I awoke I was turned quite about; I thought it was morning instead of evening; however, I was soon convinced of my error, and the sun had the good manners to wheel about and put himself in his proper position again.

Just at dark, the reinforcements having arrived and all things being put in order, we marched again, and about nine or ten o'clock we tried the waters of the Schuylkill once more, at the same place where we crossed the preceding night. It was not so cold as it was then and the crossing was not so tedious, but it was bad enough at this time.

We marched slowly the remainder of the night. At the dawn of day we found ourselves in the neighbourhood of the enemy; I mean, in the neighbourhood of where they *had* been, for when we were about to spring the net, we discovered that the birds had flown, and there was not one on the bed. There was a British guard at a little distance from the bridge, upon the opposite side of the river; they turned out to do us honour and sent off an express to the city, to inform their friends that the Yankees had come to pay them a visit, but they were so unmannerly as to take no notice of us;—after we had taken so much pains and been at so much trouble to come to see them, they might have shown a little more politeness, considering that it would not have cost them half the trouble to meet us as we had been at to meet them. But perhaps they thought, that as we had undergone so much fatigue and vexation on our journey, we might feel cross and peevish, and perchance some unlucky accidents might have happened. The British were politic, and it is good to be cautious and discreet.

We had nothing to do now but to return as we came; accordingly, we marched off slowly, hoping that the enemy would think better of it and follow us, for we were loath to return without seeing them;— however, they kept to themselves and we went on. I was hungry, tired and sleepy;—about noon we halted an hour or two, and I went a little way into the fields, where I found a black walnut tree with a plenty of nuts under it; these nuts are very nutricious, and I cracked and ate of them till I was satisfied.

We marched again. In the course of the afternoon, I somewhere procured about half a dozen turnips, which I carried all the way to camp in my hand; so much did we value any thing that we could get to eat. About sun-setting we again waded the Schuylkill, at a ford a little higher up the river. The river was not so wide here as at the former place, but the water was deeper; it was to the breast. When we had crossed, and it had become dark, we met the Quartermasters, who had come out to meet us with wagons and hogsheads of whiskey! (thinking, perhaps, that we might take cold by being so much exposed in the cold water;) they had better have brought us something more substantial, but we thought that better than nothing. The casks were unheaded, and the Quartermaster-sergeants stood in the wagons and dealt out the liquor to the platoons; each platoon halting as it came up, till served. The intention of the Quartermaster-sergeants was, to give to each man a gill of liquor, but as measuring it out by gills was tedious, it was dealt out to us in pint measures, with directions to divide a pint between four men; but as it was dark and the actions of the men could not be well seen by those who served out the liquor, each one drank as much as he pleased; some, perhaps, half a gill, some a gill, and as many as chose it drained the pint. We again moved on for the camp, distant about five miles. We had not proceeded far before we entered a lane fenced on either side with rails, in which was a water plash, or puddle. The fence was taken down on one side of the road to enable us to pass round the water. It was what is called a five rail fence, only the two upper rails of which were taken out;—here was fun. We had been on the march, since we had drank the whiskey, just long enough for the liquor to assume its height of operation;—our stomachs being empty the whiskey took rank hold, and the poor brain fared accordingly. When the men came to the fence, not being able, many or most of them, to keep a regular balance between head and heels, they would pile themselves up on each side of the fence, swearing and hallooing; some losing their arms, some their hats, some their shoes, and some themselves. Had the enemy come upon us at this time, there would have been an action worth recording; but they did not, and we, that is, such as could, arrived at camp about midnight, where "those who had remained with the stuff" had made up some comfortable fires for our accommodation. Poor fellows! it was all they could do;—as to victuals, they had none for themselves. I had then been nearly thirty hours without a mouthful of any thing to eat, excepting the wallnuts; having been the whole time on my feet (unless I happened to fall over the fence, which I do not remember to have done) and wading in, and being wet with the water of the river. I roasted some of my turnips, ate them, rolled myself up in my innocency, lay down on the leaves and forgot my misery till morning.

Soon after this affair our two Connecticut regiments (they being the only troops of that State then with the main army) were ordered off to defend the forts on the Delaware river, below the city. We marched about dark, hungry and cold, and kept on till we could proceed no further, from sheer hunger and fatigue. We halted about one o'clock at night, in a village, and were put into the houses of the inhabitants, much, I suppose, to their contentment, especially at that time of night. Sleep took such strong hold of me and most of the others, that we soon forgot our wants. Not so with some five or six of our company, who were determined not to die of hunger that night, if any means could be devised to prevent it. They, therefore, as soon as all was still, sallied out on an expedition. They could not find any thing eatable but the contents of a beehive, which they took the liberty to remove from the beehouse to a place which they thought more convenient. I had no hand in the battle and consequently no share in the spoil. One man who belonged to this foraging party had rather an uncouth visage; he had very thick lips, especially the upper one, a large flat nose, and quite a wide mouth, which gave him, as the Irishman said, really an open countenance. One of the inhabitants of the city he had helped to sack, not quite forgetting his resentment for the ill usage he had received from this paragon of beauty and his associates in the outrage, gave him a severe wound directly in the middle of the upper lip, which added very much to its dimensions. In the morning, when we came to march off, Oh! the woful figure the poor fellow exhibited!—a minister in his pulpit would have found it difficult to have kept his risible faculties in due subjection. To see him on the parade endeavouring to conceal his face from the men, and especially from the officers, was ludicrous in the extreme, and as long as it lasted it diverted our thoughts from resting on our own calamities.

We crossed the Delaware, between the town of Bristol, in Pennsylvania, and the city of Burlington, in New-Jersey. We halted for the night at the latter place, where we procured some carrion beef, (for it was no better;) we cooked it and ate some, and carried the remainder away with us. We had always, in the army, to carry our cooking utensils in our hands by turns, and at this time, as we were not overburthened with provisions, our mess had put ours into our kettle, it not being very heavy, as it was made of plated iron. Before noon, I had the carriage of the kettle and its contents, and thinking that I had carried it more than my turn, and the troops just then making a momentary halt, I put the kettle down in the road, telling my messmates that if they would not take their turns at carrying it I would carry it no further. They were cross and refused to take it up; I was as contrary as they were, so we all went on and left it. One of our company in the next platoon, in the rear of us, took it up and brought it on. We marched about half a mile and made another halt, when I turned round and saw the man who had taken care of our kettle, with one or two others helping themselves to the contents of it. I wished the kettle in their throats, but I had nothing to say, it was in part my own fault; my messmates looked rather grum, but had as little to say for themselves as I had. After the men had quieted their appetites one of them very civilly came and gave me up the kettle, but the provisions were mostly absent without leave.

We halted for the night at a village called Haddington; we had nothing to eat, nor should we have had if our kettle had kept us constant company. We were put into the houses for quarters during the night. Myself and about a dozen more of the company were put into a chamber where there was a fireplace but no fire nor any thing to make one with; it looked as if there had been no fire there for seven years; we, however, soon procured wherewithal to make a fire with and were thus enabled to keep the outside comfortable, let the inside do as it would. There was no other furniture in the room excepting an old quill-wheel and an old chair-frame; we procured a thick board and placed the ends upon the wheel and chair and all sat down to regale ourselves with the warmth, when the cat happening to come under the bench to partake of the bounty, the board bending by the weight upon it, both ends slipped off at once and brought us all slap to the floor; upon taking up the board to replace it again we found the poor cat, pressed as flat as a pancake, with her eyes started out two inches from her head. We did not eat her although my appetite was sharp enough to have eaten almost any thing that could be eaten.

After we had got regulated again, we began to contrive how we were to behave in our present circumstances, as it regarded belly-timber;—at length, after several plans had been devised, many "resolves proposed and all refused a passage," it was finally determined that two or three of the most expert at the business should sally forth and endeavour to procure something by foraging. Accordingly two of the club went out and shortly after returned with a Hissian, a cant word with the soldiers, for a goose. The next difficulty was, how to pluck it; we were in a chamber and had nothing to contain the feathers. However, we concluded at last to pick her over the fire and let that take care of the feathers. We dressed her and then divided her amongst us; if I remember rightly, I got *one wing*. Each one broiled his share and ate it, as usual, without bread or salt. After this sumptuous repast, I lay down and slept as well as a gnawing stomach would permit. In the morning we found a sad witness of our overnight's adventure to testify against us; the whole funnel of the chimney was stuck full of feathers from top to bottom, and it being a very calm night the street opposite the house was as full of them as the chimney. We would have set the chimney on fire, but having nothing to do it with, we concluded to let chimney and street unite in their testimony against us if they pleased; but as we marched off early in the morning we heard no more about the goose.

There had been an expedition of the enemy's forces against a fort of ours at a place called Redbank, near this town. Two thousand Germans under the command of Colonel-Commandant Donop, who had begged the favour of the British Commander-in-chief of having the privilege of cutting the throats of about five hundred brave Rhode-Island Yankees, under the command of Colonel Green (uncle to the General of that name) who commanded the garrison there. And here was fought as brilliant an action as was fought during the revolutionary war, considering the numbers engaged, Bunker-hill "to the contrary notwithstanding." Five hundred men defeated two thousand of the enemy, killed and wounded a large number, and mortally wounded and took prisoner their commander. So complete was the discomfiture, that the enemy threw their cannon into a creek that they might have the carriages to carry off their wounded officers on, left their provisions behind and fled for their lives. The loss of the garrison was twenty-four killed and wounded. This action happened on the 22d day of October, 1777.—I could give a full description of it and of the consequences which resulted from it, but that is foreign from my business, as I was not personally engaged in it. But why it has not been more noticed by the historians of the times I cannot tell.

This day we arrived at Woodbury, New-Jersey, which was the end of our present journey. We encamped near the village, planted our artillery in the road at each end of it, placed our guards and prepared to go into fort Mifflin, on Mud-Island. The reason of my referring to the above-mentioned battle, was, that we found several barrels of salted herrings, which the enemy had left in their flight, and as we had but a very small quantity of provisions we were glad to get these. I endeavoured to eat some of them but found them miserable food. They appeared to have been caught soon after the flood, and could neither be broiled nor boiled so as to be made eatable.

Immediately after our arrival at Woodbury, I was ordered upon an advanced guard, about half a mile in advance of a bridge which lay across a large creek, into which the tide flowed. The enemy's shipping lay in the river a little below us. They had also a fortification on the shore opposite to their shipping, at a place called Billingsport. There was a guard of the Jersey militia in advance of us. We used to make excursions in parties of three or four, from our guard, into the neighbourhood of the enemy, and often picked up stragglers from their post and shipping.

I was soon relieved from this guard, and with those who were able, of our two regiments, sent to reinforce those in the fort, which was then besieged by the British. Here I endured hardships sufficient to kill half a dozen horses. Let the reader only consider for a moment and he will be satisfied if not sickened. In the cold month of November, without provisions, without clothing, not a scrap of either shoes or stockings to my feet or legs, and in this condition to endure a siege in such a place as that, was appaling in the highest degree.

In confirmation of what I have here said I will give the reader a short description of the pen that I was confined in; confined I was, for it was next to impossible to have got away from it, if I had been so disposed. Well, the island, as it is called, is nothing more than a mud flat in the Delaware, lying upon the west side of the channel. It is diked around the fort, with sluices so constructed that the fort can be laid under water at pleasure, (at least, it *was* so when I was there, and I presume it has not grown much higher since.) On the eastern side, next the main river, was a zigzag wall built of hewn stone, built, as I was informed, before the revolution at the king's cost. At the southeastern part of the fortification (for fort it could not with propriety be called) was a battery of several long eighteen pounders. At the southwestern angle was another battery with four or five twelve and eighteen pounders and one thirty-two pounder. At the north-western corner was another small battery with three twelve pounders. There were also three block-houses in different parts of the enclosure, but no cannon mounted upon them, nor were they of any use whatever, to us while I was there. On the western side, between the batteries, was a high embankment, within which was a tier of palisadoes. In front of the stone wall, for about half its length, was another embankment, with pallisadoes on the inside of it, and a narrow ditch between them and the stone wall. On the western side of the fortification was a row of barracks, extending from the northern part of the works to about half the length of the fort. On the northern end was another block of barracks which reached nearly across the fort from east to west. In front of these was a large square two story house, for the accommodation of the officers of the garrison; neither this house nor the barracks were of much use at this time, for it was as much as a man's life was worth to enter them, the enemy often directing their shot at them in particular. In front of the barracks and other necessary places, were parades and walks, the rest of the ground was soft mud. I have seen the enemy's shells fall upon it and sink so low that their report could not be heard when they burst, and I could only feel a tremulous motion of the earth at the time. At other times, when they burst near the surface of the ground, they would throw the mud fifty feet in the air.

The British had erected five batteries with six heavy guns in each and a bomb-battery with three long mortars in it on the opposite side of the water, which separated the island from the main on the west, and which was but a short distance across; they had also a battery of six guns a little higher up the river, at a place called the Hospital point. This is a short description of the place which I was destined, with a few others, to defend against whatever force, land or marine, the enemy might see fit to bring against it.

The first attempt the British made against the place after I entered it was by the Augusta, a sixty-four gun ship. While manœuring one dark night she got on the chevaux-de-frise which had been sunk in the channel of the river. As soon as she was discovered in the morning we plied her so well with hot shot, that she was soon in flames. Boats were sent from the shipping below to her assistance, but our shot proving too hot for them, they were obliged to leave her to her fate; in an hour or two she blew up with an explosion which seemed to shake the earth to its centre, leaving a volume of smoke like a thunder cloud, which, as the air was calm, remained an hour or two. A twenty gun ship which had come to the assistance of the Augusta in her distress, shared her fate soon after.

Our batteries were nothing more than old spars and timber laid up in parallel lines and filled between with mud and dirt; the British batteries in the course of the day would nearly level our works; and we were, like the beaver, obliged to repair our dams in the night. During the whole night, at intervals of a quarter or half an hour, the enemy would let off all their pieces, and although we had sentinels to watch them and at every flash of their guns to cry, "a shot," upon hearing which every one endeavoured to take care of himself, yet they would ever and anon, in spite of all our precautions, cut up some of us.

The engineer in the fort was a French officer by the name of Fleury, the same who struck the British flag at the storming of Stony-point. He was a very austere man and kept us constantly employed day and night, there was no chance of escaping from his vigilance.

Between the stone wall and the palisadoes was a kind of yard or pen, at the southern end of which was a narrow entrance not more than eight or ten feet wide, with a ditch about four feet wide in the middle, extending the whole length of the pen. Here, on the eastern side of the wall, was the only place in the fort that any one could be in any degree of safety. Into this place we used to gather the splinters, broken off the palisadoes by the enemy's shot, and make a little fire, just enough to keep from suffering. We would watch an opportunity to escape from the vigilance of Col. Fleury, and run into this place for a minute or two's respite from fatigue and cold. When the engineer found that the workmen began to grow scarce, he would come to the entrance and call us out. He had always his cane in his hand, and woe betided him he could get a stroke at. At his approach I always jumped over the ditch and ran down on the other side, so that he could not reach me; but he often noticed me, and as often threatened me, but threatening was all, he could never get a stroke at me, and I cared but little for his threats.

It was utterly impossible to lie down to get any rest or sleep on account of the mud, if the enemy's shot would have suffered us to do so. Sometimes some of the men, when overcome with fatigue and want of sleep, would slip away into the barracks to catch a nap of sleep, but it seldom happened that they all came out again alive. I was in this place a fortnight, and can say in sincerity that I never lay down to sleep a minute in all that time.

The British knew the situation of the place as well as we did. And as their point blank shot would not reach us behind the wall, they would throw elevated grape-shot from their mortar, and when the sentries had cried, "a shot," and the soldiers, seeing no shot arrive, had become careless, the grape-shot would come down like a shower of hail about our ears.

I will here just mention one thing which will show the apathy of our people at this time. We had, as I mentioned before, a thirty-two pound cannon in the fort, but had not a single shot for it; the British also had one in their battery upon the Hospital-point, which, as I said before, raked the fort; or rather it was so fixed as to rake the parade in front of the barracks, the only place we could pass up and down the fort. The Artillery officers offered a gill of rum for each shot, fired from that piece, which the soldiers would procure. I have seen from twenty to fifty men standing on the parade waiting with impatience the coming of the shot, which would often be seized before its motion had fully ceased and conveyed off to our gun to be sent back again to its former owners. When the lucky fellow who had caught it had swallowed his rum, he would return to wait for another, exulting that he had been more lucky or more dexterous than his fellows.

What little provisions we had was cooked by the invalids in our camp and brought to the island in old flour barrels; it was mostly corned beef and hard bread, but it was not much trouble to cook or fetch what we had.

We continued here suffering cold, hunger and other miseries, till the fourteenth day of November; on that day, at the dawn, we discovered six ships of the line, all sixty-fours, a frigate of thirty-six guns and a gally in a line just below the Chevaux-de-frise; a twenty-four gun ship, (being an old ship cut down,) her guns said to be all brass twenty-four pounders, and a sloop of six guns in company with her, both within pistol shot of the fort, on the western side. We immediately opened our batteries upon them, but they appeared to take very little notice of us; we heated some shot, but by mistake twenty-four pound shot were heated instead of eighteen, which was the calibre of the guns in that part of the fort. The enemy soon began their firing upon us, and there was music indeed. The soldiers were all ordered to take their posts at the palisadoes, which they were ordered to defend to the last extremity, as it was expected the British would land under the fire of their cannon and attempt to storm the fort. The cannonade was severe, as well it might be, six sixty-four gun ships, a thirty-six gun frigate, a twenty-four gun ship, a gally and a sloop of six guns, together with six batteries of six guns each and a bomb-battery of three mortars, all playing at once upon our poor little fort, if fort it might be called.

Some of our officers endeavoured to ascertain how many guns were fired in a minute by the enemy, but it was impossible, the fire was incessant. In the height of the cannonade it was desirable to hoist a signal flag for some of our gallies, that were lying above us, to come down to our assistance. The officers inquired who would undertake it; as none appeared willing for some time, I was about to offer my services; I considered it no more exposure of my life than it was to remain where I was; the flagstaff was of easy ascent, being an old ship's mast, having shrouds to the ground, and the round top still remaining. While I was still hesitating, a sergeant of the Artillery offered himself; he accordingly ascended to the round top, pulled down the flag to affix the signal flag to the halyard, upon which the enemy, thinking we had struck, ceased firing in every direction and cheered. "Up with the flag!" was the cry of our officers in every part of the fort. The flags were accordingly hoisted, and the firing was immediately renewed. The sergeant then came down and had not gone half a rod from the foot of the staff, when he was cut in two by a cannon shot. This caused me some serious reflections at the time. He was killed! had I been at the same business I might have been killed; but it might have been otherwise ordered by Divine Providence,—we might have both lived,—I am not predestinarian enough to determine it. The enemy's shot cut us up; I saw five Artillerists belonging to one gun, cut down by a single shot, and I saw men who were stooping to be protected by the works, but not stooping low enough, split like fish to be broiled.

About the middle of the day some of our gallies and floating batteries, with a frigate, fell down and engaged the British with their long guns, which in some measure took off the enemy's fire from the fort. The cannonade continued without interruption on the side of the British throughout the day. Nearly every gun in the fort was silenced by mid-day. Our men were cut up like cornstalks; I do not know the exact number of the killed and wounded but can say it was not small, considering the numbers in the fort, which were only the able part of the fourth and eighth Connecticut regiments, with a company or two of Arillery, perhaps less than five hundred in all.

The cannonade continued, directed mostly at the fort, till the dusk of the evening. As soon as it was dark we began to make preparations for evacuating the fort and endeavouring to escape to the Jersey shore. When the firing had in some measure subsided and I could look about me, I found the fort exhibited a picture of desolation; the whole area of the fort was as completely ploughed as a field. The buildings of every kind hanging in broken fragments, and the guns all dismounted, and how many of the garrison sent to the world of spirits, I knew not. If ever destruction was complete, it was here. The surviving part of the garrison were now drawn off and such of the stores as could conveniently be taken away were carried to the Jersey shore. I happened to be left with a party of seventy or eighty men to destroy and burn all that was left in the place. I was in the northwest battery just after dark, when the enemy were hauling their shipping, on that side, higher up to a more commanding position; they were so nigh that I could hear distinctly what they said on board the sloop. One expression of theirs I well remember,—"We will give it to the d—d rebels in the morning." The thought that then occupied my mind I as well remember, 'The d—d rebels will show you a trick which the devil never will, they will go off and leave you.' After the troops had left the fort and were embarking at the wharf, I went to the waterside to find one of my messmates to whom I had lent my canteen in the morning, as there were three or four hogsheads of rum in the fort, the heads of which we were about to knock in, and I was desirous to save a trifle of their contents; there being nothing to eat I thought I might have something to drink. I found him, indeed, but lying in a long line of dead men who had been brought out of the fort to be conveyed to the main, to have the last honours conferred upon them which it was in our power to give. Poor young man! he was the most intimate associate I had in the army, but he was gone, with many more as deserving of regard as himself.

I returned directly back into the fort to my party and proceeded to set fire to every thing that would burn, and then repaired immediately to the wharf where three batteaux were waiting to convey us across the river. And now came on another trial. Before we could embark the buildings in the fort were completely in flames, and they threw such a light upon the water that we were as plainly seen by the British as though it had been broad day. Almost their whole fire was directed at us; sometimes our boat seemed to be almost thrown out of the water, and at length a shot took the sternpost out of the rear boat. We had then to stop and take the men from the crippled boat into the other two; and now the shot and water flew merrily; but by the assistance of a kind Providence we escaped without any further injury and landed, a little after midnight, on the Jersey shore.

We marched a little back into some pitch-pine woods, where we found the rest of the troops that had arrived before us. They had made up some comfortable fires and were enjoying the warmth, and that was all the comfort they had to partake of, (except rest,) for victuals was out of the question. I wrapt myself up in my blanket and lay down upon the leaves and soon fell asleep, and continued so till past noon, when I awoke from the first sound sleep I had had for a fortnight. Indeed, I had not laid down in all that time. The little sleep I had obtained was in cat-naps, sitting up and leaning against the wall; and I thought myself fortunate if I could do that much. When I awoke I was as crazy as a goose shot through the head.

We left our flag flying when we left the island, and the enemy did not take possession of the fort till late in the morning after we left it.

We left one man in the fort who had taken too large a dose of "the good creature." He was a deserter from the German forces in the British service. The British took him to Philadelphia, where (not being known by them) he engaged again in their service—received two or three guineas bounty, drew a British uniform, and came back to us again at the Valley Forge. So they did not make themselves independent fortunes by the capture of him.

Here ends the account of as hard and fatiguing a job, for the time it lasted, as occurred during the revolutionary war. Thomas Paine, in one of his political essays, speaking of the siege and defence of this post, says, "they had nothing but their bravery and good conduct to cover them." He spoke the truth. I was at the siege and capture of lord Cornwallis, and the hardships of that were no more to be compared with this, than the sting of a bee is to the bite of a rattlesnake. But there has been but little notice taken of it; the reason of which is, there was no Washington, Putnam, or Wayne there. Had there been, the affair would have been extolled to the skies. No, it was only a few officers and soldiers who accomplished it in a remote quarter of the army. Such circumstances and such troops generally get but little notice taken of them, do what they will. Great men get great praise, little men, nothing. But it always was so and always will be;—said the officers in king David's army, when going out against rebel Absolem, "thou shalt not go out with us—for if half of us die they will not care for us. But now thou art worth ten thousand of us." And this has been the burden of the song ever since, and I presume ever will be.

We now prepared to leave Redbank. I was ordered on a baggage guard; it was not disagreeable to me as I had a chance to ride in a wagon a considerable part of the night. We went in advance of the troops, which made it much easier getting along. We had been encouraged during the whole siege with the promise of relief. "Stand it out a little longer and we shall be relieved," had been the constant cry. The second day of our march we met two Regiments advancing to relieve us. When asked where they were going, they said, to relieve the garrison in the fort. We informed them that the British had done that already.

Our guard passed through Haddington in the night; heard nothing of the goose or murdered cat. We arrived early in the morning, at a pretty village called Milltown or Mount-holly. Here we waited for the troops to come up. I was as near starved with hunger, as ever I wish to be. I strolled into a large yard where was several saw mills and a grist mill, I went into the latter, thinking it probable that the dust made there was more palatable than that made in the former, but I found nothing there to satisfy my hunger. But there was a barrel standing behind the door with some salt in it. Salt was as valuable as gold with the soldiers. I filled my pocket with it and went out. In the yard and about it was a plenty of geese, turkeys, ducks, and barn-door fowls; I obtained a piece of an ear of Indian corn, and seating myself on a pile of boards began throwing the corn to the fowls which soon drew a fine battalion of them about me, I might have taken as many as I pleased, but I took up one only, wrung off its head, dressed and washed it in the stream, seasoned it with some of my salt, and stalked into the first house that fell in my way, invited myself into the kitchen, took down the gridiron and put my fowl to cooking upon the coals. The women of the house were all the time going and coming to and from the room; they looked at me but said nothing.—"They asked me no questions and I told them no lies." When my game was sufficiently broiled, I took it by the *hind* leg and made my exit from the house with as little ceremony as I had made my entrance. When I got into the street I devoured it after a *very* short grace and felt as refreshed as the old Indian did when he had eaten his crow roasted in the ashes with the feathers and entrails.

We marched from hence and crossed the Delaware again between Burlington and Bristol. Here we procured a day's ration of southern salt pork (three-fourths of a pound) and a pound of sea bread. We marched a little distance and stopped "to refresh ourselves;" we kindled some fires in the road, and some broiled their meat; as for myself I ate mine raw. We quickly started on and marched till evening, when we went into a wood for the night. We did not pitch our tents; and about midnight it began to rain very hard which soon put out all our fires, and we had to lie "and weather it out." The troops marched again before day; I had sadly sprained my ankle the day before, and it was much swelled. My lieutenant told me to stay where I was till day and then come on. Just as I was about to start off, our Brigadier-General and suite passed by and seeing me there alone, stopped his horse and asked me what I did there, I told him that Lieut. S—— ordered me to remain there till daylight. Says he, Lieut. S—— deserves to have his throat cut, and then went on. I had finished my pork and bread for supper, consequently had nothing for this day. I hobbled on as well as I could; the rain and travelling of the troops and baggage had converted the road into perfect mortar and it was extremely difficult for me to make headway. I worried on however till some time in the afternoon when I went into a house, where I procured a piece of a buckwheat slapjack. With this little refreshment I proceeded on and just before night overtook the troops. We continued our march until some time after dark, when we arrived in the vicinity of the main army. We again turned into a wood for the night; the leaves and ground were as wet as water could make them; it was then foggy, and the water dropping from the trees like a shower. We endeavoured to get fire by flashing powder on the leaves, but this and every other expedient that we could employ, failing, we were forced by our old master, Necessity, to lay down and sleep if we could, with three others of our constant companions, Fatigue, Hunger and Cold.

Next morning we joined the grand army near Philadelphia, and the heavy baggage being sent back to the rear of the army, we were obliged to put us up huts by laying up poles and covering them with leaves; a capital shelter from winter storms. Here we continued to fast; indeed we kept a continual lent as faithfully as ever any of the most rigorous of the Roman Catholics did. But there was this exception, we had no fish or eggs or any other substitute for our commons. Ours was a real fast, and depend upon it, we were sufficiently mortified.

About this time the whole British army left the city, came out, and encamped, or rather lay, on Chesnut-hill in our immediate neighbourhood; we hourly expected an attack from them; we had a commanding position and were very sensible of it. We were kept constantly on the alert, and wished nothing more than to have them engage us, for we were sure of giving them a drubbing, being in excellent fighting trim, as we were starved and as cross and illnatured as curs. The British, however, thought better of the matter, and after several days manœuvering on the hill, very civilly walked off into Philadelphia again.

Starvation seemed to be entailed upon the army and every animal connected with it. The oxen, brought from New-England for draught, all died, and the southern horses fared no better; even the wild animals that had any concern with us, suffered. A poor little squirrel who had the ill luck to get cut off from the woods and fixing himself on a tree standing alone and surrounded by several of the soldier's huts, sat upon the tree till he starved to death and fell off the tree. He, however, got rid of his misery soon. He did not live to starve by piecemeal six or seven years.

While we lay here, there happened very remarkable northern lights. At one time the whole visible heavens appeared, for some time, as if covered with crimson velvet. Some of the soldiers prognosticated a bloody battle about to be fought, but time, which always speaks the truth, proved them to be false prophets.

Soon after the British had quit their position on Chesnut-hill, we left this place, and after marching and countermarching back and forward some days, we crossed the Schuylkill in a cold rainy and snowy night, upon a bridge of wagons set end to end, and joined together by boards and planks; and after a few days more manœuvering, we at last settled down at a place called "the Gulf," (so named on account of a remarkable chasm in the hills;) and here we encamped some time, and here we had liked to have encamped forever—for starvation here *rioted* in its glory. But, lest the reader should be disgusted at hearing so much said about "starvation," I will give him something that, perhaps, may in some measure alleviate his ill humour.

While we lay here there was a Continental thanksgiving ordered by Congress; and as the army had all the cause in the world to be particularly thankful, if not for being well off, at least, that it was no worse, we were ordered to participate in it. We had nothing to eat for two or three days previous, except what the trees of the fields and forests afforded us. But we must now have what Congress said—a sumptuous thanksgiving to close the year of high living, we had now nearly seen brought to a close. Well—to add something extraordinary to our present stock of provisions, our country, ever mindful of its suffering army, opened her sympathizing heart so wide, upon this occasion, as to give us something to make the world stare. And what do you think it was, reader?—Guess.—You cannot guess, be you as much of a Yankee as you will. I will tell you: it gave each and every man *half* a *gill* of rice, and a *table spoon full* of vinegar!! After we had made sure of this extraordinary superabundant donation, we were ordered out to attend a meeting, and hear a sermon delivered upon the happy occasion. We accordingly went, for we could not help it. I heard a sermon, a "thanksgiving sermon," what sort of one I do not know now, nor did I at the time I heard it, I had something else to think upon, my belly put me in remembrance of the fine thanksgiving dinner I was to partake of when I—could get it—I remember the text, like an attentive lad at church, I can *still* remember that, it was this, "And the soldiers said unto him, And what shall we do? And he said unto them, Do violence to no man, nor accuse any one falsely." The Preacher ought to have added the remainder of the sentence to have made it complete; "And be content with your wages." But that would not do, it would be too appropos; however, he heard it as soon as the service was over, it was shouted from a hundred tongues. Well—we had got through the services of the day and had nothing to do but to return in good order to our tents and fare as we could. As we returned to our camp, we passed by our Commissary's quarters, all his stores, consisting of a barrel about two thirds full of hocks of fresh beef, stood directly in our way, but there was a sentinel guarding even that; however, one of my messmates purloined a piece of it, four or five pounds perhaps. I was exceeding glad to see him take it, I thought it might help to eke out our thanksgiving supper; but, alas! how soon my expectations were blasted!—The sentinel saw him have it as soon as I did and obliged him to return it to the barrel again. So I had nothing else to do but to go home and make out my supper as usual, upon a leg of nothing and no turnips.

The army was now not only starved but naked; the greatest part were not only shirtless and barefoot, but destitute of all other clothing, especially blankets. I procured a small piece of raw cowhide and made myself a pair of moccasons, which kept my feet (while they lasted) from the frozen ground, although, as I well remember, the hard edges so galled my ancles, while on a march, that it was with much difficulty and pain that I could wear them afterwards; but the only alternative I had, was to endure this inconvenience or to go barefoot, as hundreds of my companions had to, till they might be tracked by their blood upon the rough frozen ground. But hunger, nakedness and sore shins were not the only difficulties we had at that time to encounter;—we had hard duty to perform and little or no strength to perform it with.

The army continued at and near the Gulf for some days, after which we marched for the Valley Forge in order to take up our winter-quarters. We were now in a truly forlorn condition,—no clothing, no provisions and as disheartened as need be. We arrived, however, at our destination a few days before christmas. Our prospect was indeed dreary. In our miserable condition, to go into the wild woods and build us habitations to *stay* (not to *live*) in, in such a weak, starved and naked condition, was appaling in the highest degree, especially to New-Englanders, unaccustomed to such kind of hardships at home. However, there was no remedy,—no alternative but this or dispersion;—but dispersion, I believe, was not thought of,—at least, I did not think of it,—we had engaged in the defence of our injured country and were willing, nay, we were determined to persevere as long as such hardships were not altogether intolerable. I had experienced what I thought sufficient of the hardships of a military life the year before (although nothing in comparison to what I had suffered the present campaign) and therefore expected to meet with rubbers. But we were now absolutely in danger of perishing, and that too, in the midst of a plentiful country. We then had but little, and often nothing to eat for days together; but now we had nothing and saw no likelihood of any betterment of our condition. Had there fallen deep snows (and it was the time of year to expect them) or even heavy and long rain-storms, the whole army must inevitably have perished. Or had the enemy, strong and well provided as he then was, thought fit to pursue us, our poor emaciated carcases must have "strewed the plain." But a kind and holy Providence took more notice and better care of us than did the country in whose service we were wearing away our lives by piecemeal.

We arrived at the Valley Forge in the evening; it was dark; there was no water to be found, and I was perishing with thirst. I searched for water till I was weary, and came to my tent without finding any;—fatigue and thirst, joined with hunger, almost made me desperate. I felt at that instant as if I would have taken victuals or drink from the best friend I had on earth by force. I am not writing fiction, all are sober realities. Just after I arrived at my tent, two soldiers, whom I did not know, passed by; they had some water in their canteens which they told me they had found a good distance off, but could not direct me to the place as it was very dark. I tried to beg a draught of water from them but they were as rigid as Arabs. At length I persuaded them to sell me a drink for three pence, Pennsylvania currency, which was every cent of property I could then call my own; so great was the necessity I was then reduced to.

I lay here two nights and one day, and had not a morsel of any thing to eat all the time, save half of a small pumpkin, which I cooked by placing it upon a rock, the skin side uppermost, and making a fire upon it; by the time it was heat through I devoured it with as keen an appetite as I should a pie made of it at some other time. The second evening after our arrival here I was warned to be ready for a two days command. I never heard a summons to duty with so much disgust before or since, as I did that; how I could endure two days more fatigue without nourishment of some sort I could not tell, for I heard nothing said about "provisions." However, in the morning at roll-call, I was obliged to comply. I went to the parade where I found a considerable number, ordered upon the same business, whatever it was. We were ordered to go to the Quartermaster-General and receive from him our final orders. We accordingly repaired to his quarters, which was about three miles from camp; here we understood that our destiny was to go into the country on a foraging expedition, which was nothing more nor less than to procure provisions from the inhabitants for the men in the army and forage for the poor perishing cattle belonging to it, at the point of the bayonet. We staid at the Quartermaster-General's quarters till some time in the afternoon, during which time a beef creature was butchered for us; I well remember what fine stuff it was, it was quite transparent, I thought at the time what an excellent lantern it would make. I was, notwithstanding, very glad to get some of it, bad as it looked. We got, I think, two days allowance of it, and some sort of bread kind, I suppose, for I do not remember particularly about that, but it is probable we did. We were then divided into several parties and sent off upon our expedition. Our party consisted of a Lieutenant, a Sergeant, a Corporal and eighteen privates. We marched till night when we halted and took up our quarters at a large farm-house. The Lieutenant, attended by his waiter, took up his quarters for the night in the hall with the people of the house, we were put into the kitchen; we had a snug room and a comfortable fire, and we began to think about cooking some of our *fat* beef; one of the men proposed to the landlady to sell her a shirt for some sauce; she very readily took the shirt, which was worth a dollar at least,—she might have given us a mess of sauce, for I think she would not have suffered poverty by so doing, as she seemed to have a a plenty of *all* things. After we had received the sauce, we went to work to cook our suppers. By the time it was eatable the family had gone to rest; we saw where the woman went into the cellar, and, she having left us a candle, we took it into our heads that a little good cider would not make our supper relish any the worse; so some of the men took the water pail and drew it full of excellent cider, which did not fail to raise our spirits considerably. Before we lay down the man who sold the shirt, having observed that the landlady had flung it into a closet, took a notion to repossess it again. We marched off early in the morning before the people of the house were stirring, consequently did not know or see the woman's chagrin at having been overreached by the soldiers.

This day we arrived at Milltown, or Downingstown, a small village half way between Philadelphia and Lancaster, which was to be our quarters for the winter. It was dark when we had finished our day's march. There was a commissary and a wagon-master-general stationed here, the commissary to take into custody the provisions and forage that we collected, and the wagon-master-general to regulate the conduct of the wagoners and direct their motions. The next day after our arrival at this place we were put into a small house in which was only one room, in the centre of the village. We were immediately furnished with rations of good and wholesome beef and flour, built us up some births to sleep in, and filled them with straw, and felt as happy as any other pigs that were no better off than ourselves. And now having got into winter-quarters, and ready to commence our foraging business, I shall here end my account of my second campaign.

Chapter IV. Campaign of 1778.

> A serene and cloudless atmosphere
> Betokens that a storm is near;
> So when dame Fortune proves most kind,—
> Be sure, Miss-Fortune's close behind.

As there was no cessation of duty in the army, I must commence another campaign as soon as the succeeding one is ended. There was no going home and spending the winter season among friends, and procuring a new recruit of strength and spirits. No—it was one constant drill, summer and winter, like an old horse in a mill, it was a continual routine.

The first expedition I undertook in my new vocation, was a foraging cruise. I was ordered off into the country in a party consisting of a corporal and six men. What our success was I do not now remember; but I well remember the transactions of the party in the latter part of the journey. We were returning to our quarters on christmas afternoon, when we met three ladies, one a young married woman with an infant in her arms, the other two were maidens, for aught I knew then or since, they passed for such. They were all comely, particularly one of them; she was handsome. They immediately fell into familiar discourse with us—were very inquisitive like the rest of the sex;—asked us a thousand questions respecting our business, where we had been and where going, &c. After we had satisfied their curiosity, or at least had endeavored to do so, they told us that they (that is, the two youngest) lived a little way on our road in a house which they described: desired us to call in and rest ourselves a few minutes, and said they would return as soon as they had seen their sister and babe safe home.

As for myself, I was very unwell, occasioned by a violent cold I had recently taken, and I was very glad to stop a short time to rest my bones. Accordingly, we stopped at the house described by the young ladies, and in a few minutes they returned as full of chat as they were when we met them in the road. After a little more information respecting our business, they proposed to us to visit one of their neighbours, against whom it seemed they had a grudge, and upon whom they wished to wreak their vengeance through our agency. To oblige the ladies we undertook to obey their injunctions. They very readily agreed to be our guides as the way lay across fields and pastures full of bushes. The distance was about half a mile and directly out of our way to our quarters. The girls went with us until we came in sight of the house. We concluded we could do no less than fulfil our engagements with them, so we went into the house, the people of which, appeared to be genuine Pennsylvania farmers, and very fine folks. We all now began to relent, and after telling them our business, we concluded that if they would give us a canteen (which held about a quart) full of whiskey and some bread and cheese, we would depart without any further exactions. To get rid of us, doubtless, the man of the house gave us our canteen of whiskey, and the good woman gave us a fine loaf of wheaten flour bread and the whole of a small cheese, and we raised the seige and departed. I was several times afterwards at this house, and was always well treated. I believe the people did not recollect me, and I was glad they did not; for when I saw them I had always a twinge or two of conscience for thus dissembling with them at the instigation of persons who certainly were no better than they should be, or they would not have employed strangers to glut their vengeance upon innocent people; innocent at least as it respected us. But after all, it turned much in their favour. It was in our power to take cattle or horses, hay, or any other produce from them; but we felt that we had done wrong in listening to the tattle of malicious neighbours, and for that cause we refrained from meddling with any property of theirs ever after. So that good came to them out of intended evil.

After we had received our bread, cheese and whiskey, we struck across the fields into the highway again. It was now nearly sunset, and as soon as we had got into the road, the youngest of the girls, and handsomest and chattiest, overtook us again, riding on horseback with a gallant. As soon as she came up with us, "O here is my little Captain again," said she; (it appeared it was our corporal that attracted her attention,) "I am glad to see you again." The young man, her sweetheart, did not seem to wish her to be quite so familiar with her "little Captain," and urged on his horse as fast as possible. But female policy is generally too subtle for the male's, and she exhibited a proof of it, for they had scarcely passed us when she slid from the horse upon her feet, into the road, with a shriek as though some frightful accident had happened to her. There was nothing handy to serve as a horseblock, so the "little Captain" must take her in his arms and set her upon her horse again, much, I suppose, to their mutual satisfaction,—but not so to her gallant, who, as I thought, looked rather grum.

We had now five miles to travel to reach our quarters, and I was sick indeed, but we got to our home some time in the evening, and I soon went to sleep;—in the morning I was better.

When I was inoculated with the small pox I took that delectable disease the itch, it was given us, we supposed, in the infection. We had no opportunity, or at least, we had nothing to cure ourselves with during the whole season; all who had the small pox at Peekskill had it. We often applied to our officers for assistance to clear ourselves from it, but all we could get, was, "Bear it as patiently as you can, when we get into winter-quarters you will have leisure and means to rid yourselves of it." I had it to such a degree that by the time I got into winter-quarters I could scarcely lift my hands to my head.—Some of our foraging party had acquaintances in the Artillery and by their means we procured sulphur enough to cure all that belonged to our detachment. Accordingly, we made preparations for a general attack upon it. The first night one half of the party commenced the action by mixing a sufficient quantity of brimstone and tallow, which was the only grease we could get, at the same time not forgetting to mix a plenty of hot whiskey-toddy, making up a hot blazing fire and laying down an ox-hide upon the hearth. Thus prepared with arms and ammunition, we began the operation by plying each other's outsides with brimstone and tallow and the inside with hot whiskey sling. Had the animalcule of the itch been endowed with reason they would have quit their entrenchments and taken care of themselves, when we had made such a formidable attack upon them; but as it was we had to engage, arms in hand, and we obtained a complete victory, though it had like to have cost some of us our lives;—two of the assailants were so overcome, not by the enemy, but by their too great exertions in the action, that they lay all night naked upon the field; the rest of us got to our births somehow, as well as we could, but we killed the itch and we were satisfied, for it had almost killed us. This was a decisive victory, the only one we had achieved lately. The next night the other half of our men took their turn, but, taking warning by our mishaps, they conducted their part of the battle with comparatively little trouble or danger to what we had experienced on our part.

I shall not relate all the minute transactions which passed while I was on this foraging party, as it would swell my narrative to too large a size; I will, however, give the reader a brief account of some of my movements that I may not leave him entirely ignorant how I spent my time. We fared much better than I had ever done in the army before, or ever did afterwards. We had very good provisions all winter and generally enough of them. Some of us were constantly in the country with the wagons, we went out by turns and had no one to control us; our Lieutenant scarcely ever saw us or we him; our sergeant never went out with us once, all the time we were there, nor our corporal *but* once, and that was when he was the "little Captain." When we were in the country we were pretty sure to fare well, for the inhabitants were remarkably kind to us. We had no guards to keep, our only duty was to help load the wagons with hay, corn, meal or whatever they were to take off, and when they were thus loaded, to keep them company till they arrived at the commissary's, at Milltown, from thence the articles, whatever they were, were carried to camp in other vehicles, under other guards. I do not remember that during the time I was employed in this business, which was from christmas to the latter part of April, ever to have met with the least resistance from the inhabitants, take what we would from their barns, mills, corncribs, or stalls; but when we came to their stables, then look out for the women; take what horse you would, it was one or the other's "pony" and they had no other to ride to church; and when we had got possession of a horse we were sure to have half a dozen or more women pressing upon us, until by some means or other, if possible, they would slip the bridle from the horse's head, and then we might catch him again if we could. They would take no more notice of a charged bayonet than a blind horse would of a cocked pistol; it would answer no purpose to threaten to kill them with the bayonet or musket, they knew as well as we did that we would not put our threats in execution, and when they had thus liberated a horse (which happened but seldom) they would laugh at us and ask us why we did not do as we threatened, kill them, and then they would generally ask us into their houses and treat us with as much kindness as though nothing had happened. The women of Pennsylvania, taken in general, are certainly very worthy characters; it is but justice, as far as I am concerned, for me to say, that I was always well treated both by them and the men, especially the Friends or Quakers, in every part of the State through which I passed, and that was the greater part of what was then inhabited. But the southern ladies had a queer idea of the Yankees, (as they always called the New-Englanders,) they seemed to think that they were a people quite different from themselves, as indeed they were in many respects; I could mention many things and ways in which they differed, but it is of no consequence; they were clever and that is sufficient. I will however mention one little incident, just to show what their conceptions were of us.

I happened once to be with some wagons, one of which was detached from the party. I went with this team as its guard; we stopped at a house the mistress of which and the wagoner were acquainted. (These foraging temas all belonged in the neighbourhood of our quarters.) She had a pretty little female child about four years old. The teamster was praising the child, extolling its gentleness and quietness, when the mother observed that it had been quite cross and crying all day, "I have been threatening," said she, "to give her to the Yankees." "Take care," said the wagoner, "how you speak of the Yankees, I have one of them here with me." "La!" said the woman, "is he a Yankee? I thought he was a Pennsylvanian;—I don't see any difference between him and other people."

I have before said that I should not narrate all the little affairs which transpired while I was on this foraging party. But if I pass them all over in silence the reader may perhaps think that I had nothing to do all winter, or at least, that I *did* nothing, when in truth it was quite the reverse. Our duty was hard, but generally not altogether unpleasant;—I had to travel far and near, in cold and in storms, by day and by night, and at all times to run the *risk* of abuse, if not of injury, from the inhabitants, when *plundering* them of their property, (for I could not, while in the very act of taking their cattle, hay, corn and grain from them against their wills, consider it a whit better than plundering,— sheer privateering.) But I will give them the credit of never receiving the least abuse or injury from an individual during the whole time I was employed in this business. I doubt whether the people of New-England would have borne it as patiently, their "steady habits" to the contrary notwithstanding.

Being once in a party among the Welch mountains, there came on a tedious rain-storm which continued three or four days. I happened to be at a farmer's house with one or two of the wagon-masters;—the man of the house was from home and the old lady rather crabbed; she knew our business and was therefore inclined to be *rather* unsociable. The first day she would not give us any thing to eat but some scraps of cold victuals, the second day she grew a little more condescending, and on the third day she boiled a potfull of good beef, pork and sour crout for us.—"Never mind," said one of the wagon-masters to me, "mother comes on, she will give us roasted turkies directly." There was a little negro boy belonging to the house, about five or six years of age, who, the whole time I was there, sat upon a stool in the chimney-corner; indeed, he looked as if he had sat there ever since he was born. One of the wagon-masters said to the landlady one day, "Mother, is that your son that sits in the corner?" "My son!" said she, "why, don't you see he is a negro?" "A negro! is he?" said the man, "why I really thought he was your son, only that he had sat there until he was smoke-dried."

While the storm continued, to pass our time, several of our party went to a tavern in the neighbourhood. We here gambled a little for some liquor, by throwing a small dart or stick, armed at one end with a pin, at a mark on the ceiling of the room; while I was at this amusement I found that the landlord and I bore the same name, and upon further discourse I found that he had a son about my age, whose given name was the same as mine. This son was taken prisoner at fort Lee, on the Hudson river, in the year 1776, and died on his way home. These good people were almost willing to pursuade themselves that I was their son. There were two very pretty girls, sisters to the deceased young man, who seemed wonderfully taken up with me, called me "brother," and I fared none the worse for my name. I used often, afterwards, in my cruises to that part of the State, to call in as I passed, and was always well treated by the whole family. The landlord used to fill my canteen with whiskey, or peach or cider brandy to enable me, as he said, to climb the Welch mountains. I always went there with pleasure and left with regret. I often wished afterwards that I could find more namesakes.

I was sent one day, with another man of our party, to drive some cattle to the Quartermaster-General's quarters. It was dark when we arrived there. After we had delivered the cattle, an officer belonging to the Quartermaster-General's department asked me if I had a canteen. I answered in the negative, (I had left mine at my quarters.) "A soldier," said he "should always have a canteen," and I was sorry that I was just then deficient of that article, for he gave us a half pint tumbler full of genuine old Jamaica spirits, which was, like Boniface's ale, "as smooth as oil." It was too late to return to our quarters that night, so we concluded to go to camp, about three miles distant, and see our old messmates. Our stomachs being empty, the spirits began to take hold of both belly and brains. I soon became very faint, but, as good luck would have it, my companion happened to have a part of a dried neat's tongue, which he had plundered somewhere in his travels. We fell to work upon that and soon demolished it, which refreshed us much and enabled us to reach camp without suffering shipwreck. There was nothing to be had at camp but a little rest and that was all we asked. In the morning it was necessary to have a pass from the commander of the regiment, to enable us to pass the guards on our return to our quarters in the country. My Captain gave me one, and then it must be countersigned by the Colonel. When I entered the Colonel's hut,— "Where have you been" (calling me by name) "this winter," said he, "why, you are as fat as a pig." I told him I had been foraging in the country. "I think," said he, "you have taken care of yourself; I believe we must keep you here and send another man in your stead, that he may recruit himself a little." I told him that I was sent to camp on *particular* business and with strict orders to return, and that no one else could do so well. Finally, he signed my pass, and I soon hunted up the other man when we left the camp in as great a hurry as though the plague had been there.

But the time at length came when we were obliged to go to camp for good and all, whether we chose it or not. An order from headquarters required all stationed parties and guards to be relieved, that all who had not had the small pox might have an opportunity to have it before the warm weather came on. Accordingly, about the last of April we were relieved by a party of southern troops. The Commissary, who was a native of Connecticut, although at the commencement of the war he resided in Philadelphia, told us that he was sorry we were going away, for, said he, "I do not much like these men with one eye, (alluding to their practice of gouging,) I am acquainted with you, and if any men are wanted here I should prefer those from my own section of the country to entire strangers." Although we would have very willingly obliged him with our company, yet it could not be so, we must go to camp at all events. We accordingly marched off and arrived at camp the next day, much to the *seeming* satisfaction of our old messmates, and as much to the real dissatisfaction of ourselves; at least, it was so with me.

Thus far, since the year commenced, "Dame Fortune had been kind," but now "Miss-Fortune" was coming in for *her* set in the reel. I had now to enter again on my old system of starving;—there was nothing to eat; I had brought two or three days' rations in my knapsack, and while that lasted I made shift to get along, but that was soon gone, and I was then obliged to come to it again, which was sorely against my grain. During the past winter I had had enough to eat and been under no restraint; I had picked up a few articles of comfortable summer clothing among the inhabitants; our Lieutenant had never concerned himself about us, we had scarcely seen him during the whole time,—when we were off duty we went when and where we pleased "and had none to make us afraid;" but now the scene was changed, we must go and come at bidding and suffer hunger besides.

After I had joined my regiment I was kept constantly, when off other duty, engaged in learning the Baron de Steuben's new Prussian exercise; it was a continual drill.

About this time I was sent off from camp in a detachment consisting of about three thousand men, with four field pieces, under the command of the young General Lafayette. We marched to Barren hill, about twelve miles from Philadelphia; there are cross roads upon this hill, a branch of which leads to the city. We halted here, placed our guards, sent off our scouting parties, and waited for—I know not what.—A company of about a hundred Indians, from some northern tribe, joined us here,—there were three or four young Frenchmen with them. The Indians were stout looking fellows, and remarkably neat for that race of mortals, (but they were Indians.) There was upon the hill, and just where we were lying, an old church built of stone, entirely divested of all its entrails. The Indians were amusing themselves and the soldiers by shooting with their bows, in and about the church. I observed something in a corner of the roof which did not appear to belong to the building, and desired an Indian who was standing near me, to shoot an arrow at it; he did so and it proved to be a cluster of bats; I should think there were nearly a bushel of them, all hanging upon one another. The house was immediately alive with them, and it was likewise instantly full of Indians and soldiers. The poor bats fared hard, it was sport for all hands; they killed, I know not how many, but there was a great slaughter among them.—I never saw so many bats before nor since, nor indeed in my whole life put all together.

The next day I was one of a guard to protect the horses belonging to the detachment; they were in a meadow of six or eight acres, entirely surrounded by tall trees; it was cloudy and a low fog hung all night upon the meadow, and for several hours, during the night, there was a jack-o-lantern cruising in the edying air; the poor thing seemed to wish to get out of the meadow, but could not, the air circulating within the enclosure of trees would not permit it. Several of the guard endeavoured to catch it but did not succeed.[1]

Just at the dawn of day the officers' waiters came, almost breathless, after the horses; upon inquiring for the cause of the unusual hurry, we were told that the British were advancing upon us in our rear; how they could get there was to us a mystery, but they *were* there. We helped the waiters to catch their horses, and immediately returned to the main body of the detachment. We found the troops all under arms and in motion, preparing for an onset. Those of the troops belonging to our brigade were put into the churchyard, which was enclosed by a wall of stone and lime about breast high, a good defence against musketry

---

[1] Professor Silliman has said, on the authority of a certain Dr. Somebody, that jack-o-lanterns never move. With due submission to such high authority, I would crave their pardon for telling them that they labour under a mistake. I have seen many of these exhalations, two of which I am satisfied beyond a doubt were moving when I saw them, the one mentioned in the text and the other when I was a youngster. I was one evening walking in a lane in a sequestered place, the road crossing a low boggy piece of land, when I saw one of these meteors, if they may be so called, coming down the low ground before the wind, which was quick, it crossed the road within ten feet of me and passed on till it was lost in the distance. Now I could not be deceived in this instance; I saw it, and I could see with my natural eyes as well as a philosopher could with his. But I have lately heard of a new idea concerning them,—that is, that they are a species of glowworm in their butterfly state. If that is the case, they must of necessity move, the opinion of those scientific gentlemen to the contrary, notwithstanding.

but poor against artillery. I began to think I should soon have some better sport than killing bats. But our commander found that the enemy was too strong to be engaged in the position we then occupied, he therefore wisely ordered a retreat from this place to the Schuylkill, where we might choose any position that we pleased, having ragged woody hills in our rear and the river in front. It was about three miles to the river; the weather was exceeding warm, and I was in the rear platoon of the detachment except two platoons of Gen. Washington's guards. The quick motion in front kept the rear on a constant trot. Two pieces of artillery were in front and two in the rear. The enemy had nearly surrounded us by the time our retreat commenced, but the road we were in was very favourable for us, it being for the most part, and especially the first part of it through small woods and copses. When I was about half way to the river, I saw the right wing of the enemy through a lawn about half a mile distant, but they were too late; besides, they made a blunder here,—they saw our rear guard with the two fieldpieces in its front, and thinking it the front of the detachment, they closed in to secure their prey; but when they had sprung their net they found that they had not a single bird under it.

We crossed the Schuylkill in good order, very near the spot where I had crossed it four times in the month of October the preceding autumn. As fast as the troops crossed they formed and prepared for action, and waited for them to attack us; but we saw no more of them that time, for before we had reached the river the alarm guns were fired in our camp and the whole army was immediately in motion. The British, fearing that they should be outnumbered in their turn, directly set their faces for Philadelphia and set off in as much or more haste than we had left Barren hill. They had, during the night, left the city with such silence and secrecy, and by taking what was called the New-York road, that they escaped detection by all our parties, and the first knowledge they obtained of the enemy's movements was, that he was upon their backs, between them and us on the hill. The Indians, with all their alertness, had like to have "bought the rabit;" they kept coming in all the afternoon, in parties of four or five, whooping and hallooing like wild beasts. After they had got collected they vanished; I never saw any more of them. Our scouting parties all came in safe, but I was afterwards informed by a British deserter that several of the enemy perished by the heat and their exertions to get away from a retreating enemy.

The place that our detachment was now at was the Gulf, mentioned in the preceding chapter, where we kept the rice and vinegar thanksgiving of starving memory. We staid here till nearly night, when, no one coming to visit us, we marched off and took up our lodgings for the night in a wood. The next day we crossed the Schuylkill again and went on to Barren hill once more; we staid there a day or two and then returned to camp with keen appetites and empty purses. If any one asks why we did not stay on Barren hill till the British came up, and have taken and given a few bloody noses?—all I have to say in answer is, that the General well knew what he was about; he was not deficient in either courage or conduct, and that was well known to all the revolutionary army.

Soon after this affair we left our winter cantonments, crossed the Schulykill and encamped on the left bank of that river, just opposite to our winter-quarters. We had lain here but a few days, when we heard that the British army had left Philadelphia and were proceeding to New-York, through the Jerseys. We marched immediately in pursuit;— we crossed the Delaware at Carroll's ferry, above Trenton, and encamped a day or two between that town and Princeton. Here I was again detached with a party of one thousand men, as light troops, to get into the enemy's route and follow him close, to favour desertion and pick up stragglers.

The day we were drafted the sun was eclipsed; had this happened upon such an occasion in "olden time," it would have been considered ominous either of good or bad fortune, but we took no notice of it. Our detachment marched in the afternoon and towards night we passed through Princeton; some of the patriotic inhabitants of the town had brought out to the end of the street we passed through, some casks of ready made toddy, it was dealt out to the men as they passed by, which caused the detachment to move slowly at this place. The young ladies of the town, and perhaps of the vicinity, had collected and were sitting in the stoops and at the windows to see the noble exhibition of a thousand half starved and three quarters naked soldiers pass in review before them. I chanced to be on the wing of a platoon next to the houses, as they were chiefly on one side of the street, and had a good chance to notice the ladies, and I declare that I never before nor since saw more beauty, considering the numbers, than I saw at that time; they were *all* beautiful. New-Jersey and Pennsylvania ladies are, in my opinion, collectively handsome, the most so of any in the United States. But I hope our Yankee ladies will not be jealous at hearing this; I allow that they have as many mental beauties as the others have personal, perhaps more, I know nothing about it—they are all handsome.

We passed through Princeton and encamped on the open fields for the night, the canopy of heaven for our tent. Early next morning we marched again and came up with the rear of the British army. We followed them several days, arriving upon their camping ground within an hour after their departure from it. We had ample opportunity to see the devastation they made in their rout; cattle killed and lying about the fields and pastures, some just in the position they were in when shot down, others with a small spot of skin taken off their hind quarters and a mess of steak taken out; household furniture hacked and broken to pieces; wells filled up and mechanic's and farmer's tools destroyed. It was in the height of the season of cherries, the innocent industrious creatures could not climb the trees for the fruit, but universally cut them down. Such conduct did not give the Americans any more agreeable feelings toward them than they entertained before.

It was extremely hot weather, and the sandy plains of that part of New-Jersey did not cool the air to any great degree, but we still kept close to the rear of the British army; deserters were almost hourly coming over to us, but of stragglers we took only a few.

My risibility was always pretty easily excited at any innocent ludicrous incident;—the following circumstance gave me cause to laugh as well as all the rest who heard it. We halted in a wood for a few minutes in the heat of the day, on the ascent of a hill, and were lolling on the sides of the road, when there passed by two old men, both upon one horse that looked as if the crows had bespoken him. I did not know but Sancho Panza had lost his Dapple and was mounted behind Don Quixote upon Rosinante and bound upon some adventure with the British. However, they had not long been gone past us before another, about the same age and complexion, came steming by on foot. Just as he had arrived where I was sitting, he stopped short, and looking toward the soldiers, said, "Did you see two old horses riding a Dutchman this road up?—Hoh!" The soldiers set up a laugh, as well they might, and the poor old Dutchman finding he had gone "dail foremost" in his question, made the best of his way off out of hearing of us. We this night turned into a new ploughed field, and I laid down between two furrows and slept as sweet as though I had lain upon a bed of down.

The next morning, as soon as the enemy began their march, we were again in motion and came to their last night's encamping ground just after sunrise; here we halted an hour or two, as we often had to do, to give the enemy time to advance, our orders being not to attack them unless in self-defence. We were marching on as usual, when, about ten or eleven o'clock, we were ordered to halt and then to face to the right about. As this order was given by the officers in rather a different way than usual, we began to think something was out of joint somewhere, but what or where, our united wisdom could not explain; the general opinion of the soldiers was, that some part of the enemy had by some means got into our rear; we however retraced our steps till we came to our last night's encamping ground, when we left the route of the enemy and went off a few miles, to a place called Englishtown. It was uncommonly hot weather and we put up booths to protect us from the heat of the sun, which was almost insupportable. Whether we lay here one or two nights, I do not remember, it matters not which; we were early in the morning mustered out and ordered to leave all our baggage under the care of a guard, (our baggage was trifling,) taking only our blankets and provisions, (our provisions were less,) and prepare for immediate march and action. The officer who commanded the platoon that I belonged to was a Captain, belonging to the Rhode-Island troops, and a fine brave man he was; he feared nobody nor nothing. When we were paraded,—"Now," said he to us, "you have been wishing for some days past to come up with the British, you have been wanting to fight,—now you shall have fighting enough before night;"—the men did not need much haranguing to raise their courage, for when the officers came to order the sick and lame to stay behind as guards, they were forced to exercise their authority to the full extent before they could make even the invalids stay behind, and when some of their arms were about to be exchanged with those who were going into the field, they would not part with them,—"if their arms went," they said, "*they* would go with them at all events."

After all things were put in order, we marched, but halted a few minutes in the village, where we were joined by a few other troops and then proceeded on. We now heard a few reports of cannon ahead; we went in a road running through a deep narrow valley, which was for a considerable way covered with thick wood; we were sometime in passing this defile. While in the wood we heard a volley or two of musketry, and upon inquiry we found it to be a party of our troops who had fired upon a party of British horse; but there was no fear of horse in the place in which we then were.

It was ten or eleven o'clock before we got through these woods and came into the open fields. The first cleared land we came to was an Indian corn-field, surrounded on the east, west and north sides by thick tall trees; the sun shining full upon the field, the soil of which was sandy, the mouth of a heated oven seemed to me to be but a trifle hotter than this ploughed field; it was almost impossible to breathe. We had to fall back again as soon as we could, into the woods; by the time we had got under the shade of the trees, and had taken breath, of which we had been almost deprived, we received orders to retreat, as all the left wing of the army (that part being under the command of Gen. Lee) were retreating. Grating as this order was to our feelings, we were obliged to comply. We had not retreated far before we came to a defile, a muddy sloughy brook; while the Artillery were passing this place, we sat down by the road side;—in a few minutes the Commander-in-chief and suit crossed the road just where we were sitting. I heard him ask our officers "by whose order the troops were retreating," and being answered, "by Gen. Lee's;" he said something, but as he was moving forward all the time this was passing, he was too far off for me to hear it distinctly; those that were nearer to him, said that his words were— "d—n him;" whether he did thus express himself or not I do not know, it was certainly very unlike him, but he seemed at the instant to be in a great passion, his looks if not his words seemed to indicate as much.

After passing us, he rode on to the plain field and took an observation of the advancing enemy; he remained there sometime upon his old English charger, while the shot from the British Artillery were rending up the earth all around him. After he had taken a view of the enemy, he returned and ordered the two Connecticut Brigades to make a stand at a fence, in order to keep the enemy in check while the Artillery and other troops crossed the before-mentioned defile. [It was the Connecticut and Rhode-Island forces which occupied this post, notwithstanding what Dr. Ramsay says to the contrary; he seems willing, to say the least, to give the southern troops the credit due to the northern; a Historian ought to be sure of the truth of circumstances before he relates them.] When we had secured our retreat, the Artillery formed a line of pieces upon a long piece of elevated ground. Our detachment formed directly in front of the Artillery, as a covering party, so far below on the declivity of the hill, that the pieces could play over our heads. And here we waited the approach of the enemy, should he see fit to attack us.

By this time the British had come in contact with the New-England forces at the fence, when a sharp conflict ensued; these troops maintained their ground, till the whole force of the enemy that could be brought to bear, had charged upon them through the fence, and after being overpowered by numbers and the platoon officers had given orders for their several platoons to leave the fence, they had to force them to retreat, so eager were they to be revenged on the invaders of their country and rights.

As soon as the troops had left this ground the British planted their cannon upon the place, and began a violent attack upon the Artillery and our detachment, but neither could be routed. The cannonade continued for sometime without intermission, when the British pieces being mostly disabled, they reluctantly crawled back from the height which they had occupied, and hid themselves from our sight.

Before the cannonade had commenced, a part of the right wing of the British army had advanced across a low meadow and brook, and occupied an orchard on our left. The weather was almost too hot to live in, and the British troops in the orchard were forced by the heat to shelter themselves from it under the trees. We had a four pounder on the left of our pieces which kept a constant fire upon the enemy during the whole contest. After the British Artillery had fallen back and the connonade had mostly ceased in this quarter, and our detachment had an opportunity to look about us, Col. Cilly of the New-Hampshire line, who was attached to our detachment, passed along in front of our line, inquiring for Gen. Varnum's men, (who were the Connecticut and Rhode-Island men belonging to our command;) we answered, "Here we are;" he did not hear us in his hurry, but passed on: in a few minutes he returned, making the same inquiry,—we again answered, "Here we are." "Ah!" said he, "you are the boys I want to assist in driving those rascals from yon orchard." We were immediately ordered from our old detachment and joined another, the whole composing a corps of about five hundred men. We instantly marched towards the enemy's right wing, which was in the orchard, and kept concealed from them as long as possible, by keeping behind the bushes. When we could no longer keep ourselves concealed, we marched into the open fields and formed our line. The British immediately formed and began to retreat to the main body of their army. Col. Cilly, finding that we were not likely to overtake the enemy before they reached the main body of the army, on account of fences and other obstructions, ordered three or four platoons from the right of our corps to pursue and attack them, and thus keep them in play till the rest of the detachment could come up. I was in this party, we pursued without order; as I passed through the orchard I saw a number of the enemy lying under the trees, killed by our fieldpiece, mentioned before. We overtook the enemy just as they were entering upon the meadow, which was rather bushy. When within about five rods of the rear of the retreating foe, I could distinguish every thing about them, they were retreating in line, though in some disorder; I singled out a man and took my aim directly between his shoulders, (they were divested of their packs,) he was a good mark, being a broad shouldered fellow; what became of him I know not, the fire and smoke hid him from my sight; one thing I know, that is, I took as deliberate aim at him as ever I did at any game in my life. But after all, I hope I did not kill him, although I intended to at the time. By this time our whole party had arrived, and the British had obtained a position that suited them, as I suppose, for they returned our fire in good earnest, and we played the second part of the same tune. They occupied a much higher piece of ground than we did, and had a small piece of Artillery, which the soldiers called a grashopper; we had no Artillery with us. The first shot they gave us from this piece, cut off the thigh bone of a Captain, just above the knee, and the whole heel of a private in the rear of him. We gave it to poor Sawney (for they were Scotch troops) so hot, that he was forced to fall back and leave the ground they occupied. When our Commander saw them retreating, and nearly joined with their main body, he shouted, "come, my boys, reload your pieces, and we will give them a set-off." We did so, and gave them the parting salute, and the firing on both sides ceased. We then laid ourselves down under the fences and bushes to take breath, for we had need of it; I presume every one has heard of the heat of that day, but none can realize it that did not feel it. Fighting is hot work in cool weather, how much more so in such weather as it was on the 28th of June, 1778.

After the action in our part of the army had ceased, I went to a well, a few rods off, to get some water; here I found the wounded captain, mentioned before, lying on the ground, and begging his sergeant, who pretended to have the care of him, to help him off the field, or he should bleed to death; the sergeant, and a man or two he had with him, were taken up in hunting after plunder. It grieved me to see the poor man in such distress, and I asked the sergeant why he did not carry his officer to the surgeons; he said he would directly; directly! said I, why he will die directly. I then offered to assist them in carrying him to a meeting-house, a short distance off, where the rest of the wounded men and the surgeons were; at length he condescended to be persuaded to carry him off, I helped him to the place, and tarried a few minutes, to see the wounded and two or three limbs amputated, and then returned to my party again, where we remained the rest of the day and the following night, expecting to have another hack at them in the morning, but they gave us the slip.

As soon as our party had ceased firing, it began in the centre, and then upon the right, but as I was not in that part of the army, I had no "adventure" in it, but the firing was continued in one part or the other of the field, the whole afternoon. Our troops remained on the field all night with the Commander-in-chief; a regiment of Connecticut forces were sent to lie as near the enemy as possible and to watch their motions, but they disappointed us all. If my readers wish to know how they escaped so slyly without our knowledge, after such precautions being used to prevent it, I must tell them I know nothing about it. But if they will take the trouble to call upon John Trumbull, Esq. perhaps he will satisfy their curiosity. If he should chance to be out of the way, (and ten chances to one if he is not,) apply to McFingal, Canto 4th.

One little incident happened, during the heat of the cannonade, which I was eye-witness to, and which I think would be unpardonable not to mention. A woman whose husband belonged to the Artillery, and who was then attached to a piece in the engagement, attended with her husband at the piece the whole time; while in the act of reaching a cartridge and having one of her feet as far before the other as she could step, a cannon shot from the enemy passed directly between her legs without doing any other damage than carrying away all the lower part of her petticoat,—looking at it with apparent unconcern, she observed, that it was lucky it did not pass a little higher, for in that case it might have carried away something else, and continued her occupation.

The next day after the action each man received a gill of rum, but nothing to eat. We then joined our regiments in the line, and marched for Hudson's river. We marched by what was called "easy marches," that is, we struck our tents at three o'clock in the morning, marched ten miles and then encamped, which would be about one or two o'clock in the afternoon; every third day we rested all day. In this way we went to King's ferry, where we crossed the Hudson. Each brigade furnished its own ferrymen to carry the troops across. I was one of the men from our brigade; we were still suffering for provisions. Nearly the last trip the batteau that I was in made, while crossing the river empty, a large sturgeon (a fish in which this river abounds) seven or eight feet in length, in his gambollings, sprang directly into the boat, without doing any other damage than breaking down one of the seats of the boat. We crossed and took in our freight and recrossed, landed the men and our prize, gave orders to our several messmates as to the disposal of it, and proceeded on our business till the whole of the brigade had crossed the river, which was not long, we working with new energy in expectation of having something to eat when we had done our job. We then repaired to our messes to partake of the bounty of Providence, which we had so unexpectedly received. I found my share, which was about the seventh part of it, cooked, that is, it was boiled in salt and water, and I fell to it and ate, perhaps, a pound and a half, for I well remember that I was as hungry as a vulture and as empty as a blown bladder. Many of the poor fellows *thought* us happy in being thus supplied; for my part I *felt* happy.

From King's ferry the army proceeded to Tarrytown, and from thence to the White plains; here we drew some small supplies of summer clothing of which we stood in great need. While we lay here, I, with some of my comrades who were in the battle of the White plains in the year '76, one day took a ramble on the ground where we were then engaged with the British and took a survey of the place. We saw a number of the graves of those who fell in that battle; some of the bodies had been so slightly buried that the dogs or hogs, or both, had dug them out of the ground. The sculls and other bones, and hair were scattered about the place. Here were Hessian sculls as thick as a bomb shell;— poor fellows! they were left unburied in a foreign land;—they had, perhaps, as near and dear friends to lament their sad destiny as the Americans who lay buried near them. But they should have kept at home, we should then never have gone after them to kill them in their own country. But, the reader will say, they were forced to come and be killed here; forced by their rulers who have absolute power of life and death over their subjects. Well then, reader, bless a kind Providence that has made such a distinction between *your* condition and *theirs*. And be careful too that you do not allow yourself ever to be brought to such an abject, servile and debased condition.

We lay at the White plains some time. While here I was transferred to the Light Infantry, when I was immediately marched down to the lines. I had hard duty to perform during the remainder of the campaign. I shall not go into every particular, but only mention a few incidents and accidents which transpired.

There were three regiments of Light Infantry, composed of men from the whole main army,—it was a motly group,—Yankees, Irishmen, Buckskins and what not. The regiment that I belonged to, was made up of about one half New-Englanders and the remainder were chiefly Pennsylvanians,—two setts of people as opposite in manners and customs as light and darkness, consequently there was not much cordiality subsisting between us; for, to tell the sober truth, I had in those days, as lief have been incorporated with a tribe of western Indians, as with any of the southern troops; especially of those which consisted mostly (as the Pennsylvanians did,) of foreigners. But I *was* among them and in the same regiment too, and under their officers, (but the officers, in general, were gentlemen,) and had to do duty with them; to make a bad matter worse, I was often, when on duty, the only Yankee that happened to be on the same tour for several days together. "The bloody Yankee," or "the d—d Yankee," was the mildest epithets that they would bestow upon me at such times. It often made me think of home, or at *least* of my regiment of fellow-Yankees.

Our regiment was commanded by a Colonel Butler, a Pennsylvanian,—the same, I believe, who was afterwards Gen. Butler, and was slain by the Indians at the defeat of Gen. St. Clair, at the Miamis; but of this I am not certain. He was a brave officer, but a fiery austere hothead. Whenever he had a dispute with a brother officer, and that was pretty often, he would never resort to pistols and swords, but always to his fists. I have more than once or twice seen him with a "black eye," and have seen other officers that he had honoured with the same badge.

As I have said before, I shall not be *very* minute in relating my "adventures" during my continuance in this service. The duty of the Light Infantry is the hardest, while in the field, of any troops in the army, if there is any *hardest* about it. During the time the army keeps the field they are always on the lines near the enemy, and consequently always on the alert, constantly on the watch. Marching and guard-keeping, with all the other duties of troops in the field, fall plentifully to *their* share. There is never any great danger of Light Infantry men dying of the scurvy.

We had not been long on the lines when our regiment was sent off, lower down towards the enemy, upon a scouting expedition. We marched all night. Just at day-dawn we halted in a field and concealed ourselves in some bushes; we placed our sentinels near the road, lying down behind bushes, rocks and stoneheaps. The officers had got wind of a party of the enemy that was near us. A detachment of Cavalry which accompanied us had taken the same precaution to prevent being discovered that the Infantry had.

We had not been long in our present situation before we discovered a party of Hessian horsemen advancing up the road, directly to where we were lying in ambush for them. When the front of them had arrived "within hail," our Colonel rose up from his lurking place and very civilly ordered them to come to him. The party immediately halted, and as they saw but one man of us, the commander seemed to hesitate, and concluded, I suppose, not to be in too much of a hurry in obeying our Colonel's command, but that it was the best way for him to retrace his steps. Our Colonel then, in a voice like thunder, called out to him, "*Come here, you rascal!*" but he paid very little attention to the Colonel's summons and began to endeavour to free himself from what, I suppose, he thought a bad neighbourhood. Upon which our Colonel ordered the whole regiment to rise from their ambush and fire upon them; the order was quickly obeyed and served to quicken their steps considerably. Our horsemen had, while these transactions were in progress, by going round behind a small wood, got into their rear. We followed the enemy hard up, and when they met our horsemen there was a trifle of clashing; a part forced themselves past our Cavalry and escaped, about thirty were taken and a number killed. We had none killed and but two or three of the horsemen slightly wounded. The enemy were armed with short rifles.

There was an Irishman belonging to our Infantry, who, after the affray was over, seeing a wounded man belonging to the enemy, lying in the road and unable to help himself, took pity on him, as he was in danger of being trodden upon by the horses, and having shouldered him was staggering off with his load, in order to get him to a place of more safety; while crossing a small worn out bridge over a very muddy brook, he happened to jostle the poor fellow more than usual, who cried out "Good rebel, don't hurt poor Hushman." "Who do you call a rebel, you scoundrel?" said the Irishman, and tossed him off his shoulders as unceremoniously as though he had been a log of wood; he fell with his head into the mud, and as I passed I saw him struggling for life, but I had other business on my hands than to stop to assist him. I did sincerely pity the poor mortal, but pity him was all I could then do. What became of him after I saw him in the mud, I never knew; most likely he there made his final exit. The Infantry marched off with the prisoners, and left the horsemen to keep the field, till we were out of danger with our prize, consequently I never heard any thing more of him. But the Irishman reminded me "that the *tender* mercies of the wicked are cruel."

Soon after this I had another fatiguing job to perform. There was a Militia officer, a Colonel, (his name I have forgotten, though I think it was Jones,) who had collected some stores of flour, pork, &c. for the use of the Militia in his neighbourhood, when any small parties of them were required for actual service. A party of the enemy, denominated "Cow Boys" (Refugees) had destroyed his stores. He solicited some men from the Light Infantry, to endeavour to capture some of the gang whom he was personally acquainted with, who belonged to, or were often at Westchester, a village near King's bridge. Accordingly, a captain and two subaltern officers, and about eighty men (of which I was one) was sent from our regiment, then lying at a village called Bedford, to his assistance. We marched from our camp in the dusk of the evening, and continued our march all night. We heard repeatedly, during the night, the Tories firing on our sentrys that belonged to the horse guards, who were stationed on the lines near the enemy. This was often practised by those villains, not only upon the Cavalry but the Infantry also, when they thought they could do it with impunity. We arrived at the Colonel's early in the morning, and staid there through the day. At night the Lieutenant of our detachment with a small party of our men, guided by two or three Militia officers, were sent off in pursuit of some of those shooting gentry whom the Colonel suspected. We first went to a house where were a couple of free blacks who were strongly suspected of being of the number. The people of the house denied having any knowledge of such persons, but some of the men inquiring of a small boy belonging to the house, he very innocently told us that there were such men there and that they lay in a loft over the hogsty. We soon found their nest but the birds had flown, upon further inquiry, however, we found their skulking place and took them both. We then proceeded to another house, a mile or two distant; here we could not get any intelligence of the vermin we were in pursuit of. We, however, searched the house but found none. But we (the soldiers) desired the man who attended us with a light, to show us into the dairy-house, pretending that the supected persons might be there, and he accordingly accompanied us there,—we found no enemy in this place, but we found a friend indeed, because a friend in need. Here was a plenty of good bread, milk and butter; we were as hungry as Indians, and immediately "fell to, and spared not," while the man of the house held the candle and looked at us as we were devouring his eatables. I could not see his heart and of course could not tell what sort of thoughts "harboured there," but I could see his face and that indicated pretty distinctly what passed in his mind; he said *nothing*, but I believe he had as lief his bread and butter had been arsenic as what it was. We cared little for his thoughts or his maledictions, they did not do us half so much hurt as his victuals did us good.

We then returned to our party at the Colonel's, where we arrived before daybreak; we staid here through the day, drew some pork and biscuit, and prepared for our expedition after the Cow Boys. At dark we sat off, accompanied by the Militia Colonel and three or four subaltern Militia officers;—this was the third night I had been on my feet, the whole time without any sleep, but go we must. We marched but a short way in the road, and then turned into the fields and pastures, over brooks and fences, through swamps, mire and woods, endeavouring to keep as clear of the inhabitants as possible. About midnight we crossed a road near a house, the inmates of which, I suppose, were friendly to our cause, as the officers ordered us to stand still and not to speak nor leave our places on any account whatever, while they all entered the house for a few minutes, upon what errand I know not. As soon as the officers joined us again we marched off. One of our sergeants having disobeyed orders and gone round to the backside of the house, unobserved by the rest of us, (it being quite dark,) upon some occasion best known to himself, we marched off and left him. We had not gone fifty rods before he returned to the place where we were standing when he left us, and not finding us there he hallooed like a brave fellow; but the Militia officers said that it would not do to answer, so we marched on and left him to find the way to camp, through what might with propriety be called an enemy's country, as well as he could; he, however, arrived there, with some considerable difficulty, safe and sound.

We kept on still through the fields, avoiding the houses as much as possible. I shall never forget how tired and beat out I was; every grove of trees or piece of woods I could discern, I hoped would prove a resting place, but there was no rest. About two o'clock we took to the high road when we were between the village of Westchester and King's bridge, we then came back to the village, where we were separated into small divisions, each led by an officer, either of our own or of the Militia, and immediately entered all the suspected houses at once; what we had to do must be done quickly, as the enemy were so near that they might have been informed of us in less than half an hour; there were several men in the house into which I was led, but one only appeared to be obnoxious to the officer who led us; this man was a Tory Refugee, in green uniform; we immediately secured him. An old man as blind as a bat, came out of a bedroom, who appeared to be in great distress, for fear there would be murder committed, as he termed it. I told him it was impossible to commit murder with Refugees. We directly left the house with our prisoner, and joined the other parties and hurried off with all possible speed.

When we had got away and day light appeared, we found that we had twelve or fourteen prisoners, the most or all of whom had been concerned in the destruction of the Colonel's stores. We did not suffer the grass to grow long under our feet until we considered ourselves safe from the enemy that we had left behind us; we then slackened our pace and took to the road, where it was easier getting along than in the fields. Oh! I was so tired and hungry when we arrived at the Colonel's, which was not till sun-down or after. The most of the fellows we had taken belonged in the neighbourhood of this place. As we passed a house, just at night, there stood in the door an elderly woman, who seeing among the prisoners some that she knew, she began to open her batteries of blackguardism upon us for disturbing, what she termed, the king's peaceable subjects. Upon a little closer inspection, who should her ladyship spy amongst the herd, but one of her own sons. Her resentment was then raised to the highest pitch and we had a drenching shower of imprecations let down upon our heads. "Hell for war!" said she, "why you have got my son Josey too." Poor old simpleton! she might as well have saved her breath to cool her porridge.

We here procured another day's ration of the good Colonel's pork and bread;—we staid through the night, and got some sleep and rest. Early next morning we left our prisoners, blacks and all, to the care of the Militia, who could take care of them after we had taken them for them, and marched off for our encampment, at Bedford, where we arrived at night, sufficiently beat out and in a good condition to add another night's sleep to our stock of rest.

We lay at Bedford till the close of the season. Late in the autumn, the main army lay at New-Milford, in the northwestern part of Connecticut; while there, the Connecticut troops drew some winter clothing. The men belonging to that State, who were in the Light Infantry, had none sent them; they, therefore, thought themselves hardly dealt by. Many of them fearing they should lose their share of the clothing, (of which they stood in great need,) absconded from the Camp at Bedford and went to New-Milford. This caused our officers to keep patroling parties around the camp during the night to prevent their going off. In consequence of this, I had one evening, nearly obtained a final discharge from the army.

I had been in the afternoon, at a small brook in the rear of the camp, where the troops mostly got their water, to wash some clothes; among the rest was a handkerchief, which I laid upon a stone or stump and when I went to my tent I forgot to take it with me. Missing it after roll-call, I went to the place to get it; it was almost dark, and quite so in the bushes, when I got there. I was puzzled for some time to find the place, and longer before I could find the handkerchief; after finding it I did not hurry back, but loitered till the patrols were out, for I did not once think of *them*. It had now become quite dark and I had to pass through a place where the soldiers had cut firewood;—it was a young growth of wood, and the ground was covered with brush and the stumps about knee high, quite thick. Just as I entered upon this spot I heard somebody challenge with "Who comes there?" I had no idea of being the person hailed, and kept very orderly on my way, blundering through the brush. I, however, received a second and third invitation to declare myself, but paid no attention to the request. The next compliment I received was a shot from them; the ball passed very near to me but I still kept advancing, when instantly I had another salute. I then thought, that since I had been the cause of so much noise and alarm, it would be best for me to get off if possible, for I knew that if I was brought before our hotspur of a Colonel I should "buy the rabbit." Accordingly, I put my best foot foremost; the patrol, which consisted of twelve or fifteen men, all had a hack at me, some of the balls passing very near me indeed; one in particular, passed so near my head as to cause my ear to ring for sometime after. I now sprang to it for dear life, and I was in those days tolerable "light of foot;" but I had not made many leaps before I ran my knee with all my force against a white oak stump, which brought me up so short that I went heels over head over the stumps. I hardly knew whether I was dead or alive;—however, I got up and blundered on till I reached my tent, into which I pitched and lay as still as the pain in my knee would allow me. My messmates were all asleep and knew nothing of the affair then, nor did I ever let them or any one else know of it till after the close of the campaign, when I had joined my regiment in the line and was clear of the southern officers. But my knee was in a fine pickle,—the next morning it was swelled as big as my head, and lame enough; however, it did not long remain so. When I was questioned by the officers, or any of the men how I came by my wound, I told them I fell down, and thus far I told the truth; but when any one asked me how I came to fall down, I was compelled to equivocate a little.

I had often heard of some of the low bred Europeans, especially Irishmen, boxing with each other in good fellowship, as they termed it; but I could not believe it till I was convinced by actual demonstration. While we tarried here, I was one day at a sutler's tent, or hut, where were a number of what we Yankees call "Old countrymen;" soon after entering the hut, I observed one who was, to appearance, "pretty well over the bay." Directly there came in another who, it appeared, was an old acquaintance of the former's; they seemed exceeding glad to see each other, and so must take a drop of "the cratur" together; they then entered into conversation about former times. The first mentioned was a stout athletic fellow, the other was a much smaller man. All of a sudden the first says, "faith, Jammy, will you take a box." "Aye, and thank ye too," replied the other. No sooner said than done, out they went, and all followed to see the sport, as they thought it, I suppose; it was a cold frosty day, in the month of December, the ground all around the place, was ploughed and frozen as hard as a pavement. They immediately stripped to the buff, and a broad ring was directly formed for the combatants, (and they needed a broad one,) when they prepared for the battle. The first pass they made at each other, their arms drawing their bodies forward, they passed without even touching either; the first that picked them up was the frozen ground, which made the claret, as they called the blood, flow plentifully. They, however, with considerable difficulty, put themselves into a position for a second bout, when they made the same pass-by as at the first. The little fellow, after getting upon his feet again, as well as he could, cried out, "I am too drunk to fight," and crawled off as fast as he was able, to the sutler's hut again, the other followed, both as bloody as butchers, to drink friends again, where no friendship had been lost. And there I left them and went to my tent, thankful that Yankees, with all their follies, lacked such a *refined* folly as this.

The main army, about this time, quitted the eastern side of the Hudson river and passed into New-Jersey, to winter-quarters; the Connecticut and New-Hampshire troops went to Reading and Danbury, in the western part of Connecticut. The Light Infantry, likewise, broke up their encampment at Bedford, and separated to join their respective regiments in the line. On our march to join our regiment, some of our *gentlemen officers* happening to stop at a tavern, or rather a sort of grog-shop, took such a seasoning, that two or three of them became "quite frisky," as the old Indian said of his young squaw. They kept running and chasing each other backward and forward by the troops, as they walked along the road, acting rediculously. They soon, however, broke up the sport, for two of them at last, got by the ears, to the no small diversion of the soldiers, (for nothing could please them better than to see the officers quarrel amongst themselves.) One of the officers used his sword in the scabbard, the other a cane, and as the song says,

> At every stroke their jackets did smoke
> As though they had been all on fire.

Some of the other officers who had not dipped their bills quite so deep, parted them, at the same time representing to them the ridiculous situation they stood in, fighting like blackguards in sight of the soldiers;—at length shame, so far as they had reason to let it operate, beginning to take hold of them, the other officers persuaded them to shake hands in token of future friendship, but they carried wonderful long faces all the rest of the day.

We arrived at Reading about Christmas or a little before, and prepared to build huts for our winter-quarters. And now came on the time again between grass and hay; that is, the winter campaign of starving. We had not long been here under the command of Gen. Putnam, before the old gentleman heard, or fancied he heard that a party of the enemy were out somewhere "down below;" we were alarmed about midnight, and as cold a night as need be, and marched off to find the enemy (if he could be found.) We marched all the remaining part of the night and all the forenoon of the next day, and when we came where they were, they were not there at all at all, as the Irishman said. We now had nothing more to do but to return as we came, which we immediately set about. We marched back to Bedford, near the encamping ground I had just left. We were conducted into our bedroom, a large wood, by our landlords, the officers, and left to our repose, while the officers stowed themselves away snugly in the houses of the village, about half a mile distant. We struck us up fires and lay down to rest our weary bones, all but our jawbones, they had nothing to weary them. About midnight it began to rain which soon put out all our fires, and by three or four o'clock it came down in torrents—there *we* were, but where our careful officers were, or what had become of them we knew not, nor did we much care. The men began to squib off their pieces in derision of the officers, supposing they were somewhere amongst us, and careless of our condition; but none of them appearing, the men began firing louder and louder, till they had brought it to almost a running fire. At the dawn, the officers, having, I suppose, heard the firing, came running from their warm dry beds, almost out of breath, exclaiming, "poor fellows! are you not almost dead?" We might have been for aught they knew or cared.—However, they marched us off to the village, wet as drowned rats, put us into the houses, where we remained till the afternoon and dried ourselves. It cleared off towards night and about sundown we marched again for camp, which was about twenty miles distant; we marched till some time in the evening when we were ordered to get into the houses, under the care of the non-commissioned officers, the commissioned officers having again taken care of themselves, at an early hour of the night. Myself and ten or fifteen others of our company being under the charge of our orderly sergeant, could not get any quarters, as the people at every house made some excuse, which he thought all true. We kept pushing on till we had got three or four miles in advance of the troops; we then concluded to try for lodgings no longer, but to make the best of our way to camp, which we did, and arrived there in the latter part of the night. I had nothing to do but to endeavour to get a little rest, for I had no cooking, although I should have been very glad to have had it to do.

The rest of the troops arrived in the course of the day, and at night, I think, we got a little something to eat, but if we did not, I know what I got by the jaunt, for I got a pleurisy which laid me up for some time. When I got so well as to work I assisted in building our winter huts. We got them in such a state of readiness that we moved into them about new-year's day. The reader may take my word if he pleases, when I tell him we had nothing extraordinary, either of eatables or drinkables to keep a new-year or house warming. And as I have got into winter-quarters again, I will here bring my third campaign to a close.

Chapter V. Campaign of 1779.

You may think what you please, sir, I too can think—
I think I can't live without victuals and drink;
Your oxen can't plough, nor your horses can't draw,
Unless they have something more hearty than straw;—
If that is their food, sir, their spirits must fall—
How then can *I* labour with—nothing at all?

WE got settled in our winter-quarters at the commencement of the new year and went on in our old continental line of starving and freezing. We now and then got a little bad bread and salt beef, (I believe chiefly horse-beef, for it was generally thought to be such at the time.) The month of January was very stormy, a good deal of snow fell, and in such weather it was a mere chance if we got any thing at all to eat. Our condition, at length, became insupportable. We concluded that we *could* not or *would* not bear it any longer;—we were now in our own State, and were determined that if our officers would not see some of our grievances redressed, the State should. Accordingly, one evening after roll-calling, the men generally turned out, (but without their arms,) and paraded in front of their huts. We had no need of informing the officers, we well knew that they would hear of our muster without our troubling ourselves to inform them. We had hardly got paraded before all our officers, with the Colonel at their head, came in front of the regiment, expressing a deal of sorrow for the hardships we were compelled to undergo, but much more for what they were pleased to call our mutinous conduct; this latter expression of their sorrow only served to exasperate the men, which the officers observing, changed their tone and endeavoured to sooth the Yankee temper they had excited, and, with an abundance of fair promises, persuaded us to return to our quarters again. But hunger was not to be so easily pacified, and would not suffer many of us to sleep, we were therefore determined that none others should sleep. Martial law was very strict against firing muskets in camp, nothing could, therefore, raise the officers' "lofty ideas" sooner, or more, than to fire in camp; but it was beyond the power or vigilance of all the officers to prevent the men from "making void the law" on that night. Finding they were watched by the officers, they got an old gun barrel which they placed in a hut that was unfinished; this they loaded a third part full and putting a slow match to it, would then escape to their own huts, when the old barrel would speak for itself, with a voice that would be heard. The officers would then muster out, and some running and scolding would ensue; but none knew who made the noise, or where it came from. This farce was carried on the greater part of the night, but at length the officers getting tired of running so often to catch Mr. Nobody, without finding him, that they soon gave up the chase, and the men seeing they could no longer gull the officers, gave up the business likewise.

We fared a little better for a few days after this memento to the officers; but it soon became an old story, and the old system commenced again as regular as fair weather to foul. We endeavoured to bear it with our usual fortitude, until it again became intolerable, and the soldiers determined to try once more to raise some provisions, if not, at least to raise another dust. Accordingly, one evening, after dark, we all turned out again with our arms, appointed a commander and were determined that time, if we could not be better accommodated, to march into the centre of the State and disperse to our homes, in presence of as many of our fellow-citizens as chose to be spectators. After we had organized ourselves and regulated the plan for our future operations, it was the design of our regiment to have marched to our field-officers' quarters, and through them to demand of our country better usage; but before we had got all our little matters of etiquette settled, our Adjutant came up, (he having been over at the village, on some errand best known to himself,) and seeing us in arms upon the parade at that time of night, mistrusted something was in the wind; he passed us without saying a word and went directly and informed the other officers, all of whom were soon upon the parade. Our Major was the first that arrived, he was a fine bold looking man, and made a fine appearance. He came on to the right of the regiment, and soon after the Colonel and other officers came in front; the commanding seargeant ordered the men to shoulder arms, and then to present, (which is a token of respect,) and then to order them again. The Major then addressed the sergeant thus: "Well, sergeant —— you have got a larger regiment than we had this evening at roll-call, but I should think it would be more agreeable for the men to be asleep in their huts this cold night, than to be standing here on the parade, for I remember that they were very impatient at roll-call on account of the cold." "Yes, sir," said the sergeant, "Solomon says that 'the abundance of the rich will not suffer *him* to sleep;' and we find that the abundance of poverty will not suffer us to sleep." By this time the Colonel had come to where the Major and serjeant were arguing the case, and the old mode of flattery and promising was resorted to and produced the usual effect; we all once more returned to our huts and fires, and there spent the remainder of the night, muttering over our forlorn condition.

It was now the beginning of February; many of the men had obtained furloughs to go home and visit their friends, before I had left the Light Infantry, and many since; I now made application and obtained one for fifteen days' absence. I prepared for the journey (which was about thirty miles) and started from the camp about nine o'clock in the morning, intending to go the whole distance that day. I had not a mouthful of any thing to eat or to carry with me. I had, it is true, two or three shillings of old continental money, worth about as much as its weight in rags. I, however, sat off for home; the hopes of soon seeing my friends and the expectation of there filling my belly once more, buoyed up my spirits until I had got within about five miles of home;—when coming to a tavern about sunset, I consulted with myself whether I had not better call and get me a glass of spirits, as I did not possess wherewith to procure me a meal of victuals, concluding that I should soon be where I could get that gratis; I accordingly did call and drank a glass of spirits and water, and immediately pursued my journey. I soon came to where I was obliged to leave the high road and take to one that struck across the country and a ferry. By the time I had got to this road I had become so faint that I thought I could not reach the nearest house, which was more than a mile distant. I was acquainted with this road, but the main road which led to a large village, I was unacquainted with any further than where I then was. I sat down and rested myself a few minutes, and I had need of it. I concluded to keep on the main road, being confident that I should find a house in a less distance than on the other. I went on, often having to rest myself from mere faintness; I travelled, however, nearly a mile and a half without seeing the least sign of a house. At length, after much fatigue, I came to an old house, standing, as the Irishman said, out of doors. I made up to it and knocked at the door,—"Who's there?" cried an old woman from within. "A friend," I replied. "What do you want?" said she,—"I want to rest here to-night." "I cannot entertain you," said she, "I am alone and cannot let a stranger in." I told her I could not, and would not go any further. After some inquiring on her part and answering on mine, she condescended to admit me. She needed not to have feared me, for had she been a virgin, and as beautiful as Hellen, I should have had no inclination to have soiled her chastity that night, I had something else to employ my thoughts upon; however loath the old lady was to admit me, she used me extremely well, for she provided me with a good supper and a field bed before the fire, where I slept soundly till the morning, nor would she let me depart in the morning till I had breakfasted. While she was preparing my breakfast, I chopped off a backlog and put it on the fire, which was all the compensation she required, nor even that, it was my own will; we then parted with mutual thanks, and I proceeded on my journey.

On the evening before, the ground was quite clear of snow, but during the night, there fell nearly a foot in depth of light snow and I had to return to the road I had left the preceding evening. There was no track in the new fallen snow until I came to the cross road, when I found a footman had passed before me. He appeared, by his track and the mark of a cane he used, to be an old man. I could not help being diverted by observing at every few rods distance, that the poor fellow had slipped down on the ice, which was covered by the snow, when he would spatter the snow about like a horse. I soon overtook him, he was an old black man. When I came to the ferry it was frozen over, and covered with snow a foot deep; I went into the ferryman's house, one of who's daughters was wife to the drummajor of our regiment; she made a bitter complaint to me against her husband, said he came home from the army and spent all her earnings, gave the whole family the itch, and then went off to camp, leaving her and her children to shift for themselves as well as they could. I could have told her a little more of his *amiable* conduct than she knew, but I thought she might as well get her information from some other quarter. The people here told me that it was dangerous crossing the river, as the ice was full of holes which were mostly covered by the snow. There was no way for me but to venture on the ice, or go five or six miles lower down the river to another ferry. I did not like the first and the second I could not agree to at all. I therefore ventured upon the ice and passed over to the opposite shore in safety, with some danger and trouble; when I arrived at the other side I found the tide up and the edge of the ice a rod or two from the shore; I then had to travel up the river on the ice, three times the distance that it was to cross the river, and with more danger, before I could get off; I got off however without drowning. I then had two miles to go, and frequently met people belonging to the town, but very few recollected me; I arrived at my good old grandsire's about eight or nine o'clock in the morning, with a keen appetite for my breakfast, although I had ate one that day. I believe the old people were glad to see me, they appeared to be much so, and I am quite sure I was glad to see them and all my other friends, if I had any. I had now an opportunity of seeing the place of my boyhood, visit old acquaintance, and ramble over my old haunts; but my time was short, and I had of course, to employ every minute to the best advantage.

I remained at home till my furlough had fully expired; I intended my country should give me a day to return to camp. The day before I intended to set off for the army, my Lieutenant arrived at home to spend a week with his family. He called upon me and told me that if I chose I might stay and accompany him to camp, and he would be responsible for me. I did not want much persuasion to comply with his desire, and accordingly remained another week, and then went with the Lieutenant to camp, and had no fault found.

I had not been at camp more than a week, before I was sent off with a large detachment to New-London, to guard the fortifications in and about that town. On our march we passed through the place of my residence when at home; the detachment tarried a night there, so I had an opportunity of being at home another night. We marched in the morning and remained the following night at New-Haven. I was quartered for the night in a house in the skirts of the town; there was a young lady belonging to the house, who, as it was Sabbath eve, had gone out to see the "daughters of the land," like Dinah of old. Just as we were about to lie down, I went to the back door of the house, where was a small field of dry cornstalks, I met the young lady with a gallant, just at the door; the moment he saw me he left his sweetheart and went off through the cornstalks, making as much noise as if a whirlwind had passed through them. I thought he was a brave fellow, thus to leave his mistress in the power of those he was afraid of himself, and not stop so long as to ask quarters for her, but, upon the first alarm, to desert her to save his own four quarters from receiving damage. Many pretended heroes have done the same, perhaps worse.

We went by easy marches and nothing of consequence occurred until we arrived at New-London; here we were put into houses, and here too we almost starved to death, and I believe should have quite starved, had we not found some clams which kept us from absolutely dying. We had nothing to eat except now and then a little miserable beef or a little fresh fish, and a very little bread, baked by a baker belonging to the town, which had some villainous drug incorporated with it that took all the skin off our mouths. I sincerely believe it was done on purpose to prevent our eating. I was not free from a sore mouth the whole time I staid there. Just before we left this place a privateer brig arrived from a cruise; she was hauled up and dismantled. One day I went on board her, and in the bread room I found one or two bushels of sea-biscuit; at night I again went on board and filled my knapsack, which was a relief to my hungry stomach. But this bread had nearly as much flesh as bread, being as full of worms as ever the dry sap-wood of a white ash pole was; consequently, it required a deal of circumspection in eating it;—however, it was better than snow balls. The other men in my room, likewise, used to avail themselves of the opportunity to procure some, after I had told them where it might be obtained.

Several funny, and some serious accidents occurred while I remained here, but as they would be tedious to narrate, and, perhaps, uninteresting to the reader, I shall pass them by unnoticed.

We staid here, starving, until the first of May, when we received orders to march to camp and join our regiments. The troops belonging to New-Hampshire marched sometime before we did. While on our march, we halted in a village; here I went into a house, with several other soldiers, which happened to be a deacon's;—while there some of the men chanced to swear, (a circumstance extremely uncommon with the soldiers,) upon which the good woman of the house checked them. "Is there any harm in it?" said one of them. "Yes," said she. "Well," said he, "may I not say swamp it." "No," said she, "nor maple log roll over me, neither." She then turned to me and said, "I do not like you soldiers." I asked her why? "Because," said she, "there came some along here the other day and they stole every morsel of my dinner from the pot, while it was boiling over the fire, pudding bag and all." I told her that her case was, upon the whole, rather a calamitous one, but, said I, "I suppose the soldiers thought your pot could be easier replenished than their kettles." She made me no answer, whatever she thought.

We went on to New-Haven where we arrived upon a Sabbath eve and staid till Wednesday; on the Tuesday following there was to be a muster of the Militia. On Monday we washed our clothes, and as we understood we were to remain here during the next day, we put ourselves into as decent a condition as we possibly could, to witness the Militia exhibition the next day. Early next morning there was a general stir in the town, a regiment of foot and a troop of horse were paraded on the green, and they made a very good appearance, (considering the times,) to speak the truth; but they seemed to be rather shy of displaying their knowledge of military tactics before regular troops. However, they did very well and deserved praise, whether they received it or not.

The next morning we marched again, I then applied to our commander and obtained permission to go on in advance of the troops and see my grand-parents again, I would have done this sooner, but I could not forego the pleasure of seeing the Militia muster. I remained at home that day and the next, and then started for camp. I was acquainted with the country, and consequently could reach camp by a much shorter way than the troops went, as they kept the country roads, by which means I arrived there within a few hours after them.

On some duty, I do not recollect what, I was deprived of my rest for a night or two; the next day I took a ramble into the woods near the camp, determined, if I could, to take a nap; the trees had just began to leave out and "all nature was gay;" I walked about half a mile, when I came to a flat ledge of rocks covered with soft thick moss, as smooth as a carpet; I laid myself down and soon fell into a sound sleep; I had not slept long before I was attacked by that delectable disorder, the night mare, I recovered partly from the first attack, but before I could fully overcome it, it took a second gripe upon me more serious than the first. I had often heard people say, when they had been under the influence of this disorder, that they were confident they were awake, and had the full possession of their faculties, and I had many times thought so myself; recollecting this, tormented as I was, I thought I would now satisfy myself whether it was so or not; accordingly, I took a survey of the trees about me, which I imagined I saw distinctly; one tree in particular I noticed, a large black birch tree, which had a limb broken off, leaving a stump some five or six feet long and a foot in diameter; but when I was fully recovered there was no such tree there, which convinced me that I was not awake, and had not so full command of my reason as I thought I had. I should not have mentioned so trivial a matter, but to satisfy those that read this, that they may be as much deceived in their conjectures as I was at the time I have mentioned.

We remained here a short time after my return from New-London, when we received information that the British were moving up the Hudson river in force, had taken possession of Stoney point, and were fortifying it. We were immediately ordered to march, which order was quickly put in execution. We went directly to the Fishkill, on the Hudson, and from thence down nearly opposite to West point. We remained here some days, I was the most of that time on a stationed guard, keeping the horses that belonged to the army at pasture. I procured some damaged cartridges, and after converting the balls into shot, and getting out of hearing from the camp, diverted myself by killing birds or squirrels, or any such game; this I often practised, though I ran the risk of a keelhaling, if detected. Here I had a good opportunity to exercise myself at the business, being at a considerable distance from camp; pigeons were plenty, and we fared pretty comfortably with what provisions we were allowed otherwise.

After being relieved from this guard, I was detached with a small party to the Peekskill, in the southern edge of the Highlands. We took up our quarters in some old barracks; there was a number of bombshells and some old damaged wagon wheels lying near the barracks; one day, after diverting ourselves by filling the shells with water, pluging them up, and setting them on the fire, while the water boiling, the steam would force the plug out with a report as loud as that of a pistol. Tired with exercising ourselves at this diversion, we began to contrive some other mischief, when four or five of us took one of the old wagon wheels, and after considerable trouble and fatigue, we carried the wheel about thirty or forty rods up the mountain, at the back of the barracks and a considerable distance from them, when we gave the wheel the liberty to shift for itself and find its own way back. It went very regular for a few turns, when taking a glancing stroke against something, it took a course directly for the barracks and just in that part too where the men were, who we could hear distinctly laughing and talking—Ah me! what would I not have given had I never meddled with the ugly thing, but it was then too late to repent, the evil one had come. I confess, I felt myself in a forlorn case; the barracks were only a single board thick, and those rotten and old, and the wheel might have gone through them and the men too, that stood in its route, without scarcely retarding its progress. We all stood breathless, waiting the result, when, as it happened (and well for us there was such a thing as chance) the wheel, when within about fifteen feet of the barracks, and with the motion almost of a cannon-ball, struck something that gave it an elevation of twenty or thirty feet into the air, and passed over the barracks and several rods beyond them before it struck the ground again. The reader may rest satisfied that this last circumstance did not cause many tears of grief to fall.

The Americans had a fortification upon Verplank's point, on the eastern side of the Hudson, opposite Stoney point, garrisoned by a Captain and about one hundred men. The British took this place and made the garrison prisoners, after a close siege of about a week, and fortified the point. They appeared, by their conduct, to have a strong inclination to possess West point. To make a diversion in their own favour and draw off some of our forces from the vicinity of that fortress, they sent the infamous Gov. Tryon into Connecticut with his banditti, who took possession first of New-Haven and plundered it, and then embarked and went and plundered and burnt Fairfield and Norwalk. The two Connecticut brigades were then sent in pursuit of them. We marched nearly down to the seacoast, when the enemy getting scent of us they took to their shipping and made the best of their way back to New-York. We returned as soon as possible. Being on our march the fifteenth day of July, and destitute of all kinds of eatables, just at night I observed a cheese in a press before a farmer's door, and we being about to halt for the night, I determined to return after dark and lay siege to it; but we went further than I expected before we halted, and a smart shower of rain with thunder happening at the time, the cheese escaped. It cleared off with a brisk wind at northwest and cold; we were all wet to the skin, and had no tents with us, lying on the western side of a cleared hill. I never came nearer perishing with the cold in the middle of summer in all my life, either before or since.

In the night we heard the cannon at Stoney point, and early next morning had information of the taking of that place, by the Light Infantry of our army, under the command of Gen. Wayne. Our officers were all on tiptoe to show their abilities in executing some extraordinary exploit. Verplank's point was the word; "shall the Light Infantry get all the honour, and we do nothing!" said they. Accordingly, we sat off, full tilt, to take Verplank's point; we marched directly for the Peekskill, and arrived near there early in the day. We there received information that the British at Verplank's point were reinforced, and advancing to attack *us*. We were quite knocked on the head by this news. However, we put ourselves in as good a condition as our circumstances would admit, and waited their approach; they were afraid of us, or we of them, or both, for we did not come in contact that time. And thus ended the taking of Verplank's point, and our honourable expectations.

We then fell back and encamped, but soon after we broke up our encampment and fell back to Robinson's farm, just below West-point, on the eastern side of the river; here we lay the rest of the season, employed in building two strong bomb-proof redoubts, on two hills near the river. Sometime, late in the fall, the British evacuated all their works and retired to New-York. A large detachment (of which I was one) was sent to Verplank's point to level the British works. We were occupied in this business nearly two weeks, working and starving by day, and at night having to lie in the woods without tents. Some of our men got some pease which had been left there by the British, but one might as well have boiled gravel stones soft. Some affirmed that they had seen them growing where the British soldiers had dropt them after they had passed through them. After we had finished levelling these works we returned to camp.

While lying at, or near the Peekskill, a man belonging to the Cavalry was executed for desertion to the enemy, and as none of the corps to which he belonged were there, no troops were paraded, as was customary on such occasions, except a small guard. The ground on which the gallows was erected was literally covered with pebble stones. A Brigade-Major attended the execution; his duty on these occasions being the same as the High-Sheriff's in civil matters. He had, somewhere, procured a raggamuffin fellow for an executioner, to preserve his own immaculate reputation from defilement. After the culprit had hung the time prescribed by law, or custom, the hangman began stripping the corpse; the clothes being his perquisite. He began by trying to pull off his boots, but for want of a boot-jack he could not readily accomplish his aim; he kept pulling and hauling at them, like a dog at a root, until the spectators, who were very numerous, (the guard having gone off,) growing disgusted, began to make use of the stones, by tossing several at his pretty carcass. The Brigade-Major interfering in behalf his aid-de-camp, shared the same usage; they were both quickly obliged "to quit the field;" as they retreated the stones flew merrily. They were obliged to keep at a proper distance until the soldiers took their own time to disperse, when they returned and completed their honourable business.

We remained at and near Peekskill till some time in the month of December. The cold weather having commenced earlier than usual, we had hard combatting with hunger, cold, nakedness and hard duty, but were obliged to grapple with them all as well as we could. As the old woman said by her husband, when she baked him instead of his clothes, to kill the vermin, "You must grin and bear it."

About the middle of this month (December) we crossed the Hudson, at King's ferry, and proceeded into New-Jersey, for winter-quarters. The snow had fallen nearly a foot deep.—Now I request the reader to consider what must have been our situation at this time, naked, fatigued and starved, forced to march many a weary mile in winter, through cold and snow, to seek a situation in some (to us, unknown) wood to build us habitations to starve and suffer in. I do not know how the hearers of this recital may feel, but *I* know how I felt at the time, and I know how I yet feel at the recollection of it; but there was no remedy, we *must* go through it, and we did go through it, and I am yet alive.

Our destination was at a place in New-Jersey, called Baskinridge. It was cold and snowy, we had to march all day through the snow and at night take up our lodgings in some wood, where, after shovelling away the snow, we used to pitch three or four tents facing each other, and then join in making a fire in the centre. Sometimes we could procure an armful of buckwheat straw to lie upon, which was deemed a luxury. Provisions, as usual, took up but a small part of our time, though much of our thoughts.

We arrived on our wintering ground in the latter part of the month of December, and once more, like the wild animals, began to make preparations to build us a "city for habitation." The soldiers, when immediately going about the building of their winter huts, would always endeavour to provide themselves with such tools as were necessary for the business, (it is no concern of the reader's, as I conceive, by what means they procured their tools,) such as crosscut-saws, handsaws, frows, augers, &c. to expedite the erection and completion of their dwellingplaces. Do not blame them too much, gentle reader, if you should chance to make a shrewd Yankee guess how they *did* procure them; remember, they were in distress, and you know when a man is in that condition, he will not be over scrupulous how he obtains relief, so he does obtain it.

We encamped near our destined place of operation and immediately commenced. It was upon the southerly declivity of a hill; the snow, as I have already observed, was more than a foot deep, and the weather none of the warmest. We had to level the ground to set our huts upon; the soil was a light loam. When digging just below the frost, which was not deep, the snow having fallen early in the season, we dug out a number of toads, that would hop off when brought to the light of day as lively as in summer time. We found by this where toads take up their winter-quarters, if we can never find where swallows take up theirs.

As this will be the last time that I shall have occasion to mention my having to build huts for our winter habitations, I will, by the reader's leave, just give a short description of the fashion and manner of erecting one of those log towns.

After the ground was marked out by the Quartermasters, much after the same manner as for pitching tents in the field, we built the huts in the following manner.—Four huts, two in front and two in the rear, then a space of six or eight feet, when four more huts were placed in the same order, and so on to the end of the regiment, with a parade in front and a street through the whole, between the front and rear, the whole length, twelve or fifteen feet wide. Next in order, in the rear of these huts the officers of the companies built theirs with their waiters in the rear of them. Next, the Field officers in the same order; every two huts, that is, one in front and one in the rear, had just their width in front indefinitely, and no more, to procure the materials for building; the officers had all in the rear. No one was allowed to transgress these bounds on any account whatever, either for building or firewood. The next thing is the erecting of the huts; they were generally about twelve by fifteen or sixteen feet square, (all uniformly of the same dimensions,) the building of them was thus; after procuring the most suitable timber for the business, it was laid up by notching them in at the four corners. When arrived at the proper heighth, about seven feet, the two end sticks which held those that served for plates were made to jut out about a foot from the sides and a straight pole made to rest on them, parellel to the plates; the gable ends were then formed by laying on pieces with straight poles on each, which served for ribs to hold the covering, drawing in gradually to the ridge pole. Now for the coving; this was done by sawing some of the larger trees into cuts about four feet in length, splitting them into bolts, and riving them into shingles, or rather staves; the covering then commenced by laying on those staves, resting the lower ends on the poles by the plates, they were laid on in two thicknesses, carefully breaking joints; these were then bound on by a straight pole with withes, then another double tier with the butts resting on this pole and bound on as before, and so on to the end of the chapter. A chimney was then built at the centre of the backside, composed of stone as high as the eves and finished with sticks and clay, if clay was to be had, if not, with mud. The last thing was to hew stuff and build us up cabins or births to sleep in, and then the buidings were fitted for the reception of *gentlemen soldiers,* with all their *rich* and *gay* furniture.

Such were the habitations we had to construct at this time. We got into them about the beginning of the year, when the weather became intensely cold. Cold weather and snow were plenty, but beef and bread were extremely scarce in the army. Let it be recollected that this was what has been termed the "hard winter," and hard it was to the poor soldiers, as will appear in the sequel. So here I will close the narrative of my campaign of 1779. And happy should I then have thought myself if that had ended the war, but I had to see a little more trouble before that period arrived.

Chapter VI. Campaign of 1780.

The soldier defending his country's rights,
Is griev'd when that country his services slights;
But when he remonstrates and finds no relief,
No wonder his anger takes place of his grief.

THE winter of 1779 and '80 was very severe; it has been denominated "the hard winter," and hard it was to the army in particular, in more respects than one. The period of the revolution has repeatedly been styled "the times that tried men's souls." I often found that those times not only tried men's souls, but their bodies too; I know they did mine, and that effectually.

Sometime in the month of January there happened a spell of remarkably cold weather; in the height of the cold, a large detachment from the army was sent off on an expedition against some fortifications held by the British on Staten Island. The detachment was commanded by Major-General John Sullivan. It was supposed by our officers that the bay before New-York was frozen sufficiently to prevent any succours being sent to the garrisons in their works. It was therefore determined to endeavour to surprise them and get possession of their fortifications before they could obtain help. Accordingly, our troops were all conveyed in sleighs and other carriages; but the enemy got intelligence of our approach (doubtless by some tory) before our arrival on the island. When we arrived we found Johnny Bull prepared for our reception; he was always complaisant, especially when his own honour or credit was concerned; we accordingly found them all waiting for us—so that we could not surprise them, and to take their works by storm looked too hazardous; to besiege them in regular form was out of the question, as the bay was not frozen so much as we expected. There was an armed brig lying in the ice not far from the shore, she received a few shots from our fieldpieces for a morning's salutation; we then fell back a little distance and took up our abode for the night upon a bare bleak hill, in full rake of the northwest wind, with no other covering or shelter than the canopy of the heavens, and no fuel but some old rotten rails which we dug up through the snow, which was two or three feet deep; the weather was cold enough to cut a man in two.

We lay on this accommodating spot till morning when we began our retreat from the island. The British were quickly in pursuit; they attacked our rear guard and made several of them prisoners, among whom was one of my particular associates. Poor young fellow! I have never seen or heard any thing from him since. We arrived at camp after a tedious and cold march of many hours, some with frozen toes, some with frozen fingers and ears, and half starved into the bargain. Thus ended our Staten Island expedition.

Soon after this there came on several severe snowstorms. At one time it snowed the greater part of four days successively, and there fell nearly as many feet deep of snow, and here was the keystone of the arch of starvation. We were absolutely, literally starved;—I do solemnly declare that I did not put a single morsel of victuals into my mouth for four days and as many nights, except a little black birch bark which I gnawed off a stick of wood, if that can be called victuals. I saw several of the men roast their old shoes and eat them, and I was afterwards informed by one of the officer's waiters, that some of the officers killed and ate a favourite little dog that belonged to one of them.—If this was not "suffering" I request to be informed what can pass under that name; if "suffering" like this did not "try men's souls," I confess that I do not know what could. The fourth day, just at dark, we obtained a half pound of lean fresh beef and a gill of wheat for each man, whether we had any salt to season so delicious a morsel, I have forgotten, but I am sure we had no bread, (except the wheat,) but I will assure the reader that we had the best of sauce; that is, we had keen appetites. When the wheat was so swelled by boiling as to be beyond the danger of swelling in the stomach, it was deposited there without ceremony.

After this, we sometimes got a little beef, but no bread; we, however, once in a while got a little rice, but as to flour or bread, I do not recollect that I saw a morsel of either (I mean wheaten) during the winter, all the bread kind we had was Indian meal.

We continued here, starving and freezing, until, I think, some time in the month of February, when the two Connecticut Brigades were ordered to the lines near Staten Island. The small parties from the army which had been sent to the lines, were often surprised and taken by the enemy or cut to pieces by them. These circumstances, it seems, determined the Commander-in-chief to have a sufficient number of troops there to withstand the enemy even should they come in considerable force. And now a long continuance of our hardships appeared unavoidable. The first brigade took up its quarters in a village called Westfield, and the second in another called Springfield;—we were put into the houses with the inhabitants. A fine addition we were, doubtless, to their families, but as we were so plentifully furnished with necessaries, especially in the article of food, we could not be burdensome to them, as will soon appear.

I think it necessary before I proceed further, to prevent much repetition, to give some information of the nature and kind of duty we had to perform while here, that the reader may form a clearer idea of the hardships we had to encounter in the discharge of it. Well, then, I shall speak only of the first brigade, as I belonged to that; as to the second, I know no more of it, than that those who belonged to it doubtless had as hard duty and hard times as we had in the first. I say, as I belonged to the first brigade, I shall endeavour to describe some of the hardships and troubles we had to contend with.

We were stationed about six miles from Elizabethtown, which is situated near the waters which separate Staten Island from the main. We had to send a detachment to this place which continued on duty there several days, it consisted of about two hundred men, and had to form several guards while there. We had another guard, which consisted of about one hundred men, at a place called Woodbridge; this guard staid there two days before they were relieved, and was ten miles from our quarters. Woodbridge also lay by the same waters. We likewise kept a quarter guard in every regiment at home, besides other small guards. Our duty all the winter and spring was thus—suppose I went upon the Woodbridge guard, I must march from the parade at eight o'clock in the morning, go a distance of ten miles and relieve the guard already there, which would commonly bring it to about twelve o'clock; stay there two days and two nights, then be relieved and take up the afternoon of that day to reach our quarters at Westfield,—where, as soon as I could get into my quarters, and, generally, before I could lay by my arms, warned for Elizabethtown the next day; thus it was the whole time we lay here, which was from the middle of February to the latter part of May following. It was Woodbridge and Elizabethtown, Elizabethtown and Woodbridge alternately, till I was absolutely sick of hearing the names mentioned.

And now I will relate some of the incidents and accidents that occurred during this *very pleasant* tour, that is, as far as I was concerned.

The first thing I shall mention is one that has so very seldom been heard of by the reader, that, it may be, he has forgotten it; I mean, we had next to nothing to eat. As I have just before observed, we had no wheat flour, all the bread stuff we got was Indian corn meal and Indian corn flour. Our Connecticut Yankees were as ignorant of making this meal or flour into bread, as a wild Indian would be of making pound cake; all we had any idea of doing with it was, to make it into hasty-pudding, and sometimes (though very rarely) we would chance to get a little milk, or, perhaps, a little cider, or some such thing to wash it down with; and when we could get nothing to qualify it, we ate it as it was. The Indian flour was much worse than the meal, being so fine it was as clamy as glue, and as insipid as starch. We were glad to get even this, for nothing else could be had; flesh meat was nearly as scarce as wheaten bread, we had but very little of the former, and not any of the latter; there was not the least thing to be obtained from the inhabitants, they being so near the enemy, and many of them seemed to be as poor as ourselves.

The guard kept at Woodbridge, being so small, and so far from the troops, and so near the enemy that they were obliged to be constantly on the alert. We had three different houses that we occupied alternately, during the night; the first was an empty house, the second the parson's house, and the third a farmer's house; we had to remove from one to the other of these houses three times every night, from fear of being surprised by the enemy. There was no trusting the inhabitants, for many of them were friendly to the British, and we did not know who were or who were not, and consequently, were distrustful of them all, unless it were one or two. The parson was a staunch whig, as the friends to the country were called in those times, and the farmer, mentioned before, was another, and perhaps more that we were not acquainted with; be that as it would, we were shy of trusting them. Here, especially in the night, we were obliged to keep about one half of the guard upon sentry, and besides these, small patroling parties on all the roads leading towards the enemy; but with all the vigilance we could exercise, we could hardly escape being surprised and cut off by the enemy; they exerted themselves more than common, to take some of our guards, because we had challenged them to do it, and had bid them defiance.

I was once upon this guard, it was in the spring, after the snow had gone off the ground; myself and another young man took for our tour of duty to patrol upon a certain road during the night. About midnight or a little after, our guard being then at the farmer's house, which was the farthest back from the water's side of any of the houses we occupied; this distance caused some of our sentinels to be three miles from the guard. We patroled from the guard to the farthest sentries which, were two, (or in military phrase, a double sentinel,) who were standing upon a bridge. After we had visited these sentinels and were returning, we passed the parson's house; there was a muddy plash in the road nearly opposite the house, and as it happened, the man with me passed on the side next to the house, and I passed on the other; after we had got clear of the water and had come together again, he told me there were British soldiers lying in the garden and door yard; I asked him if he was sure of it, he said he was, for, said he, "I was near enough to have reached them with my hand, had there been no fence between." We stopped and consulted what was best for us to do. I was for going back and giving them a starter, but my comrade declined, he thought it would be best to return to the guard and inform the officers what we had discovered, and let them act their pleasure. We accordingly did so, when the Captain of the guard sent down two horsemen that attended upon the guard to serve in such circumstances and to carry and fetch intelligence, to ascertain whether it was as we had reported; the horsemen finding it true, instead of returning and informing the officers, as they were ordered to, fired their carbines, one into the house, the ball lodging in the bedpost where the parson and his wife were in bed, and the other into the garden or door yard; the British finding they were discovered, walked off with themselves without even returning a single shot. We were sorry then that we had not given them a loving salute as we passed them, and thus saved the horsemen the trouble. This was one among many of the sly methods the British took to surprise and take our guards.

At another time I was upon the Elizabethtown station; being one night on my post as sentinel, I observed a stir among the troops composing the detachment; I inquired the cause, of a passing officer, who told me the British were upon Holstead's point, which was a point of land about two miles from the main body of the detachment, where we had a guard consisting of a sergeant, a corporal, and ten privates. The circumstances were as follows, the guard informed the man of the house where the guard was kept (a Mr. Holstead, the owner of the land that formed the point) that they had heard boats pass and repass at some distance below, during the night. He said they were the British, and that they had landed some of the Refugees, as that neighbourhood abounded with such sort of cattle, but that it would be next to impossible to detect them, as they had so many friends in that quarter, and many of the enemy belonging to those parts, they knew every lurking place in all the neighbouring country; the only way for the guard was, to be vigilant and prevent a surprise. When the guard was relieved in the morning, the new one was informed of these circumstances, and cautioned to be on the look out.

Accordingly at night, they consulted with Mr. Holstead, who advised them to place a sentinel at a certain spot that had been neglected, for, said he, "they know your situation better than you do yourselves; and if they come, they will enter your precincts by the way I have pointed out to you, and," continued he, "they will come about the time of the setting of the moon." Agreeable to his advice the sergeant stationed a sentinel at that place, and prepared for them. Just as had been predicted, about the time the moon was setting, which was about ten o'clock, they came, and at the same point. The first sentinel that occupied that post had not stood out his trick, before he saw them coming; he immediately hailed them by the usual question, "who comes there?" they answered him, that if he would not discharge his piece, they would not hurt him, but if he did they would kill him. The sentinel being true to his trust, paid no regard to their threats, but fired his piece and ran for the house to alarm the guard; in his way he had to cross a hedge fence, in passing which, he got entangled in the bushes, as it was supposed, and the enemy coming up thrust a bayonet through him, they then inflicted twelve more wounds upon him with bayonets, and rushed on for the house, to massacre the remainder of the guard, but they had taken the alarm and left the house. The Refugees (for such they were) entered the house, but found none of the men to murder. Mr.

Holstead had two young daughters in the house, one of which secreted herself in a closet and remained throughout the whole transaction undiscovered; the other they caught, and compelled to light a candle, and attend them about the house in search of the Rebels, but without finding any, or offering any other abuse to the young lady, (which was indeed a wonder.) When they could find none to wreak their vengeance upon, they cut open the knapsacks of the guard, and strewed the Indian meal about the floor, laughing at the poverty of the Yankee soldiery, who had nothing but hog's fodder, as they termed it, to eat; after they had done all the mischief they could in the house, they proceeded to the barn and drove off five or six head of Mr. Holstead's young cattle, took them down upon the point and killed them, and went off in their boats, that had come across from the island for that purpose, to their den among the British.

There was another young man belonging to the guard, on his post at the extremity of the point; when the Refugees came down to embark, they cut off this man's retreat, there being a sunken marsh on each side of the point, covered with dry flags and reeds; when he challenged them, they answered him the same as they did the other sentinel; but he paid as little attention to their threats as the other had done, although, apparently, in a much worse situation, but fired his musket, and sprang into the marsh among the reeds, where he sunk to his middle in the mud, and there remained unperceived, till they went off, and thus preserved his life.

Such manœuvres the British continued to exhibit the whole time we were stationed here, but could never do any other damage to us than killing poor Twist, (the name of the young man.) Unfortunate young man! I could not restrain my tears, when I saw him next day, with his breast like a sieve, caused by the wounds. He lost his own life by endeavouring to save the lives of others; massacred by his own countrymen, who ought to have been fighting in the common cause of the country, instead of murdering him. I have been more particular in relating this circumstance, that the reader may be informed what people there were in the times of the revolution. Mr. Holstead told me that almost the whole of his neighbourhood had joined the enemy and that his next door neighbour was in this very party. There was a large number in this place and its vicinity by the name of Hetfield who were notorious rascals. A certain Captain of Militia, resident in these parts, who, upon some occasion, had business to transact within the reach of these miscreants, they caught and hanged him up without ceremony, judge or jury. General Washington demanded the perpetrators of this infernal deed, of the British authorities in New-York, but they declined complying with his demand, he, therefore, selected a British Captain, a prisoner,—a son, and I believe an only son, of an opulent English lady, and put him in close confinement, threatening to execute him unless the murderers were given up to justice. But his distressed mother by her strong maternal intercession with the King and court of France prevailed on them; and their remonstrances to Gen. Washington, joined with his own benevolent feelings, so far wrought upon him that he set the Captain at liberty and thus these murderous villains escaped the punishment due to their infernal deeds.

We remained on this tedious duty, getting nothing to eat but our old fare, Indian meal, and not over much of that, till the middle of May, when we were relieved, but we remained at our quarters eight or ten days after that. Our duty was not quite so hard now as it had been, but that faithful companion, hunger, stuck as close to us as ever; he was a faithful associate, I will not say friend, for, indeed, poverty is no friend, nor has *he* many admirers, though he has an extensive acquaintance;— the soldiers were well acquainted with him during the whole period of the revolutionary war.

We were here at the time the "dark day" happened, (19th of May;) it has been said that the darkness was not so great in New-Jersey as in New-England. How great it was there I do not know, but I know that it was very dark where I then was in New-Jersey; so much so that the fowls went to their roosts, the cocks crew and the whip-poor-wills sung their usual serenade; the people had to light candles in their houses to enable them to see to carry on their usual business; the night was as uncommonly dark as the day was.

We left Westfield about the twenty-fifth of May, and went to Baskinridge to our old winter cantonments; we did not reoccupy the huts which we built, but some others that the troops had left, upon what account I have forgotten. Here, the monster Hunger, still attended us; he was not to be shaken off by any efforts we could use, for here was the old story of starving, as rife as ever. We had entertained some hopes that when we had left the lines and joined the main army, we should fare a little better, but we found that there was no betterment in the case. For several days after we rejoined the army, we got a little musty bread, and a little beef, about every other day, but this lasted only a short time and then we got nothing at all. The men were now exasperated beyond endurance; they could not stand it any longer; they saw no other alternative but to starve to death, or break up the army, give all up and go home. This was a hard matter for the soldiers to think upon; they were truly patriotic; they loved their country, and they had already suffered every thing short of death in its cause; and now, after such extreme hardships to give up all, was too much; but to starve to death was too much also. What was to be done?—Here was the army starved and naked, and there their country sitting still and expecting the army to do notable things while fainting from sheer starvation. All things considered, the army was not to be blamed. Reader, suffer what we did and you will say so too.

We had borne as long as human nature could endure, and to bear longer we considered folly. Accordingly, one pleasant day, the men spent the most of their time upon the parade, growling like soreheaded dogs; at evenening roll-call they began to show their dissatisfaction, by snapping at the officers, and acting contrary to their orders; after their dismissal from the parade, the officers went, as usual, to their quarters, except the Adjutant, who happened to remain, giving details for next day's duty to the orderly sergeants, or some other business, when the men (none of whom had left the parade) began to make him sensible that they had something in train; he said something that did not altogether accord with the soldiers' ideas of propriety, one of the men retorted, the Adjutant called him a mutinous rascal, or some such epithet, and then left the parade. This man, then stamping the butt of his musket upon the ground, as much as to say, I am in a passion, called out, "who will parade with me?" The whole regiment immediately fell in and formed. We had made no plans for our future operations, but while we were consulting how to proceed, the fourth regiment, which lay on our left, formed, and came and paraded with us. We now concluded to go in a body to the other two regiments that belonged to our brigade, and induce them to join with us; these regiments lay forty or fifty rods in front of us, with a brook and bushes between. We did not wish to have any one in particular to command, lest he might be singled out for a Court Martial to exercise its demency upon; we therefore gave directions to the drummers to give certain signals on the drums; at the first signal we shouldered our arms, at the second we faced, at the third we began our march to join with the other two regiments, and went off with music playing. By this time our officers had obtained knowledge of our military manœuvreing, and some of them had run across the brook, by a nearer way than we had taken, (it being now quite dark,) and informed the officers of those regiments of our approach and supposed intentions. The officers ordered their men to parade as quick as possible *without* arms; when that was done, they stationed a camp guard, that happened be be near at hand, between the men and their huts, which prevented them from entering and taking their arms, which they were very anxious to do. Col. Meigs of the sixth regiment, exerted himself to prevent his men from obtaining their arms, until he received a severe wound in his side by a bayonet in the scuffle, which cooled his courage at the time. He said he had always considered himself the soldier's friend and thought the soldiers regarded him as such; but had reason now to conclude he might be mistaken. Col. Meigs was truly an excellent man and a brave officer;—the man, whoever he was, that wounded him, doubtless, had no particular grudge against him, it was dark, and the wound was given, it is probable, altogether unintentionally. Col. Meigs was afterwards Governor of Ohio, and Postmaster General.

When we found the officers had been too crafty for us we returned with grumbling instead of music, the officers following in the rear growling in concert. One of the men in the rear calling out, "halt in front," the officers seized upon him like wolves on a sheep, and dragged him out of the ranks, intending to make an example of him, for being a "mutinous rascal," but the bayonets of the men pointing at their breasts as thick as hatchel teeth, compelled them quickly to relinquish their hold of him. We marched back to our own parade and then formed again; the officers now began to coax us to disperse to our quarters, but that had no more effect upon us than their threats. One of them slipped away into the bushes, and after a short time returned, counterfeiting to have come directly from head-quarters; said he, "there is good news for you, boys, there has just arrived a large drove of cattle for the army;" but this piece of finesse would not avail; all the answer he received for his labour was, "go and butcher them," or some such slight expression. The Lieutenant-Colonel of the fourth regiment now came on to the parade; he could persuade *his* men, he said, to go peaceably to their quarters; after a good deal of palaver, he ordered them to shoulder their arms, but the men taking no notice of him or his order, he fell into a violent passion, threatening them with the bitterest punishment, if they did not immediately obey his orders; after spending a whole quiver of the arrows of his rhetoric, he again ordered them to shoulder their arms, but he met with the same success that he did at the first trial, he therefore gave up the contest as hopeless, and left us and walked off to his quarters, chewing the cud of resentment all the way, and how much longer I neither knew nor cared. The rest of the officers, after they found that they were likely to meet with no better success than the Colonel, walked off likewise to their huts.

While we were under arms, the Pennsylvania troops, who lay not far from us, were ordered under arms and marched off their parades upon, as they were told, a secret expedition; they had surrounded us, unknown to either us or themselves, (except the officers,) at length, getting an item of what was going forward, they inquired of some of the stragglers, what was going on among the Yankees? Being informed that they had mutined on account of the scarcity of provisions,—"Let us join them," said they, "let us join the Yankees, they are good fellows, and have no notion of lying here like fools and starving." Their officers needed no further hinting; the troops were quickly ordered back to their quarters, from fear that they would join in the same song with the Yankees.—We knew nothing of all this for some time afterwards.

After our officers had left us to our own option, we dispersed to our huts, and laid by our arms of our own accord, but the worm of hunger knawing so keen kept us from being entirely quiet, we therefore still kept upon the parade in groups, venting our spleen at our country and government, then at our officers, and then at ourselves for our imbecility, in staying there and starving in detail for an ungrateful people, who did not care what became of us, so they could enjoy themselves while we were keeping a cruel enemy from them. While we were thus venting our gall against we knew not who, Colonel Stewart of the Pennsylvania line, with two or three other officers of that line came to us and questioned us respecting our unsoldierlike conduct, (as he termed it;) we told him he needed not to be informed of the cause of our present conduct, but that we had borne till we considered further forbearance pusillanimity; that the times, instead of mending, were growing worse, and finally, that we were determined not to bear or forbear much longer. We were unwilling to desert the cause of our country, when in distress; that we knew her cause involved our own; but what signified our perishing in the act of saving her, when that very act would inevitably destroy us, and she must finally perish with us. "Why do you not go to your officers?" said he, "and complain in a regular manner;" we told him we had repeatedly complained to them, but they would not hear us. "Your officers," said he, "are gentlemen, they *will* attend to you, I know them, they cannot refuse to hear you. But," said he, "your officers suffer as much as you do, we all suffer, the officers have no money to purchase supplies with any more than the private men have, and if there is nothing in the public store we must fare as hard as you. I have no other resources than you have to depend upon; I had not a sixpence to purchase a partridge, that was offered me the other day. Besides," said he, "you know not how much you injure your own characters by such conduct.—You Connecticut troops have won immortal honour to yourselves the winter past, by your perseverance, patience, and bravery, and now you are shaking it off at your heels. But I will go and see your officers, and talk with them myself." He went, but what the result was, I never knew.—This Colonel Stewart was an excellent officer, much beloved and respected by the troops of the line he belonged to. He possessed great personal beauty, the Philadelphia ladies stiled him *the Irish Beauty.*

Our stir did us some good in the end, for we had provisions directly after, so we had no great cause for complaint for some time.

About this time there were about three thousand men ordered out for a particular field day, for the Prussian General Baron de Stuben to exercise his manœuvreing functions upon. We marched off our regimental parades at dawn of day, and went three or four miles, to Morristown, to a fine plain, where we performed a variety of military evolutions. We were furnished with a plenty of blank cartridges, had eight or ten fieldpieces, and made a great noise, if nothing more. About one or two o'clock we ceased, and were supplied with a gill of rum each; having had nothing to eat since the night before, the liquor took violent hold, and there were divers queer tricks exhibited both by officers and men. I saw a Pennsylvania soldier staggering off with three espontoons on his shoulder, that he had gleaned up after some of his officers. This day was nearly equal to the whiskey scrape at the Schuylkill, in 1777.

In the month of June five thousand British and Hessian troops advanced into New-Jersey, burnt several houses in Elizabethtown and the Presbyterian meeting house and most of the village of Springfield; they also barbarously murdered, by shooting, Mrs. Caldwell, the wife of the Minister of that place;—what their further intentions were could not be ascertained by our commanders. Sometimes it was conjectured that they were aiming at a quantity of public stores deposited in Morristown; sometimes that it was for a diversion in favour of their main army, by endeavouring to amuse us till their forces could push up the North river and attack West point. Our army was accordingly kept in a situation to relieve either in case of an attack. While we remained in this situation our army was infested by spies from the British;—I saw three of those vermin, one day, hanging on one gallows. The enemy soon after recoiled into their shell again at New-York.

During these operations, we were encamped at a place called the Short-hills. While lying here, I came near taking another final discharge from the army in consequence of my indiscretion and levity. I was one day upon a camp guard; we kept our guard in the fields, and to defend us from the night dew, we laid down under some trees which stood upon the brink of a very deep gully; the sides and tops of the banks of this gully were covered with walnut or hickory saplings, three, four, or five inches diameter at their butts, and many of them were fifty or sixty feet in height. In the morning before the guard was relieved, some of the men (and I among the rest, to be sure, I was never far away when such kind of business was going forward) took it into our heads to divert ourselves by climbing these trees as high as they would bear us, and then swinging off our feet, the weight would bring us by a gentle flight to the ground, when the tree would resume its former position. After exercising ourselves some time at this diversion, I thought I would have one capital swing; accordingly, I climbed one of the tallest trees that stood directly on the verge of the gully, and swung off over the gully; when the tree had bent to about an horizontal position, it snapped off as short as a pipestem; I suppose I was nearly or quite forty feet from the ground, from which distance I came, feet foremost, to the ground at quick time; the ground was soft, being loamy and entirely free from stones, so that it did me but little hurt, but I held the part of the tree I had broken off firmly in my grasp, and when I struck the ground with my feet, I brought it with all the force of my weight and its own directly upon the top of my unthinking skull, which knocked me as stiff as a ringbolt. It was several minutes before I recovered recollection enough to know or remember what I had been about, but I weathered the point, although it gave me a severe headache for several days afterwards, as a memento to keep upon the ground, and not attempt to act the part of a flying squirrel.

Another affair happened soon after this which did not set very well on my stomach at the time. I had been on a detached party for four or five days and had had nothing to eat, for at least eight and forty hours of the latter part of the time. When I came to camp there was nothing there; I strolled off to where some butchers were killing cattle, as I supposed, for the General officers, (for they must have victuals, let the poor men fare as they would,) and by some means procured an old ox's liver; I then went home and soon had a quantity of it in my kettle; the more I seethed it the harder it grew, but I soon filled my empty stomach with it, and, it being night, I turned in; I had not slept long before I awoke, feeling much like Jonathan when he had the dry bellyache for want of some fourth proof Jamaica spirits; that is, I felt "dreadfully." I worried it out till morning, when, as soon as I thought I could call upon the doctors, without too much disturbing their honours, I applied to one for relief; he gave me a large dose of tartar-emetic, the usual remedy in the army for all disorders, even sore eyes, though he could not have given me a better one for my then present malady. He gave me ample directions how to proceed, a part of which was, to take one half or two thirds of the potion, and wait a given time, and if it did not operate, then to swallow the remainder; it did not work till I had the whole in my crop, nor then neither. I waited sometime for it, but growing impatient, I wandered off into the fields and bushes to see what effect exercise would have; I had not strolled a half or three fourths of a mile from camp, when it took full hold of my gizzard; I then sat down upon a log, or stone, or something else, and discharged the hard junks of liver like grapeshot from a fieldpiece. I had no water or any other thing to ease my retchings. O, I thought I *must* die in good earnest. The liver still kept coming, and I looked at every heave for my own liver to come next, but that happened to be too well fastened to part from its moorings. Perhaps the reader will think this a trifling matter, happening in the ordinary course of things, but I think it a "suffering," and not a small one neither, "of a revolutionary soldier."

After the British had retreated to New-York, our army marched for West point. We passed through the Highlands, by the Clove, a remarkable chasm in the mountains, and came out on the bank of the Hudson river, at a place called Buttermilk-falls, where a small stream falls into the river over a high craggy bank, forming a pretty cascade. We halted here, it was in the morning, and I well remember our Colonel's orders on the occasion, "men," said he, "you have one hour allowed you to refresh yourselves!" Had we been herbaceous animals, we might have refreshed ourselves on browse, for there was no deficiency of that, but as to victuals fit for human beings, I question if there was five pounds weight in the whole regiment; I had none, nor had I had any for twenty-four hours; we were, at this time, ruminating animals, but our ruminating was mentally, not by the teeth. Had the falls been real buttermilk, the Colonel's order might have been given with some propriety, but as it was not so, we were forced to be patient, for we did not expect to be fed by a miracle.

We passed on to West point; the Connecticut forces crossed the river to the eastern side, and encamped opposite to West point, upon what was called Nelson's point. It was now very hot weather, being the latter part of June; here, for a considerable length of time, our rations, when we got any, consisted of bread and salt shad; this fish, as salt as fire, and dry bread, without any kind of vegetables, was hard fare in such extreme hot weather as it was then. We were compelled to eat it as it was; if we attempted to soak it in a brook that ran close by the camp, we were quite sure to lose it; there being a great abundance of Otters and Minks in and about the water, four legged and two legged, (but much the largest number of the latter,) so that they would be quite sure to carry off the fish, let us do what we would to prevent it.

Soon after we were encamped here I was sent off with a working party to work upon some fortifications on Constitution Island, a mile or two higher up the river. We had our allowance of salt shad and bread, and were to remain there a week; our duty was, chiefly, wheeling dirt upon a stone building intended for a magazine. We had to wheel to the top of the wall, which was about twenty feet high, upon a way two planks wide, and in the passage we had to cross a chasm in the rocks thirty or forty feet wide and perhaps as many deep. None of us happened to take a dive into it, but it often made my head swim when crossing it at such a rate, and I thought it would not be strange if some of us should feel the bottom before we left there. From the planks, which we wheeled upon, to the bottom of the hole, could not be less than sixty feet; if any one had fallen into it he would have received his discharge from the army without further trouble. We continued at this business two or three days, when the weather became so hot that it was difficult to breathe; the rays of the sun reflected from the bare rocks (all that part of the island where we were, being mostly so) was stifling in the extreme, and to complete a bad business, there was not a drop of water on the island, except the brackish water of the river, and that was as warm as milk and almost as nauseous as the waters of the Nile after it had felt the effects of Moses' rod. There was no shade, and we had no tents; we could get no refreshment but in a place where were two high points of rocks butting upon the shore, which caused a small draught of wind (when there was any air stirring) from the river; here we repaired two or three hours, in the heat of the day, and then went to work again till dark.

After we had been two or three days at this invigorating business, the troops were inspected by General Stuben; when he found out our situation, he ordered us off immediately. "You may as well knock those men on the head," said he, "as keep them there, they will die if kept there much longer, and they can do no more if you knock their brains out." He had more sense than our officers; but they did not feel the hardships which we had to undergo, and of course, cared but little, if any thing at all, about us. We were called off, and I never was so glad to get clear of any duty as I was to get clear of that. A state-prison would be preferable to it, for there one might chance to get something to eat, or at least to drink.

And now there was to be a material change in my circumstances, which, in the long run, was much in my favour. There was a small corps to be raised by enlistments, and in case of the failure of that, by drafts from the line; these men were called "Sappers and Miners," to be attached to the engineer's department. I had known of this for some time before, but never had a thought of belonging to it, although I had heard our Major (to whose company I belonged) tell some of our officers (after I had neatly marked his name upon his chest) that if there was a draft from our regiment, he intended I should go, although, he added, he did not wish to part with me. I, however, thought no more about it, till a Captain of that corps applied for a draft of one man from each regiment throughout the whole army present. This Captain was personally acquainted with our Major and told him he would like to have him furnish him with a man from the regiment that he knew was qualified for a non-commissioned officer; the Major then pitched upon me. How far he was to be justified in his choice the reader may, perhaps, be enabled to judge by the construction of this present work; I give him my free consent to exercise his judgment upon it.

I was accordingly, transferred to this corps and bid a farewell forever to my old comrades, as it respected any further associating with them, or sharing in their sufferings or pleasures. I immediately went off with this (now my) Captain and the other men drafted from our brigade, and joined the corps in an old meetinghouse at the Peekskill. It was after dark when we arrived there. I had now got among a new set, who were, to a man, entire strangers to me; I had, of course, to form new acquaintances, but I was not long in doing that; I had a pretty free use of my tongue, and was sometimes apt to use it when there was no occasion for it. However, I soon found myself at home with them. We were all young men and therefore easy to get acquainted.

I found nothing more here for bellytimber than I had in the line, and got nothing to eat till the second day after I had joined the corps. I have heard it remarked by the old farmers, that when beasts are first transferred from one place to another, that if they keep them without food for two or three days, it will go far towards wonting them to their new situation. Perhaps it might be so thought by our commanders. Be that as it would, I got nothing, as I have said, till the second day I had been with them; we then drew, if I remember right, two days rations of our good old diet, salt shad, and as we had not, as yet, associated ourselves into regular messes, as is usual in the army, each man had his fish divided out by himself. We were on the green before the meetinghouse, and there were several cows feeding about the place, I went into the house to get something to put my fish into, or some other business, and staid longer than I intended, or rather ought to have done, for when I came out again, one of the cows was just finishing her meal on my shad, the last I saw of it was the tail of a fish sticking out of the side of her mouth. I was vexed enough to have eaten the weight of it off her carcass, but she took care of that, and I had another opportunity (if well improved) of mortifying my body by fasting two days longer; but I got something among the men, as poorly as they were off, to sustain nature till I could get more by some means or other. Such shifts were nothing strange to us.

This corps of Miners was reckoned an honourable one; it consisted of three companies. All the officers were required to be acquainted with the sciences, and it was desirable to have as intelligent young men as could be procured to compose it, although some of us fell considerably short of perfection. Agreeable to the arrangement between my former commander and my new Captain, I was appointed a sergeant in this corps, which was as high an office as I ever obtained in the army; and I had some doubts in my own mind, at the time, whether I was altogether qualified for that; however, I was a sergeant, and I think I *did* use my best abilities to perform the duties of the office according to my best knowledge and judgment. Indeed, I can say at this late hour of my life, that my conscience never did, and I trust never will accuse me of any failure in my duty to my country, but, on the contrary, I always fulfilled my engagements to her, however she failed in fulfilling her's with me. The case was much like that of a loyal and faithful husband, and a light heeled wanton of a wife. But I forgive her and hope she will do better in future.

Soon after I had joined this corps, the army moved down on the west side of the Hudson to Orangetown, commonly called by the inhabitants of those parts, Tappan, (pronounced Tap-pawn.) Just before arriving at our encamping ground, we halted in the road an hour or two; some four or five of our men, knowing that the regiments to which they formerly belonged were near, slipped off for a few minutes to see their old messmates. When we came to march again, they not having returned, I was ordered to remain with their arms and knapsacks till they came and then bring them on and join the corps again. I accordingly waited an hour or two before they all returned. As soon as I had got them all together we set off; but the troops arriving and passing in almost every direction, I knew not where to go to find our corps. After much trouble and vexation (being constantly interrogated by the passing officers, who we were, and how we came to be behind our troops,) I concluded, that as most or all the troops had passed us, to stay where I then was, and wait the coming up of the baggage of our troops, thinking that the guard or drivers might have directions where to find them. Our baggage happening to be quite in the rear, while we were waiting we had an opportunity to see the baggage of the army pass. When that of the middle States passed us, it was truly amusing to see the number and habiliments of those attending it; of all specimens of human beings, this group capped the whole; a carravan of wild beasts could bear no comparison with it. There was "Tag, Rag and Bobtail;" "some in rags and some in jags," but none "in velvet gowns." Some with two eyes, some with one, and some, I believe, with none at all. They "beggared all description;" their dialect, too, was as confused as their bodily appearance was odd and disgusting; there was the Irish and Scotch brogue, murdered English, flat insipid Dutch and some lingos which would puzzle a philosopher to tell whether they belonged to this world or some "undiscovered country." I was glad to see the tail end of the train, and waited with impatience for the arrival of our baggage, which soon after made its appearance; but the men with the wagons knew no better than myself where to go;—we, however, proceeded and soon after met one of the sergeants coming to meet and conduct us to where our people were, which was at Dobb's ferry, and about three miles from any part of the rest of the army;—most of the Artillery belonging to the army was at the same place.

Here we lay till the close of the campaign. We built a strong blockhouse near the ferry, in which we were assisted by detachments from the main army, and erected a battery near it; but that fiend, scarcity, followed us here; and when we chanced to get any meat we had no salt. For a long time we had to go three fourths of a mile to the river to get water, which was somewhat salt, before we could cook our breakfasts,—this was trifling, however, compared with the trouble of having nothing to cook, which was too often the case with us. There was, indeed, a plenty of fruit to be had, and we being few in number, and so far from the main army, this resource was not soon or easily exhausted; but there were musquetoes enough to take a pound of blood from us, while we could make an ounce. We had some plague or other always to torment us;—says the reader, "who is without?"

Soon after our arrival here, a British brig passed up the river; the same that conveyed the unfortunate Major Andre to his bane. Poor man! he had better have staid where he was better acquainted.

I was about this time ordered to return up the river, in company with one of our Lieutenants, after some clothing for our men. The Lieutenant rode in company with an officer of the Artillery, who was going that way upon business of his own, and I went on foot, and started early in the morning with only my blanket and provisions, (that is, if I had any;) it was very hot weather; and when I had travelled about ten miles on my way, being on a good road, in the heat of the day, and passing through a considerable wood, a young lady made her appearance at a turn of the road about forty rods ahead of me. The heat had induced her to divest herself of some of her outside garments. But upon discovering me in her immediate neighbourhood, she slipped on her clothes and came on towards me seemingly quite unconcerned; but, on thinking better of the matter, (as I supposed,) she concluded that it would not be quite safe to encounter a soldier in such a place; she accordingly turned about and made her escape as fast as possible through the bushes. When she first started from the road I saw her drop something and she partly turned about to take it up, but thinking that it would not do to stop for trifles when the enemy was so near, she resumed her race. I then hallooed to her which caused her to hasten her departure in double quick time. Upon coming to the place where she turned off from the road, I had the curiosity to see what she had dropped, it proved to be a knot of black ribbon, of about a yard and a half. Not knowing but the poor thing might take another fright if she came back after it, I concluded to save her the trouble, and accordingly took it with me. She seemed to be in a violent panic. But every Miss that I saw while in the army was not so easily frightened.

I crossed King's ferry and went on to the foot of the Highlands, where there was a commissary, and wagoners, boatmen, &c. Here I again joined my Lieutenant, and obtained a ration or two of provisions, consisting of corned beef and hard bread, borrowed a pot, cooked my meat, ate my supper, turned in under an old wagon and slept soundly till about an hour before day, when the Lieutenant called me up to go on to Newburgh, about twenty miles further up the river. He had procured a batteau and five or six men to convey us up and bring down the clothing which we were after. We had a mile or two to go to reach the boat, over ledges, through brush, and as dark as Egypt. We then proceeded to Newburgh, where we got our clothing. While I was packing it away in empty hogsheads the Lieutenant gave me a hint to take care of my own interest, I accordingly picked from the best of each article what was allowed to each man and bundled them up by themselves; afterwards, when a distribution was made, some of the sergeants were a little inclined to cavil with me for my partiality to myself, but the Lieutenant interfered in my favour, telling them that I deserved the preference, as I had been at so much pains and trouble while they had remained at home at their ease.

We returned down the river on our way to camp until we came to where we took the boat, when I was set on shore to take the Lieutenant's and the other officer's horses to King's ferry, while the

Lieutenant went down in the boat. I took the horses and went on alone to the ferry; on the way, being hungry, my provisions, if I had any, being in the boat, I saw some fine looking apples in a field and dismounted and filled my pockets with them and ate a considerable quantity; they were sweet and of rather a tough texture, and caused me considerable trouble, as I shall relate by and by. I crossed the ferry in a large scow; there were ten or twelve head of cattle, besides my horses, in the boat. About midway of the river a cow jumped out and took her departure directly down the river, it being ebb tide and the water rapid, she was soon out of sight. There was not the least exertion made to save her; she was continental property and *consequently* thought of but little *consequence.*

I landed and soon found my officer, who had arrived some time before me; he had got our baggage into a wagon, which had gone on, and he was waiting for me. We should have gone down to Dobb's ferry with the boat had it not been for the British brig Vulture, which was lying just below King's ferry, waiting upon Arnold and Andre. There was a large number of wagons, teamsters and soldiers at the ferry; every thing destined to the army, coming down the river, was obliged to be landed here on account of the abovementioned brig. When I had found the Lieutenant he took his horse, leaving the other with me, and sent me back to the river's side on an errand; I did as ordered and then went on after him and our baggage. I had gone but a small distance before my apples began to operate; I had felt their effects some time before. I now began to think the game was up with me; my head ached as though it was splitting into ten thousand pieces and my sight entirely failed. I got, or rather tumbled, off my horse and lay on the ground, giving myself up for lost. The Lieutenant, finding I did not make my appearance, came back to seek me. He found me in a sad condition. I asked him to give me some water; he got some that was quite warm, and it was well for me that it was so, for I had no sooner swallowed it than it caused me to discharge the contents of my stomach, which quickly gave me ease. I then got upon *his* horse, which had a soft deer's skin for a saddle-cloth, and he walked by my side and led my horse. I again asked him for water; he went into a house a little distance from the road, in which was no person except an old man; the Lieutenant asked him for a vessel to dip some water from a spring near by, which was six or eight feet deep; but the old man refused, saying that he would not let a soldier have a cup to drink from if it were to save his life. The officer then took a glass pint mug and came out to me, the old man following him raving like a madman; the Lieutenant gave me some water and, after I had drank, he flung the mug into the spring with a motion that seemed to indicate that he was not well pleased; upon which the old man redoubled his abuse, when the Lieutenant, drawing his sword, swore that if he did not immediately shut his mouth, he would bleed him. The old man seeing the sword glitter, thought it best to shut up whilst his skin was whole, and walked off to the house, and we went on. This officer was a very mild man, but the old man had "raised his ideas" by abusing the soldiers, which he would not bear from any one.

We went on and overtook the wagons; but I felt very meagre all day. I never before thought myself so near death, and it was all occasioned by eating a few apples; but less things than these may deprive a man of life.—This was one "suffering" of a Revolutionary Soldier.

There were more than fifty wagons in company with us, bound to the army. We halted at night at a cluster of houses; the Lieutenant took up his abode for the night in a farmer's house;—I staid out with the wagons. In the evening I strolled into a cornfield, upon some occacasion or other, where I discovered a large patch of watermelons; I took one and went to the wagon and ate it, although the Lieutenant had given me a strict charge not to meddle with any kind of fruit until I had fully digested the apples. He insisted upon my lodging in the house from fear of taking cold, but I chose to keep out with the baggage, which I did till supper time, he then sent out to me to come in and get supper, I could not well refuse this invitation, and went in; the lady of the house provided me a rarity, homminy and milk; the Lieutenant again urged me to stay in the house, but I pretended that our clothing might be in danger unless I attended to it; he said no more to me but left me to regulate my own conduct. It was not the clothing I had so much at heart, though that bore some weight on my mind, but the thought of the luscious watermelons was what so strongly attracted my mind in that direction. Accordingly, when all was still, I went and took as many as I thought necessary, stowed them into the wagon and then lay down under it, and slept very contentedly till morning, without once thinking of the danger of the baggage. We started early next morning and arrived at Dobb's ferry about noon.

Soon after this journey, one night, the British brig came down the river with her precious cargo—Arnold—on board. There were several shots discharged at her as she passed the block-house, but she went by without paying us much attention. The next day it was reported that Gen. Arnold had deserted; I should as soon have thought West point had deserted as he; but I was soon convinced that it was true. Had I possessed the power of foreknowledge, I might twice have put Arnold asleep without any one knowing it and saved the life of, perhaps, a better man, and my country much trouble and disgrace. The first time was at the Peekskill in a barn, just before Andre came to his quarters and while their clandestine negotiation was in progress. I was upon a guard. "There are men," says Shakespear, "who, in their sleep mutter all their conceits." Such an one was Arnold, and therefore afraid to sleep near any one lest he should "babble his conceits" in his sleep. He ordered me and my guard out of the barn, that he might have his bed upon the floor; I was so put out of my bias at the time, that had I known what plans he had in his head, I should have needed but little persuasion to have had a reckoning with him. The other time was but three or four days before his desertion; I met him upon the road a little distance from Dobb's ferry, he was then taking his observations and examing the roads, I thought that he was upon some deviltry; we met at a notch of the roads and I observed he stopped, and sitting upon his horse, seemed minutely to examine each road. I could not help taking notice of him, and thought it strange to see him quite alone in such a lone place. He looked guilty, and well he might, for Satan was in as full possession of him at that instant as ever he was of Judas; it only wanted a musket ball to have driven him out. I had been acquainted with Arnold from my childhood and never had too good an opinion of him.

The British had a block-house below, said to be garrisoned by a gang of fugitive Negroes, commanded by a black by the name of Cuff—Col. Cuff.—One night a black man, a runaway, came to one of our sentinels at our block-house; when he came up he addressed the sentinel with, "is this Col. Cuffee's brock-house?" The sentinel called the commander of the guard, who quickly undeceived poor Ceasar and sent him back to his master, where, no doubt, he got a striped jacket as part of his uniform suit, to remember Col. Cuff by.

Our people had a number of spy boats lying a little distance above the ferry. One night one of these boats went down the river and anchored not far from the western shore, which was there very high, placed a sentinel in the boat and lay down to rest. A British boat, getting intelligence of them, rowed up with muffled oars, keeping close under the highland, in the shadow of the mountains, (the moon being in that quarter,) till they had got above them, and then came directly down upon them. The sentinel immediately roused up the men in the boat; one of them having his musket charged with buckshot, (Yankee pease, as the British used to call them,) challenged them with, "who comes there?" they answered, "we will quickly let you know." The man in our boat, answered, "here's give you Shelar McGira then," and gave them the contents of his musket, which caused a bitter lamentation in the British boat. Our people had now cut their cable and got to their oars, they rowed a small distance, and lay to for the enemy's boat to come up, when they all fired into her and again sprang to their oars. Our boat could row much faster than the other, which still followed her. They kept up a constant fire upon each other till they got nearly up to the ferry, where there were a few troops encamped, who, running down upon the bank of the river, prepared to give the English boat a seasoning, but the enemy, seeing them, gave over the chase and went back down the river. What execution our people did among them was not known, but one of our men received a musket ball directly in the middle of his forehead, which passed out behind his head; this was done about eleven o'clock at night, and I saw him at nine next morning, alive, and breathing just like a man in a sound sleep; he died in about an hour after.

About this time Major Andre was brought from the Highlands to head-quarters, where he was examined, condemned and executed. I saw him before his execution, but was on duty on that day and could not attend; otherwise I should. He was an interesting character. There has been a great deal said about him, but he was but a man, and no better, nor had he better qualifications than the brave Captain Hale, whom the British commander caused to be executed as a spy, upon Long-Island, in 1776, without the shadow of a trial; denying him the use of a Bible or the assistance a clergyman in his last moments, and destroying the letters he had written to his widowed mother and other relations. Andre had every indulgence allowed him that could be granted with propriety;—see the contrast—let all who pity Andre so much, look at it and be silent.

We were frequently alarmed while lying at Dobb's ferry; being so few and at a distance from the main army, we had constantly to be on the look out, but never happened to come in contact with the enemy, although they very frequently made us believe we should.

While lying here I was almost persuaded, once, that I should have to take a trip to New-York, but was quite agreeably disappointed. One day my Captain sent me across the country to the western part of Connecticut, to bring him some mathematical instruments he had left there. He directed me which way to take, as it was dangerous travelling there on account of the small parties of British, or rather Refugees and Cowboys in their service. I knew the way very well, but I knew too, there was a way lower down, that was shorter. I determined after I had crossed the river, to take that road and hazard the consequences. I had got about half way on my journey, when just at night, I passed a house, which before the war had been a tavern. I passed by the house, thoughtlessly, and saw nobody, but as I passed the horse shed, I observed several horses standing under it, caparisoned like dragoon horses. I hurried on as fast as I could to get out of sight, but I had not got many rods by the house, when I saw a man come out with a fusee in his hand, and otherwise equipped like a soldier, who calling after me, bid me stop. I was so near him and entirely unarmed, that I dare not refuse his demand. He stepped along slowly a few paces towards me, inquiring where I was going and where I came from. I now inwardly cursed my indiscretion in not obeying my Captain's directions respecting the road I ought to have taken. I asked him the same questions he had asked me; he said that was nothing to the purpose, he had first interrogated me and I must answer him. He kept all the time advancing slowly towards me; I wished we were further apart. By this time two or three more of his party had come out of the house and were standing looking at us. I then told him to tell me who he was and where from, and keep me no longer in suspense. As he advanced I receded as much as I dared to, till he peremptorily told me not to go any further till I had satisfied him who I was and where I was going. By this time I began to gather courage; I thought that if he belonged to the enemy he would not stand so long without my knowing who he was by stronger arguments than words. I at last told him frankly who I was and where bound; well, said he, I thought you were upon some particular business, or you would not have been seen on this dangerous road. He then asked me to go back to the house and take some refreshment; but I declined his invitation, being glad to find myself safe and in my own hands. I went on and accomplished my business, but took care to return on a safer road.

We lay at Dobb's ferry till the latter part of the month of October, when we marched to West point for winter-quarters. I left this place with regret, more so than any other during my continuance in the army. It was upon an account which I need not mention. Many young men have, doubtless, felt the same upon similar occasions. If they have, they know my feelings at the time I speak of. But that time has long since gone by and my affections with it, both "gone with the years beyond the flood," never more to return.

We marched for West point.—At the Peekskill we procured batteaux to convey ourselves and baggage up the river to the point, where we arrived in safety and went into the old barracks, until new ones could be built for us, which we immediately commenced. We had to go six miles down the river, and there hew the timber, then carry it on our shoulders to the river, and then raft it to West point. We, however, soon completed this part of the business ourselves, when the carpenters took it in hand, and by newyear's day they were ready to receive us; till then, we had been living in the old barracks, where there were rats enough, had they been men, to garrison twenty West points.

Our barracks being completed, and we safely stowed away in them, I shall here conclude the campaign of 1780.

Chapter VII. Campaign of 1781.

I saw the plundering British bands,
Invade the fair Virginian lands.
I saw great WASHINGTON advance
With Americans and troops of France;
I saw the haughty Britons yield,
And stack their muskets on the field.

NOTHING material occurred to me till the month of February, nor any thing then *very* material. About the twentieth of that month I took it into my head to apply to my Captain for a recommendation to our Colonel for a furlough, that I might once more visit my friends; for I saw no likelihood that the war would ever end. The Captain told me that the Colonel was about sending a non-commissioned officer into Connecticut after two men belonging to our corps, who had been furloughed but had staid beyond the time allowed them, and that he would endeavour to have me sent on this business, and that after I had sent the delinquents to camp, I might tarry a space at home. Accordingly, I soon after received a passport, signed by the Colonel, in these terms, "Permit the bearer, —— ——, to pass into the country after some deserters, and to come back."—The time, "to come back," not being fixed, I set off, thinking I would regulate that as would best suit my own convenience.

When I arrived at home I found that my good old grandmother was gone to her long home, and my grandsire gone forty miles back into the country, to his son's, and I never saw him afterwards. My sister was keeping the house, and I was glad to see her, as I had not seen her for several years. There was likewise a neighbour's daughter there, who kept as much as she possibly could with my sister, and generally slept with her, whom I had seen more than once in the course of my life. Their company and conversation made up for the absence of my grandparents, it being a little more congenial to my age and feelings. I staid at home two or three days, to recruit after my journey, when a man belonging to our company (going home on furlough) called and informed me that one of the men I was after had arrived at camp, and as he should pass through the town where the other resided, he agreed to do my errand for me. With this arrangement I was much pleased, as it would save me about sixty miles travel in all, going and coming, and I gave him a dollar to help him along, which was all the money I had;— he then went on and did as he agreed. I had nothing now to do but to recreate myself, for, as the time of my return to the army was indefinitely set, I did not trouble myself about it.

I spent my time as agreeble as possible among the young people of my acquaintance, for I thought I was old enough to choose my own method of employing my time, being now nearly twenty-one years of age. I did, indeed, enjoy myself about ten days as agreeably as ever I did in the same space of time in my life; but as I had no set time to return to camp, I was loath to trespass upon my good Colonel's indulgence, and therefore began to think about my return; and as there was two men, one an old associate and the other a private citizen, who were going to camp, I thought, for company's sake, I would go with them, and accordingly did; but I confess that I never left my home with so much regret before; I need not tell the reason, perhaps the reader can guess.

When I arrived within sight and hearing of the army, or rather the garrison of West point, it again harrowed up my melancholy feelings that had, in a manner, subsided on my journey; but upon reaching the barracks where I had left my companions, I could hardly contain myself when I considered my folly in returning so soon, when I might have remained at home a month longer as well as not, and I just then began to think it was my Colonel's intention that I should do so; but what added to my perturbation mostly was, that I found our barracks entirely unoccupied, our men all gone, and not a soul could tell me where. What to do I knew not; I had a great mind to set off for home again, but at length concluded that I would try a little longer to find which way the men had gone. I therefore went to the issuing commissary of the garrison, who was my quondam schoolmate, and he soon informed me that they had gone to Virginia with General Lafayette; I was thunderstruck at this intelligence, and blamed myself tenfold for leaving home so soon. The commissary observing my chagrin, told me that my Captain and eight or ten of our people were in the country, about twenty miles off, where they were undergoing the operation of the small pox. The next day I went out to them and remained with them two or three days; but that would not do for me; I told the Captain that I would go after the men; he said I might act my pleasure as it respected that, but that he should advise me to stay with him till he had got through with the small pox, and the other men that were with him had recovered, and then they should all go together; but that would not content me, I was as uneasy as a fish out of the water. The Captain then told me that if I was determined to follow the corps that my arms were with him, and I might take them and go. I took them and went back to West point, to the commissary, where I procured three or four rations of provisions, and an order for five or six more, in case I could find any commissary on the way. The commissary filled my canteen with liquor, and thus equipped I set off on my journey alone, not expecting to find the men within less than four hundred miles.

I encountered nothing very material on my journey, except it were fatigue and some want, until I arrived at Annapolis, in Maryland; there I found what I had so long sought after, the Sappers and Miners, they were returning to West point. They were on board vessels, and were blocked in at Annapolis by some British ships at the mouth of the river. Shortly after I joined them an opportunity offered, and we escaped with our little fleet, by sweeping out in a dark night, and went up the bay.

We went directly on to West point and took possession of our new barracks again and remained there till sometime in the month of May, when we (with the rest of the army in the Highlands) moved down and encamped at the Peekskill. We remained here awhile and then moved down near King's bridge, fifteen miles from New-York. A part of the army, under the command of Gen. Lincoln, fell down the river in batteaux and landed near old fort Independence, where they were soon attacked by the enemy, when a smart skirmish ensued; our corps, among others, immediately marched to reinforce Gen. Lincoln, but the action ceased and the enemy had retired before we could arrive.

We lay on the ground we then occupied till after midnight, when we advanced further down towards Morrisonia. At the dawn of day we were in close neighbourhood with a British redoubt, and saw a single horseman of the enemy reconnoitering us; we sent a platoon of men around a hill to cut of his retreat, but mistrusting our scheme he kept off out of our reach, although he was seen near us the greater part of the day, "cutting his capers." As soon as it was fairly light we halted, and remained there all day and the night following.—The next morning we were joined by the French army from Rhode-Island. Between us and the British redoubt there was a large deep gully. Our officers gave leave to as many as chose, of our men, to go over the gully and skirmish with the small parties of horsemen and footmen that kept patroling from the redoubt to the gully, watching that none of us took shelter there to annoy them. Accordingly, a number of us kept disturbing their tranquillity all day; sometimes only four or five of us, sometimes ten or twelve; sometimes we would drive them into the redoubt, when they would reinforce and sally out and drive us all over the gully. We kept up this sport till late in the afternoon, when myself and two others of our non-commissioned officers went down near the creek that makes the island upon which New-York is situated. The two other men that were with we stopped under an apple tree that stood in a small gully. I saw four or five British horsemen on their horses a considerable distance from me, on the island. When they saw me they hallooed to me, calling me, "a white livered son of a b—h," (I was dressed in a white hunting shirt, or was without my coat, the latter, I think, as it was warm, and I wore a white under dress.) We then became quite sociable; they advised me to come over to their side and they would give me roast turkeys. I told them that they must wait till we left the coast clear, ere they could get into the country to steal them, as they used to do. They then said they would give me pork and lasses; and then inquired what execution some cannon had done, just before fired from the island, if they had not killed and wounded some of our men; and if we did not want help, as our surgeons were a pack of ignoramuses. I told them, in reply, that they had done no other execution with their guns than wounding a dog, (which was the case,) and as they and their surgeons were of the same species of animals, I supposed the poor wounded dog would account it a particular favour to have some of his own kind to assist him. While we were carrying on this very polite conversation, I observed at a house on the Island, in a different direction from the horsemen, a large number of men,—but as they appeared to be a motley group, I did not pay them much attention. Just as I was finishing the last sentence of my conversation with the horsemen, happening to cast my eyes toward the house (and very providentially too) I saw the flash of a gun; I instinctively dropped, as quick as a loon could dive, when the ball passed directly over me and lodged in the tree under which my comrades were standing. They saw the upper part of my gun drop as I fell, and said, "They have killed him;" but they were mistaken. The people at the house set up a shouting, thinking they had done the job for one poor Yankee, but they were mistaken too, for I immediately rose up, and slapping my backsides to them, slowly moved off. I do not know that I ever ran a greater risk for my life while I was in the army, indeed, I could not, for I verily believe that if I had not "dove at the flash," the ball would have gone directly through my body, but "a miss is as good as a mile," says the proverb. I kept a bright look out for them as I walked off. They sent another shot after me, and I again dropped, but that did not come so near me as the other, nor did they huzza again. These shots must have come from a rifle, as the distance was more than a quarter of a mile. It is poor business to stand thus a single mark.

This afternoon I had like to have picked up another of their shots. I was standing with another of our men in a narrow gateway talking; a man from the redoubt had crept down behind an old battery near us and fired at us; the ball passed between our noses which were not more than a foot apart. The fellow walked off and we sent him something to quicken his pace, but our shots did as little execution as his had done.

The horseman that I mentioned having seen early in the morning, kept prancing about and blackguarding the sentinels, who often fired at him without effect, until late in the afternoon, when one of the sentinels gave him something that seemed to cool his courage. He reached the redoubt, how he fared afterwards I know not; but I heard no more of his yelping.

There were two British soldiers hanging in chains here; I was standing near them with some others of our men, when two French officers rode up and inquired whether they were Americans or English; we told them they were English; upon which one of the officers laid his cane several times across one of the bodies, making the dry bones rattle, at the same time exclaiming, "Fotre d' Anglaise." A bold action! says the reader.

Our people fired several shots from their fieldpieces at some boats crossing the water to the redoubt, but never fired a single shot at the redoubt, or they at us, although we were lying all day in open sight of each other and within half a mile distant; there seemed to be a tacit agreement between them not to injure one another.

We lay all night upon the ground which we had occupied during the day. I was exceedingly tired, not having had a wink of sleep the preceding night, and had been on my feet during the last twenty-four hours, and this night, to add to my comfort, I had to take charge of the quarter guard. I was allowed to get what rest I could consistently with our safety. I fixed my guard, placed two sentinels, and the remainder of us laid down. We were with our corps, who were all by dark, snug in the arms of Morpheus; the officers slept under a tree near us. My orders were, if there was any stir or alarm during the night, to awake the officers, and if any strangers attempted to pass, to stop them and bring them to the officers to be examined by them. Some time in the night, the sentry by the guard, stopped two or three officers who were going past us; the sentry called me up, and I took the strangers to our officers, where they went through an examination and were then permitted to pass on; I returned to my guard and lay down till called up again to relieve the sentinels; all this time I was as unconscious of what was passing as though nothing of the kind had happened, nor could I remember any thing of the matter when told of it the next day; so completely was I worn down by fatigue.

We now fell back a few miles and encamped, (both Americans and French,) at a place called Phillip's Manor. We then went to making preparations to lay siege to New-York; we made facines and gabions, the former, bundles of brush and the latter are made in this manner, viz.—after setting sticks in the ground in a circle, about two feet or more in diameter, they are interwoven with small brush in form of a basket, they are then laid by for use, which is in entrenching; three or more rows of them are set down together, (breaking joints,) the trench is then dug behind and the dirt thrown into them, which, when full, together with the trench, forms a complete breastwork; the word is pronounced gab-beens. The fascines (pronounced fas-heens) are, as I said, bundles of brush bound snugly together, cut off straight at each end; they are of different lengths, from five to twelve feet; their use is in building batteries and other temporary works.

We now expected soon to lay close siege to New-York. Our Sappers and Miners were constantly employed with the Engineers in front of the army, making preparations for the siege. One day I was sent down towards the enemy with a corporal and twelve men, upon a reconnoitring expedition, the Engineers having heard that there was a party of Refugees, or Cowboys, somewhere not far from their premises. Mr orders were to go to a certain place and if I did not see or hear any thing of the enemy to return; or if I *did* find them to return as soon as possible and bring word to the officers, unless I thought we were able to cope with them ourselves. We set off upon our expedition early in the afternoon and went as far as directed by our officers, but saw no enemy. We stopped here awhile and rested ourselves.—When we had refreshed ourselves, we thought it a pity to return with our fingers in our mouths and report that we had seen nothing; we therefore agreed *unanimously,* to stretch our orders a trifle, and go a little further. We were in the fields,—about a mile ahead were three or four houses at which I and some others of our party had been before. Between us and the houses there was a narrow wood, mostly of young growth and quite thick. We concluded to go as far as the houses, and if we could not hear any thing of the Cowboys there, to return contented to camp.

Agreeably to our plan we set out, and had but just entered the wood when we found ourselves flanked by thirty or forty Cowboys, who gave us a hearty welcome to their assumed territories and we returned the compliment; but a kind Providence protected every man of us from injury although we were within ten rods of the enemy. They immediately rushed from their covert, before we had time to reload our pieces; consequently, we had no other alternative but to get off as well and as fast as we could. They did not fire upon us again, but gave us chase, for what reason I know not. I was soon in the rear of my party, which had to cross a fence composed of old posts and rails with trees plashed down upon it. When I arrived at the fence, the foremost of the enemy was not more than six or eight rods distant, all running after us helter-skelter, without any order; my men had all crossed the fence in safety, I alone was to suffer. I endeavoured to get over the fence across two or three of the trees that were plashed down; some how or other, I blundered and fell over, and caught my right foot in a place where a tree had split partly from the stump, here I hung as fast as though my foot had been in the stocks, my ham lying across the butt of another tree, while my body hung down perpendicularly; I could barely reach the ground with my hands, and, of course, could make but little exertion to clear myself from the limbs. The commander of the enemy came to the fence and the first compliment I received from him was a stroke with his hanger across my leg, just under or below the knee-pan, which laid the bone bare. I could see him through the fence and knew him; he was, when we were boys, one of my most familiar playmates, was with me, a messmate, in the campaign of 1776, had enlisted during the war in 1777, but sometime before this, had deserted to the enemy, having been coaxed off by an old harridan, to whose daughter he had taken a fancy; the old hag of a mother, living in the vicinity of the British, easily inveigled him away. He was a smart active fellow, and soon got command of a gang of Refugee-cowboy plunderers. When he had had his hack at my shins, I began to think it was "neck or nothing," and making one desperate effort, I cleared my foot by leaving my shoe behind, before he could have the second stroke at me. He knew me as well as I did him, for as soon as he saw me clear of the fence and out of the reach of his sword, he called me by name, and told me to surrender myself and he would give me good quarters;—thought I, you will wait till I ask them of you. I sprang up and run till I came to my party who were about a hundred rods ahead, waiting to see how I should come off. The enemy never fired a shot at me all the time I was running from them, although nearly the whole of their party was standing on the other side of the fence when I started from it. Whether his conscience smote him and he prevented them from firing at me; or, whether they were unprepared, not having had time to reload their pieces in their pursuit of us, or from what other cause, I know not, but they never interfered with me while I was running across the field, fifty or sixty rods, in open sight of them. Thus I escaped; and this was the only time the enemy drew blood from me during the whole war. This same Refugee was the youngster that was with me at the salt hay poleing, mentioned in the first chapter of this narrative.

We remained at Phillips' Manor till the last of July. I had a lame leg, caused by the wound given me by Mr. Refugee, but I lost only a short time from duty. I was favoured with easy duty by my officers, on account of my wound.

The first of August, I think it was the first day of that month, we all of a sudden marched from this ground and directed our course towards King's ferry, near the Highlands, crossed the Hudson and lay there a few days, till the baggage, artillery, &c. had crossed, and then proceeded into New-Jersey. We went down to Chatham, where were ovens built for the accommodation of the French troops. We then expected we were to attack New-York in that quarter, but after staying here a day or two, we again moved off and arrived at Trenton by rapid marches. It was about sunset when we arrived here, and instead of encamping for the night, as we expected, we were ordered immediately on board vessels, then lying at the landing place, and a little after sunrise found ourselves at Philadelphia. We, that is, the Sappers and Miners, staid here some days, proving and packing off shells, shot and other military stores. While we staid here we drew a few articles of clothing, consisting of a few tow shirts, some overalls and a few pairs of silk-and-oakum stockings; and here, or soon after, we each of us received a MONTH'S PAY, in specie, borrowed, as I was informed, by our French officers from the officers in the French army. This was the first that could be called money, which we had received as wages since the year '76, or that we ever did receive till the close of the war, or indeed, ever after, as wages.

When we had finished our business at Philadelphia, we, (the Miners,) left the city. A part of our men, with myself, went down the Delaware in a schooner which had her hold nearly full of gunpowder. We passed Mud Island, where I had experienced such hardships in Nov. '77. It had quite a different appearance to what it had then, much like a fine, fair, warm and sunny day succeeding a cold, dark, stormy night. Just after passing Mud Island, in the afternoon, we had a smart thunder shower; I did not feel very agreeably, I confess, during its continuance, with such a quantity of powder under my feet; I was not quite sure that a stroke of the electric fluid might not compel me to leave the vessel sooner than I wished,—but no accident happened, and we proceeded down the river to the mouth of Christiania Creek, up which we were bound. We were compelled to anchor here on account of wind and tide; here we passed an uneasy night from fear of British cruisers, several of which were in the Bay. In the morning we got under weigh, the wind serving, and proceeded up the creek, fourteen miles, the creek passing, the most of its course, through a marsh, as crooked as a snake in motion,—there was one place in particular, near the village of Newport, where you sail four miles to gain about forty rods. We went on till the vessel grounded for lack of water, we then lightened her, by taking out a part of her cargo, and when the tide came in we got up to the wharves and left her at the disposal of the Artillerists.

We then crossed over land to the head of the Elk, or the head, or rather bottom, of Chesapeak bay. Here we found a *large* fleet of *small* vessels, waiting to convey us and other troops, stores, &c. down the bay. We soon embarked, that is, such of us as went by water, the greater part of the army having gone on by land. I was in a small schooner, called the Birmingham; there was but a small number of our corps of Sappers and Miners in this vessel, with a few Artillerists, six or eight officers, and a Commissary, who had a small quantity of stores on board, among which was a hogshead containing twenty or thirty gallons of rum. To prevent the men from getting more than their share of the liquor, the officers (who loved a little of the "good creature" as well as the men) had the bulkhead between the hold and the cabin taken down and placed the hogshead in the cabin, carefully nailing up the partition again, when they thought that they had the exclusive disposal of the precious treasure; but the soldiers were as wiley as they, for the very first night after the officers had snugly secured it, as they thought, the head of the cask being crouded against the bulkhead, the soldiers contrived to loosen one of the boards at the lower end, so as to swing it aside, and broached the hogshead on the other head; so that while the officers in the cabin thought they were the sole possessors of its contents, the soldiers in the hold had possession of at least as good a share as themselves.

We passed down the bay, making a grand appearance with our mosquetoe fleet, to Annapolis, (which I had left about five months before for West point,) here we stopped, fearing to proceed any further at present, not knowing exactly how matters were going on down the bay. A French cutter was despatched to procure intelligence. She returned in the course of three or four days, bringing word that the passage was clear; we then proceeded and soon arrived at the mouth of James' river, where were a number of armed French vessels and two or three fifty gun ships. We passed in sight of the French fleet, then lying in Lynnhaven bay; they resembled a swamp of dry pine trees. We had passed several of their men-of-war higher up the bay.

We were obliged to stay here a day or two on account of a severe North-East rain storm; the wind was quite high, and in the height of the storm, some officers on board a vessel lying near ours, sent off a soldier in a small punt, hardly capable of carrying a man in calm weather, to another vessel to procure them some spirituous liquor, one of the officers had furnished him with his hat as a token for something. The man had done his errand and was returning, when the sea running so high that it upset his underpinning, which floated from him and left him to shift for himself in the water. The storm was so severe that the people were below deck in all the vessels near, except ours. The Captain of our company happened at that instant to be on deck (peeping into some concern that was none of his own, as he generally was) and saw him upset. We had no better boat belonging to our vessel than the one the man in the water had just been thrown from. Our Captain seized a musket that happened to be near by, and discharged it several times before he could rouse any of the people in the nearest vessels. At length he was heard and observed by some on board a French armed vessel, who sent a boat and took the man up and put him on board the vessel he went from. I saw him in the water and he exhibited rather a ludicrous figure; with an officer's large cocked hat upon his head, paddling away with one hand, and holding his canteen in the other. He was nearly exhausted before the boat reached him. Our officers pretended to blame the others greatly, for sending the poor fellow upon such an errand in a storm. But it is to be remembered that they had a plenty of liquor on board their vessel, and therefore had no occasion to send any one on such business.

After the storm had ceased, we proceeded up the river to a place called Burwell's ferry, where the fleet all anchored; it was sunset when we anchored and I was sent across the river with two men in a borrowed boat, to fill a cask with water; it was quite dark before I got ready to return, and I had to cross almost the whole river, (which is pretty wide here,) and through the whole fleet before I reached our vessel. I could not find her in the dark among so many, and when I hailed her the soldiers in almost every vessel in the river would answer me. What could I do? why, just what I did do; keep rowing one way and another till nine or ten o'clock at night, weary, and wishing every man in the fleet, except ourselves, had a toad in his throat; at length by mere good luck I found our vessel, which soon put an end to my trouble and fatigue, together with their mischievous fun.

We landed the next day in the afternoon, when our quartermaster sergeant sat off to procure something for us to eat; we had to go nearly two miles for it. Myself and another sergeant, a messmate of mine, concluded to go after the provisions, to stretch our legs, after so long confinement on board the vessel; we took our cook with us, for he, as usual, had nothing to do at home. When we arrived at the place, we found it would be quite late before we could be served; we therefore bought a beef's harslet of the butchers, and packed off our cook with it, that we might have it in readiness against our return to camp. The cook, who had been a bank fisherman, and of course loved to wet his whistle once in a while, sat off for home and we contented ourselves till after dark, before we could get away, in expectation of having something to eat on our return. When we came home we went directly to our tent to get our suppers, when, lo, we found Mr. Cook fast asleep in the tent, and not the least sign of cookery going on. With much ado we waked him and inquired where our victuals were; he had got none, he mumbled out as well as he could. "Where is the pluck you brought home?" "I sold it," said he; "sold it! what did you sell it for?" "I don't know," was the reply. "If you have sold it, what did you get for it?" "If you will have patience," said he, "I will tell you." "Patience," said the sergeant, "it is enough to vex a saint; here we sent you home to get something in readiness against our return, and you have sold what we ordered you to provide for us and got drunk, and now we must go all night without any thing to eat, or else set up to wait a division of the meat and cook it ourselves. What, I say, did you get for it? if any thing we can eat at present, say so." "I will tell you," said he; "first, I got a little rum, and next, I got a little pepper, and—and—then I got a little more rum." "Well, and where is the rum and pepper you got"—"I drank the rum," said he, "there is the pepper." "Pox on you," said the sergeant, "I'll pepper you," and was about to belabor the poor fellow, when I interfered and saved him from a basting. But, truly, this was one among the "sufferings" I had to undergo, for I was hungry and impatient enough to have eaten the fellow had he been well cooked and peppered.

Soon after landing we marched to Williamsburg, where we joined Gen. Lafayette, and very soon after, our whole army arriving, we prepared to move down and pay our old acquaintance, the British at

Yorktown, a visit. I doubt not but their wish was, not to have so many of us come at once, as their accommodations were rather scanty. They thought "The fewer the better cheer." We thought "The more the merrier." We had come a long way to see them, and were unwilling to be put off with excuses; we thought the present time quite as convenient (at least for us) as any future time could be, and we accordingly persisted, hoping, that as they pretended to be a very courtly people, they would have the politeness to come out and meet us, which would greatly shorten the time to be spent in the visit, and save themselves and us much labour and trouble; but they were too impolite at this time to do so.

We marched from Williamsburg the last of September. It was a warm day; when we had proceeded about half way to Yorktown we halted and rested two or three hours. Being about to cook some victuals, I saw a fire which some of the Pensylvania troops had kindled a short distance off; I went to get some fire while some of my messmates made other preparations; (we having turned our rum and pepper cook adrift;) I had taken off my coat and unbuttoned my waistcoat, it being (as I said before) very warm; my pocketbook, containing about five dollars in money, and some other articles, in all about seven dollars, was in my westcoat pocket. When I came among the strangers they appeared to be uncommonly complaisant, asking many questions, helping me to fire, and chatting very familiarly. I took my fire and returned, but it was not long before I perceived that those kind hearted helpers had helped themselves to my pocketbook and its whole contents. I felt mortally chagrined but there was no plaster for my sore but patience, and my plaster of that, at this time, I am sure was very small and very thinly spread, for it never covered the wound.

Here, or about this time, we had orders from the Commander-in-chief, that in case the enemy should come out to meet us, we should exchange but one round with them and then decide the conflict with the bayonet, as they valued themselves at that instrument. The French forces could play their part at it, and the Americans were never backward at trying its virtue. The British, however, did not think fit at that time to give us an opportunity to soil our bayonets in their carcases; but why they did not we could never conjecture; we as much expected it, as we expected to find them there.

We went on, and soon arrived and encamped in their neighbourhood, without let or molestation. Our Miners lay about a mile and a half from their works, in open view of them. Here again we encountered our old associate, hunger; affairs, as they respected provisions, &c. were not yet regulated,—no eatable stores had arrived, nor could we expect they should until we knew what reception the enemy would give us. We were, therefore, compelled to try our hands at foraging again. We, that is, our corps of Miners, were encamped near a large wood; there was a plenty of shoats all about this wood, fat and plump, weighing, generally, from fifty to a hundred pounds apiece. We soon found some of them, and as no owner appeared to be at hand, and the hogs not understanding our enquiries (if we made any) sufficiently to inform us to whom they belonged, we made free with some of them to satisfy the calls of nature till we could be better supplied, if better we could be. Our officers countenanced us, and that was all the permission we wanted; and many of us did not want even that.

We now began to make preparations for laying close siege to the enemy. We had holed him and nothing remained but to dig him out. Accordingly, after taking every precaution to prevent his escape, settled our guards, provided fascines and gabions, made platforms for the batteries, to be laid down when needed, brought on our battering pieces, ammunition, &c.; on the fifth of October we began to put our plans into execution.

One third part of all the troops were put in requisition to be employed in opening the trenches. A third part of our Sappers and Miners were ordered out this night to assist the Engineers in laying out the works. It was a very dark and rainy night. However, we repaired to the place and began by following the Engineers and laying laths of pine wood end to end upon the line marked out by the officers, for the trenches. We had not proceeded far in the business, before the Engineers ordered us to desist and remain where we were, and be sure not to straggle a foot from the spot while they were absent from us. In a few minutes after their departure, there came a man alone to us, having on a surtout, as we conjectured, (it being exceeding dark,) and inquired for the Engineers. We now began to be a little jealous for our safety, being alone and without arms, and within forty rods of the British trenches. The stranger inquired what troops we were; talked familiarly with us a few minutes, when, being informed which way the officers had gone, he went off in the same direction, after strictly charging us, in case we should be taken prisoners, not to discover to the enemy what troops we were. We were obliged to him for his kind advice, but we considered ourselves as standing in no great need of it; for we knew as well as he did, that Sappers and Miners were allowed no quarters, at least, are entitled to none, by the laws of warfare, and of course should take care, if taken, and the enemy did not find us out, not to betray our own secret.

In a short time the Engineers returned and the afore-mentioned stranger with them; they discoursed together sometime, when, by the officers often calling him "Your Excellency," we discovered that it was Gen. Washington. Had we dared, we might have cautioned him for exposing himself so carelessly to danger at such a time, and doubtless he would have taken it in good part if we had. But nothing ill happened to either him or ourselves.

It coming on to rain hard, we were ordered back to our tents, and nothing more was done that night. The next night, which was the sixth of October, the same men were ordered to the lines that had been there the night before. We this night completed laying out the works. The troops of the line were there ready with entrenching tools and began to entrench, after General Washington had struck a few blows with a pickaxe, a mere ceremony, that it might be said "Gen. Washington with his own hands first broke ground at the siege of Yorktown." The ground was sandy and soft, and the men employed that night eat no "idle bread," (and I question if they eat any other,) so that by daylight they had covered themselves from danger from the enemy's shot, who, it appeared, never mistrusted that we were so near them the whole night; their attention being directed to another quarter. There was upon the right of their works a marsh; our people had sent to the western side of this marsh a detachment to make a number of fires, by which, and our men often passing before the fires, the British were led to imagine that we were about some secret mischief there, and consequently directed their whole fire to that quarter, while we were entrenching literally under their noses.

As soon as it was day they perceived their mistake, and began to fire where they ought to have done sooner. They brought out a fieldpiece or two, without their trenches and discharged several shots at the men who were at work erecting a bomb-battery; but their shot had no effect and they soon gave it over. They had a large bull-dog, and every time they fired he would follow their shots across our trenches. Our officers wished to catch him and oblige him to carry a message from them into the town to his masters, but he looked too formidable for any of us to encounter.

I do not remember, exactly, the number of days we were employed before we got our batteries in readiness to open upon the enemy, but think it was not more than two or three. The French, who were upon our left, had completed their batteries a few hours before us, but were not allowed to discharge their pieces till the American batteries were ready. Our commanding battery was on the near bank of the river and contained ten heavy guns; the next was a bomb-battery of three large mortars; and so on through the whole line; the whole number, American and French, was, ninety-two cannon, mortars and howitzers. Our flagstaff was in the ten gun battery, upon the right of the whole. I was in the trenches the day that the batteries were to be opened; all were upon the tiptoe of expectation and impatience to see the signal given to open the whole line of batteries, which was to be the hoisting of the American flag in the ten gun battery. About noon the much wished for signal went up. I confess I felt a secret pride swell my heart when I saw the "star spangled banner" waving majestically in the very faces of our implacable adversaries; it appeared like an omen of success to our enterprize, and so it proved in reality. A simultaneous discharge of all the guns in the line followed; the French troops accompanying it with "Huzza for the Americans!" It was said that the first shell sent from our batteries, entered an elegant house, formerly owned or occupied by the Secretary of State under the British government, and burnt directly over a table surrounded by a large party of British officers at dinner, killing and wounding a number of them;—this was a warmday to the British.

The siege was carried on warmly for several days, when most of the guns in the enemy's works were silenced. We now began our second parellel, about half way between our works and theirs. There were two strong redoubts held by the British, on their left. It was necessary for us to possess those redoubts, before we could complete our trenches. One afternoon, I, with the rest of our corps that had been on duty in the trenches the night but one before, were ordered to the lines. I mistrusted something extraordinary, serious or comical, was going forward, but what, I could not easily conjecture. We arrived at the trenches a little before sunset; I saw several officers fixing bayonets on long staves. I then concluded we were about to make a general assault upon the enemy's works; but before dark I was informed of the whole plan, which was to storm the redoubts, the one by the Americans and the other by the French. The Sappers and Miners were furnished with axes, and were to proceed in front and cut a passage for the troops through the abatis, which are composed of the tops of trees, the small branches cut off with a slanting stroke which renders them as sharp as spikes. These trees are then laid at a small distance from the trench or ditch, pointing outwards, and the butts fastened to the ground in such a manner that they cannot be removed by those on the outside of them;— it is almost impossible to get through them. Through these we were to cut a passage before we or the other assailants could enter. At dark the detachment was formed and advanced beyond the trenches, and lay down on the ground to await the signal for advancing to the attack, which was to be three shells from a certain battery near where we were lying. All the batteries in our line were silent, and we lay anxiously waiting for the signal. The two brilliant planets, Jupiter and Venus, were in close contact in the western hemisphere, (the same direction that the signal was to be made in,) when I happened to cast my eyes to that quarter, which was often, and I caught a glance of them, I was ready to spring on my feet, thinking they were the signal for starting. Our watchword was "Rochambeau," the commander of the French forces' name, a good watchword, for being pronounced Ro-sham-bow, it sounded, when pronounced quick, like rush-on-boys. We had not lain here long before the expected signal was given, for us and the French, who were to storm the other redoubt, by the three shells with their fiery trains mounting the air in quick succession. The word up, up, was then reiterated through the detachment. We immediately moved silently on toward the redoubt we were to attack, with unloaded muskets. Just as we arrived at the abatis, the enemy discovered us and directly opened a sharp fire upon us. We were now at a place where many of our large shells had burst in the ground, making holes sufficient to bury an ox in; the men having their eyes fixed upon what was transacting before them, were every now and then falling into these holes. I thought the British were killing us off at a great rate. At length one of the holes happening to pick me up, I found out the mystery of the huge slaughter. As soon as the firing began, our people began to cry, "the fort's our own!" and it was "rush on boys." The Sappers and Miners soon cleared a passage for the Infantry, who entered it rapidly. Our Miners were ordered not to enter the fort, but there was no stoping them. "We will go," said they; "then go to the d—l," said the commanding officer of our corps, "if you will." I could not pass at the entrance we had made, it was so crowded; I therefore forced a passage at a place where I saw our shot had cut away some of the abatis; several others entered at the same place. While passing, a man at my side received a ball in his head and fell under my feet, crying out bitterly. While crossing the trench, the enemy threw hand grenades, (small shells) into it; they were so thick that I at first thought them cartridge papers on fire; but was soon undeceived by their cracking. As I mounted the breastwork, I met an old associate hitching himself down into the trench; I knew him by the light of the enemy's musketry, it was so vivid. The fort was taken, and all quiet in a very short time. Immediately after the firing ceased, I went out to see what had become of my wounded friend and the other that fell in the passage—they were both dead. In the heat of the action I saw a British soldier jump over the walls of the fort next the river and go down the bank, which was almost perpendicular, and twenty or thirty feet high; when he came to the beach he made off for the town, and if he did not make good use of his legs I never saw a man that did.

All that were in the action of storming the redoubt were exempted from further duty that night; we laid down upon the ground and rested the remainder of the night as well as a constant discharge of grape and canister shot would permit us to do; while those who were on duty for the day completed the second parallel by including the captured redoubts within it. We returned to camp early in the morning, all safe and sound, except one of our Lieutenants, who had received a slight wound on the top of the shoulder by a musket shot. Seven or eight men belonging to the Infantry were killed, and a number wounded.

Being off duty one day, several of us went into the woods and fields in search of nuts; returning across the fields, which lay all common, we came across a number of horses at pasture; thinking to make a little fun for myself, I caught one of the horses and mounting him, as the Dutchman did his bear, without saddle or bridle, set off full speed for camp, guiding my nag with a stick. After I had proceeded thus for nearly a mile, my charger appeared to possess a strong inclination to return to his associates. I could not persuade him from his determination, but rather affronted him in all my endeavours to stop him. He at length set off back with himself and me too, at full spring, I clung to him till I found he was directing his course straight under the limbs of a large spreading oak tree; fearing I might meet with something like Absalom's fate, I thought it best to quit my situation in season, and accordingly jumped off; I happened to get but little personal injury, but I bounded like a foot-ball; this cooled my courage for such sort of exercises ever after.

Our duty was hazardous but not very hard. As to eatables, what we could not get from the public stores, we could make up in the woods. We had a large dog that we had brought from West point; we had no more to do than to go into the woods, which were quite handy, and when we came across the trail of a shoal of hogs, to set off old Bose, when we soon heard a crying out, and it was generally made by a black one, he having a particular regard or antipathy (he never told us which) for that colour. After the knife had passed the throat of the victim, we carried it to a frog pond, in the rear of our camp, and near our bakehouse, where, after evening roll call, we could fit it for eating, convey it to the baker where it was baked in prime order. We were on duty in the trenches twenty-four hours, and forty-eight hours in camp. The invalids did the camp duty, and we had nothing else to do, but to attend morning and evening roll calls, and recreate ourselves as we pleased the rest of the time, till we were called upon to take our turns on duty in the trenches again. The greatest inconvenience we felt, was the want of good water, there being none near our camp but nasty frog ponds, where all the horses in the neighbourhood were watered, and we were forced to wade through the water in the skirts of the ponds, thick with mud and filth, to get at water in any wise fit for use, and that full of frogs. All the springs about the country, although they looked well, tasted like copperas water, or like water that had been standing in iron or copper vessels. I was one day rambling alone in the woods, when I came across a small brook of very good water, about a mile from our tents; we used this water daily to drink, or we should almost have suffered. But it was "the fortune of war." I was one night in the trenches, erecting a bomb-battery, the enemy (it being very dark) were directed in their firing by a large tree. I was ordered by our officers to take two or three men and fell the tree with some old axes as dull as hoes; the tree was very large and we were two hours in cutting it, although we took Solomon's advice in handling dull tools, by "putting to the more strength," the British all the time urging us to exert ourselves with round and grape shot; they struck the tree a number of times while we were at work at it, but chanced to do us no harm at all.

In the morning, while the relieves were coming into the trenches, I was sitting on the side of the trench, when some of the New-York troops coming in, one of the sergeants stepped up to the breastwork to look about him, the enemy threw a small shell which fell upon the outside of the works, the man turned his face to look at it; at that instant a shot from the enemy (which doubtless was aimed for him in particular, as none others were in sight of them) passed just by his face without touching him at all; he fell dead into the trench; I put my hand on his forehead and found his skull was shattered all in pieces, and the blood flowing from his nose and mouth, but not a particle of skin was broken. I never saw an instance like this among all the men I saw killed during the whole war.

After we had finished our second line of trenches there was but little firing on either side. After lord Cornwallis had failed to get off, upon the seventeenth day of October, (a rather unlucky day for the British) he requested a cessation of hostilities for, I think, twenty-four hours, when commissioners from both armies met at a house between the lines, to agree upon articles of capitulation. We waited with anxiety the termination of the armistice, and as the time drew nearer our anxiety increased. The time at length arrived,—it passed, and all remained quiet.—And now we concluded that we had obtained what we had taken so much pains for,—for which we had encountered so many dangers, and had so anxiously wished. Before night we were informed that the British had surrendered and that the siege was ended.

The next day we were ordered to put ourselves in as good order as our circumstances would admit, to see (what was the completion of our present wishes) the British army march out and stack their arms. The trenches, where they crossed the road leading to the town, were levelled and all things put in order for this grand exhibition. After breakfast, on the nineteenth, we were marched on to the ground and paraded on the righthand side of the road, and the French forces on the left. We waited two or three hours before the British made their appearance; they were not always so dilatory, but they were compelled at last, by necessity, to appear, all armed, with bayonets fixed, drums beating, and faces lengthening; they were led by Gen. O'Harra, with the American Gen. Lincoln on his right, the Americans and French beating a march as they passed out between them. It was a noble sight to us, and the more so, as it seemed to promise a speedy conclusion to the contest. The British did not make so good an appearance as the German forces; but there was certainly some allowance to be made in their favour; the English felt their honour wounded, the Germans did not greatly care whose hands they were in. The British paid the Americans, seemingly, but little attention as they passed them, but they eyed the French with considerable malice depicted in their countenances. They marched to the place appointed and stacked their arms; they then returned to the town in the same manner they had marched out, except being divested of their arms. After the prisoners were marched off into the country, our army separated, the French remaining where they then were and the Americans marching for the Hudson.

During the siege, we saw in the woods herds of Negroes which lord Cornwallis, (after he had inveigled them from their proprietors,) in love and pity to them, had turned adrift, with no other recompense for their confidence in his humanity, than the small pox for their bounty and starvation and death for their wages. They might be seen scattered about in every direction, dead and dying, with pieces of ears of burnt Indian corn in the hands and mouths, even of those that were dead. After the siege was ended many of the owners of these deluded creatures, came to our camp and engaged some of our men to take them up, generally offering a guinea a head for them. Some of our Sappers and Miners took up several of them that belonged to a Col. Banister; when he applied for them, they refused to deliver them to him unless he would promise not to punish them. He said he had no intention of punishing them, that he did not blame them at all, the blame lay on lord Cornwallis. I saw several of those miserable wretches delivered to their master; they came before him under a very powerful fit of the ague. He told them that he gave them the free choice, either to go with him or remain where they were; that he would not injure a hair of their heads if they returned with him to their duty. Had the poor souls received a reprieve at the gallows, they could not have been more overjoyed than they appeared to be at what he promised them; their ague fit soon left them. I had a share in one of them by assisting in taking him up; the fortune I acquired was small, only one dollar; I received what was then called its equivalent, in paper money, if money it might be called, it amounted to twelve hundred (nominal) dollars, all of which I afterwards paid for one single quart of rum; to such a miserable state had all paper stuff, called—money—depreciated.

Our corps of Sappers and Miners were now put on board vessels to be transported up the bay; I was on board a small schooner, the Captain of *our* company and twenty others of our men were in the same vessel. There was more than twenty tons of beef on board, salted in bulk in the hold; we were obliged to remain behind to deal out this beef in small quantities to the troops that remained here. I remained part of the time on board, and part on shore, for eighteen days after all the American troops were gone to the northward, and none remaining but the French. It now began to grow cold, and there were two or three cold rain storms; we suffered exceedingly while we were compelled to stay on shore, having no tents nor any kind of fuel, the houses in the town being all occupied by the French troops. Our Captain at length became tired of this business and determined to go on after the other troops at all events; we accordingly left Yorktown and set our faces towards the

Highlands of New-York. It was now the month of November, and winter approaching; we all wished to be nearer home, or at least to be with the rest of our corps, who were—we knew *not* where, nor did they know where we were; they had heard before this that our schooner was cast away, and we were drowned. After we left Yorktown we had head winds for several days and made but little progress, getting no farther than Petuxant river in Maryland, in that time; we came to anchor at the mouth of that river about sunset, and as we had been some time on board the vessel, we obtained permission from our Captain to go on shore and sleep, as we saw a shelter on shore, put up by some of the troops who had gone on before us. And here again I had like to have taken a short discharge from the army. It was noised around that there was a small pirate boat in the bay. Just after we had anchored with several other small vessels in the river; there came sweeping in a boat that answered the description given of the vessel in question. Our Captain charged a musket that was on deck, belonging to one of our men, and hailed the boat; but as the people proved to be friendly, and acquaintance too, the musket was laid by and no further notice taken of it for the present. When we had landed and kindled a fire, and were most of us sitting down by it, one of our men took up the loaded musket (not knowing it to be so) and placing the butt of the piece on the ground between his legs, asked the owner if his musket was in good order, and cocked and snapped it. I was standing by his side with the muzzle of the piece close by my ear, when it proved to be in good order enough to go off, and nearly sent me off with its contents; the fire from it burnt all the hair off the side of my head, and I thought at the instant, that my head had gone with it.

In the morning there were signs of a southerly wind; we hastened on board and the wind breezing up, we got under weigh and steered for the head of the bay; it was about sunrise when we started, and when we anchored at the head of the bay, the sun had just set, having run in that time upwards of a hundred and thirty miles. The flats about our anchoring place were almost covered with wild water fowl. I do not remember ever seeing so many at one time, before or since, although I have often seen large numbers of them. One of our men discharged his piece at a flock on the wing, when they appeared like a cloud, and were spread over a space of a quarter of a mile every way. The ball passed almost through the flock before it chanced to hit one, and it hit *but* one.

The next morning we landed at what is called the head of Elk, where we found the rest of our corps, and some of the Infantry, also a few French. Our people seemed very glad to see us again, as they had been informed that we were certainly all drowned.—We remained here a few days and then marched for Philadelphia. We encamped one night, while on our march, at Wilmington, a very handsome borough town on the Christiana creek, in the State of Delaware. I was quartered for the night, at a gentleman's house, who had, before the war, been a sea captain. He related to me an anecdote, that gave me rather a disagreeable feeling, as it may, perhaps, my readers. It was thus,—"At the battle of Germantown, in the year 1777, a Dutchman (an inhabitant of that town) and his wife fired upon some of the British during the action; whether they killed any one or not, he did not say; but after the battle some one informed against them and they were both taken and confined in the provost-guardhouse, in the city, and there kept with scarcely any thing to sustain nature, and not a spark of fire to warm them. On the morning that the Augusta was blown up at fort Mifflin, on Mud Island, the poor old man had got to the prison-yard, to enjoy the warm sunbeams, with a number of other prisoners, (my informant among them, he being a prisoner at the time,) when they heard the report of the ship's magazine, the poor creature exclaimed, "Huzza for Gen. Washington! to-morrow he comes." The villain Provost Marshal, upon hearing this, put him into the cellar of the prison, and kept him there, without allowing him the least article of sustenance, till he died. The prisoners cut a small crevice in the floor, with a knife, through which they poured water and sometimes a little spirits, while he held up his mouth to the place to receive it."—Such inhuman treatment was often shown to our people when prisoners, by the British, during the revolutionary war. But it needs no comment.

In the morning before we marched, some of us concluded to have a stimulater. I went to a house, near by, where I was informed they sold liquors; when I entered the house, I saw a young woman in decent morning dishabille; I asked her if I could have any liquor there; she told me that her husband had just stepped out and would be in directly, and very politely desired me to be seated. I had sat but a minute or two when there came in from the back yard, a great potbellied negro man, rigged off in his superfine broadcloth, ruffled shirt, bow-shin and flat foot, and as black and shining as a junk bottle. "My dear," said the lady, "this soldier wishes for a quart of rum." I was thunderstruck; had not the man taken my canteen from me and measured me the liquor, I should certainly have forgotten my errand. I took my canteen and hastened off as fast as possible, being fearful that I might hear or see more of their "dearing," for had I, I am sure it would have given me the ague. However agreeable such "twain's becoming one flesh," was in that part of the Union, I was not acquainted with it in that in which I resided.

We went on to Philadelphia, crossed the river Schuylkill on a pontoon bridge, entered the city and took up our abode in the barracks. The Infantry passed on for the Hudson, but the regiments of Artillerists, (Col. Lamb's,) who were at the siege of Yorktown, stopped with us. We staid here several days. The barracks in this city are, or were then, very commodious; they were two stories high, with a gallery their whole length, and an ample parade in front; they were capable of sheltering two or three thousand men. One night, while we were lying here, one of my comrades having occasion to go out, it being very dark, he soon came back in a shocking fright, hardly able to speak; he was asked what was the matter, when, having recovered himself so far as to be able to speak, he said there was a ghost in the gallery. The greater part of the men in the room turned out to see the ghost, a thing often talked of but very rarely seen. We could hardly persuade the man to go out with us, to direct us to the object of his terror; however, we went out, when lo! what should the spirit be but an old white horse, which had walked up the stairs to the gallery, probably in search of something to eat, as, judging by his appearance, he very much needed it, for he had rather a ghostly aspect, but did not seem a very formidable foe.

After staying in Philadelphia about a fortnight, we left the city and proceeded to the city of Burlington, in New-Jersey, twenty miles above Philadelphia, on the Delaware; which place we understood was to be our winter-quarters. We marched about noon, went about ten miles and halted for the night. We took up our lodgings in the houses of the inhabitants; the house where I was quartered seemed to belong to a man well off for this world's goods. We were allowed the kitchen and a comfortable fire, and we happened to have, just then, what a soldier of the revolution valued next to the welfare of his country, and his own honour, that is, something to eat, and being all in good health, and having the prospect of a quiet night's rest; all which comforts happening to us at this time, put us in high spirits. We had received some fresh beef and bread that morning, and, after being settled in our quarters, we set about cooking our suppers. There were three or four small boys belonging to the house, who were so taken up with their new guests, that they kept with us the whole evening. We traded with these boys for some potatoes to cook with our meat; we gave them two or three cartridges and they gave us as many potatoes as we needed. Just as we had got our supper upon the table, the man of the house passed through the room, and seeing that we had potatoes, asked us where we procured them; some of the men replied, "in Philadelphia." He took up one from the dish and broke it: "miserable things," said he, "my potatoes are worth double the value of these." We laughed in our sleeves at his simplicity—his own boys skinned their teeth to think how their father was deceived, but said nothing. When we turned out in the morning to resume our march, upon examination we found these roguish urchins had undertaken to serve us with the same sauce they had their father, for they had, during the night, nearly emptied all our cartridge boxes. We saw where they deposited those we gave them; when, upon examining the place, we found our lost goods which we did not fail to secure: and likewise those which we had given them, as a punishment for their roguery.

We marched again and crossed a narrow ferry, called Penny ferry; arrived at Bristol and crossed the Delaware, to Burlington, where the Artillerists went into barracks, and our corps of Miners were quartered in a large elegant house, which had formerly been the residence of the Governour, when the State was a British province. The non-commissioned officers, with a few others had a neat room in one of the wings, and the men occupied the rest of the house, except the rooms in the third story, which were taken up by the officers and their attendants. Now we thought ourselves well situated for the winter, (as indeed we were, as it respected shelter,) after a tedious campaign; but it turned out quite the reverse with several, and myself among the rest, as in the next chapter will appear. Being once more snugly stowed away in winter-quarters, it of course ends my sixth campaign.

Chapter VIII. Campaign of 1782.

A man with morbid pains oppress'd
Who feels the nightmare in his breast;
Rejoices when the pressure's o'er,
And the distress is felt no more:
So wars and tumults, when they cease
Bring comfort in the thoughts of peace.

THE arm of British power in America being dislocated by the capture of lord Cornwallis and his myrmidons, we had not much to disturb us on account of the enemy; I fared rather better than I did when I was here on my journey to Mud Island in 1777. Our duty was not very hard, but I was a soldier yet, and had to submit to soldier's rules and discipline, and soldier's fare.

Either here, or just before, our officers had enlisted a recruit; he had lately been discharged from the New-Jersey line. After enlisting with us, he obtained a furlough to visit his friends; but receiving no money when he engaged with us (which was, I believe, the sole motive of his entering the service at this time) and obtaining his ends in getting home, he took especial care to keep himself there; at least, till he could get another opportunity to try his luck again, which he accordingly did, by enlisting in a corps of new levies in his own State—New-Jersey. My Captain hearing where he was, and how engaged, sent me with two men to find him out, and bring him back to his duty.

And now, my dear reader, excuse me for being so minute in detailing this little excursion, for it yet seems to my fancy, among the privations of that war, like one of those little verdant plats of ground, amid the burning sands of Arabia, so often described by travellers.

One of our Captains and another of our men being about going that way on furlough, I and my two men sat off with them. We received, that day, two or three rations of fresh pork and hard bread. We had no cause to call this pork "carrion," or "hogmeat," for, on the contrary, it was so fat, and being entirely fresh, we could not eat it at all. The first night of our expedition, we boiled our meat; and I asked the landlady for a little sauce, she told me to go to the garden and take as much cabbage as I pleased, and that, boiled with the meat, was all we could eat. The next morning we proceeded; it was cool weather, and about six inches deep of snow on the ground. After two or three days journeying, we arrived in the neighbourhood of the game that we were in pursuit of. It was now sundown; and our furloughed Captain and man, concluded to stop for the night; here we fell in with some soldiers of the corps that our man belonged to. Our captain inquired if they knew such a man, naming him; they equivocated and asked many questions concerning our business. Our officious Captain answered them so much to their satisfaction that Mr. Deserter took so good care of himself that I could not find him, and I cared but little about it. I knew he would get nothing with us, if we caught him, but a striped jacket; and as we concluded the war was nearly ended, we thought it would be but of little service to *him*, nor his company any to *us*.

The Captain put me and my two men into the open cold kitchen of a house that they said, had sometime or other, been a tavern; but as it was in the vicinity of the place where I passed the winter of 1779—80, I was acquainted with several of the inhabitants in the neighbourhood, and accordingly sent one of my men to a house hard by, the master of which I knew to be a fine man, and obtained his leave to lodge there. We had a good warm room to sit and lodge in, and as the next day was thanksgiving, we had an excellent supper. In the morning, when we were about to proceed on our journey, the man of the house came into the room and put some bread to the fire to toast; he next produced some cider, as good and rich as wine, then giving each of us a large slice of his toasted bread, he told us to eat it and drink the cider,—observing that he had done so for a number of years and found it the best stimulater imaginable. We again prepared to go on, having given up the idea of finding the deserter. Our landlord then told us that we must not leave his house till we had taken breakfast with him; we thought we were very well dealt by already, but concluded not to refuse a good offer. We therefore staid and had a genuine New-Jersey breakfast, consisting of buckwheat slapjacks, flowing with butter and honey, and a capital dish of chockolate. We then went on, determined not to hurry ourselves, so long as the thanksgiving lasted. We found a good dinner at a farmer's house; but I thought that both the good man and his lady looked at us as if they would have been as well pleased with our room as our company; however, we got our dinners and that was quite sufficient for us. At night we applied for lodging at a house near the road; there appeared to be none but females in the house, two matronly ladies and two misses. One of the women said she should have no objection to our staying there through the night, were it not that a woman in the house was then lying at the point of death, (I had often heard this excuse made before;) we readily perceived her drift, and, when turning to go away, one of the men told her that he did not wish to stay, "for," said he, "if old Corpus should chance to come in the dark, for the sick woman, he might in his haste mistake and take me." The woman smiled and we went on. The next house which looked as if hospitality was an inmate, I applied to and obtained admittance. Here, again, we found a plenty of thanksgiving fare. The people of this house were acquainted with numbers of the Connecticut soldiers, who had been here during the winter of '79, and made many inquiries respecting them; they seemed to have a particular regard for the Connecticut forces, as that section of the State was originally settled by Connecticut people, and it still retains the name of "the Connecticut Farms." The good man of the house would not let us depart in the morning, until we had breakfasted. We then bid our kind host farewell and proceeded on; about noon we called at a house, and while we were warming ourselves in the kitchen and chatting with the young people, the good old housewife came into the room and entered into conversation with us upon the hardships of a soldier's life; she lamented much that we had no mothers nor sisters to take care of us; she said she knew what it was, in a measure, to endure the fatigues and hardships of a camp, by the sufferings her sons had undergone in the drafted militia; they had told her how they had suffered hunger and cold, and to cap all, said she, they came home ragged, dirty and lousy as beggars. The young men, who were present, did not seem to relish the latter part of her narrative, for they leered like cross colts. The good woman, all the while, did not say a word to us about eating, but went off to her room and shut the door; we staid a few minutes longer, and were just going away, when the old lady opened her door and said, "Come to your dinners, soldiers," with as much ease and familiarity as though we had belonged to the family. Agreeably to invitation, we went in and found the master of the house sitting in his elbow chair by the fire, who gave us a hearty welcome to the remains of his thanksgiving cheer; we ate a hearty dinner, and an excellent one it was; when, after returning them our sincere thanks for their hospitality, we pursued our journey.

This afternoon we passed a place where, on our march to Virginia, the past summer, a funny incident occurred, which at the time it happened, and at this time, excited considerable merriment. Our Captain (who we always took pains to discommode) had placed himself on the top of an old rail fence, during a momentary halt of the troops; the rail upon which he sat was very slender;—behind him was a meadow, and from the fence, for about a rod, was a bank almost perpendicular. I was sitting on the other end of the rail, when our

Sergeant-Major, observing the weakness of the fence, came and seated himself by my side, and giving me a hint, we kept wriggling about till we broke the rail and let the Captain take his chance down the bank, among the bushes, quite to the bottom, taking good care ourselves not to go with him. When he came back he did not look very well pleased with his Irish hoist; whether he mistrusted that we had been the cause of his overturn, I do not know; he said but little, whatever he might think.

At night we stopped at a large elegant brick house, to which the owner bid us welcome. He told me that his house was lord Cornwallis' quarters, during part of the time he was in the Jerseys, in '76 and '77. He said, that Cornwallis was a morose, cross man, always quarrelling with and beating his servants; that he was glad his pride was humbled, but had much rather have heard that he was killed than taken. Here we again regaled ourselves on thanksgiving viands, which was nearly, or quite, the last; however, we had fared something better than I did at the rice and vinegar thanksgiving, in Pennsylvania, in the year 1777. We took breakfast here and went on.

We this forenoon passed through a pretty village, called Maidenhead; (don't stare, dear reader, I did not name it,) an hour or two before we came to this place, I saw a pretty young lady standing in the door of a house, just by the road side. I very innocently inquired of her how far it was to Maidenhead; she answered, "five miles." One of my men, who, though young, did not stand in very imminent danger of being hanged for his beauty, observed to the young lady, "that he thought the commodity scarce in the market, since he had to go so far to seek it." "Don't trouble yourself," said she, "about that, there is no danger of its being more scarce on your account." The fellow leered, and, I believe, wished he had held his tongue.

The next day we arrived at Trenton, where was a commissary and some public stores. I concluded, although we were in a thanksgiving country, yet, as we should soon be where we should not find so much to be thankful for, that I would endeavour to supply the deficiency in some degree. Accordingly I made out a return for three men for three days rations. We went to the commissary's, who told us that he had no kind of meat on hand nor any other provisions but flour, that if we chose to take that, he would allow us a pound and a quarter of flour for a pound of beef. We took it and exchanged it at the baker's, pound for pound, and went on; we arrived at our quarters in Burlington, some time in the evening.

Soon after this came on my trouble, and that of several others of the men belonging to our corps; some time in the month of January, two of our men were taken down with a species of yellow fever; one recovered and the other died. Directly after, one belonging to our room was seized with it and removed to the hospital, where he recovered;

next I was attacked with it, this was in February, it took hold of me in good earnest. I bled violently at the nose, and was so reduced in flesh and strength in a few days, that I was as helpless as an infant;—O! how much I suffered, although I had as good attendance as circumstances would admit. The disorder continued to take hold of our people till there were more than twenty sick with it. Our officers made a hospital in an upper room in one of the wings of the house, and as soon as the men fell sick they were lodged there. About the first of March I began to mend, and recovered what little reason I ever possessed, of which I had been entirely deprived from nearly the first attack of the fever. As soon as I could bear it, I was removed from my room to the hospital among those that were recently taken; for what reason I was put with the sick and dying, I did not know, nor did I ask; I did not care much what they did with me, but nothing ill resulted from it that I know of. The doctor belonging to the Artillery regiment (who attended upon us, we having no doctor in our corps) went home on furlough, and it was a happy circumstance for us, for he was not the best of physicians; besides, he was badly provided to do with; the apothecary's stores in the Revolutionary army were as ill furnished as any others; the doctor, however, left us under the care of a physician belonging to the city, who was a fine man, and to his efforts, under Providence, I verily believe I owed my life; he was a skilful, tender-hearted and diligent man. There was likewise, in the city, a widow woman that rendered us the most essential service during our sickness. As we were unable to eat any thing, and had only our rations of beef and bread to subsist upon, this widow, this pitying angel, used almost every evening to send us a little brass kettle, containing about a pail full of posset, consisting of wine, water, sugar and crackers. O, it was delicious, even to our sick palates. I never knew who our kind benefactress was; all I ever knew concerning her was, that she was a widow. The neighbours would not tell us who she was nor where she lived; all that I, or any others who had been sick, could learn from them was, that she was a very fine, pious and charitable lady. Perhaps she did not wish to have a trumpet sounded before her alms, and therefore kept concealed; I hope heaven will bless her pious soul; yes, she *will* be rewarded, where it will be said to her, "I was hungry and you gave me meat; I was sick and you visited me," although she did not visit us personally, she ministered more to our comfort than thousands of idle visits, which are oftener of more detriment to sick people than they are benefit.

Four men died in the room into which I was removed, after I was carried there. One occurrence (though nothing strange in such circumstances as I was then in) I took notice of, although I could take notice of little else. We lay on sacks filled with straw, and our beds mostly upon the floor, in a rank on each side of the room, with an alley between. The first man that died, after my being conveyed there, was the first in order from the entering door of the room, on the side I lay; next, the fourth man from him died, there was then four men between this last that died and me. In my weakness I felt prepossessed with a notion, that every fourth man would die, and that, consequently, I should escape, as I was the fifth from the one that died last; and just so it happened, the man next me on the side of those that had died, died next. I believe this circumstance contributed a great deal in retarding my recovery, until the death of this last man, and that after his death, when I thought myself exempted, it helped as much toward my recovery.—Such strange whims will often work great effects both in hindering and forwarding in such cases. When the body is feeble and the head weak, small causes often have great effect upon the sick; I know it by too frequent experience.

Eight men died at this time, the rest recovered, though the most of them very slowly; some were as crazy as coots for weeks after they had gained strength to walk about. My hair came off my head, and I was as bald as an eagle; but after I *began* to gain strength I soon got about. But it was a grievous sickness to me, the sorest I had ever undergone. Although death is much nearer to *me* now than it was then, yet I never had thought myself so near *death* as I did then.

The spring had now began to open and warm weather soon came on. We remained here till the month of May, when one of our sergeants and myself obtained permission to go down to Philadelphia for a couple of days, to visit some of our acquaintance in that city, but particularly to carry some little clothing to one of our men in the hospital there, who was wounded at the siege of Yorktown, and had had his leg amputated above the knee. I carried him, among other things, a pair of stockings and shoes; his nurse told him, that he was more lucky than most other people, for when they got one pair of shoes and stockings, he got two. Poor fellow! I never saw nor heard of him afterwards. Thus poor soldiers pass out of notice.

My comrade and I staid over two days at Philadelphia, intending to return the next day in the packet. That evening, one of our non-commissioned officers came down, who informed us that our corps had marched for Hudson's river, and that our arms and clothing were gone on in the baggage wagons, and that we must immediately follow. We all, however, staid there that night, and early next morning, we sat off by land. We had nothing to burden us, not even provisions or money; consequently, had nothing to hinder us from proving our adroitness at travelling. We walked that day about forty miles, and stopped at night at a small snug house in the State of New-Jersey. We were obliged to take the soft side of the floor for our lodging, having no blankets or any other kind of bedding. I was tired and could have slept almost any where, had I been undisturbed; but there was, belonging to the house, a likely young huzzy; she, with her parents, composed the whole family;

at least, they were all I saw. They all went to rest in a back room, and we were left to sleep in the outer room. I had hardly fallen asleep, when some one came bawling at the door; the girl, I suppose, knowing who it was, got up and came blundering over the chairs, through the room where I was lying, making as much noise as a thunder storm, she at length got to the door and talked some time with the man; when she came rattling back and went muttering to her bed. I had but just dropped asleep again, when the same jockey, I supposed, as it appeared to be the same voice, came back and began his yelping again; the poor girl had to scratch open her eyes once more, and come through our territories, making as much confusion as at the first time; they talked pretty loud for nearly an hour, which kept us awake all the time they were there. I wished he had taken an opportunity to visit his Miss when I was farther off. She came in again and went to her room, growling like an old bear. "What did he want?" said the mother to her; "He wanted me to go with him to ——," she mentioned some place. "Why did you not go?" said the good woman; "I should look well going with him at this time of night,—I should—so I should," said she. Before I could get to sleep again it was daybreak;—I wished the girl had been asleep and her wooer gagged, before I had seen or heard either of them. As soon as the day dawned, the man of the house came into the room where we were, and took a large jug, that had stood all night just at my head, and poured out a morning stimulater for himself and then put the jug into a closet; I was sorry I did not know it was so near me, that I might have taken a comforter for the trouble they had caused me.

We started before sunrise this morning, and walked forty-nine miles, when, just before sunset, we overtook our corps. I had eaten nothing all day, but drank several draughts of buttermilk which I begged of the farmer's ladies on the road. The next day we arrived at a large house near King's ferry, usually denominated by the army "The white house," belonging to —— Smith, the man who conducted Major Andre on his way towards New-York, when he was taken. Our troops staid here that night, and the next day and night, the officers in the house and the men in the barns. In the evening of the last day we were here, just at dark, one of our officers came and told me that two of the men had deserted, and had compelled another man to go with them. As they were all what we called "Old Countrymen," it was conjectured that they had gone to the enemy, and I was accordingly ordered to take nine men, who were then in readiness, and endeavour to overtake them before they could reach New-York. I immediately set off, having received my orders, which were, to go to what was called the "English neighbourhood," and if I could not find them, or hear of them, to return. The English neighbourhood was from forty-five to fifty miles distant from the place we were then at. We travelled so hard, that at daylight I had but three men of the nine left with me, the other six having given out by the way. We were now near our journey's end, when the men with me beginning to grow slack, and hearing no tiding of the deserters, we concluded to return. When we had got eight or ten miles on our retrograde movement, we met one of our Lieutenants, on his way to visit his friends who lived in that quarter. He had with him three men for an escort, and had picked up those of my party who had given out by the way. We met him just as he arrived at his father's house, a lucky circumstance for us, as we stopped and got something to eat. He then sent me off alone, to a place on the river, where some spy boats (as they were called) were stationed, with directions to request the officers commanding them to take up the three deserters, should they see them. I executed this commission and returned to the Lieutenant, who then told me to take all the men and return to our corps. The country all about here was infested by Tories, especially a certain district through which I had to pass on my return. The Lieutenant charged me not to stop at this place through the night, but to rest short of it, or proceed beyond it. I again set out with my twelve men, little heeding the Tories. It being some time to night when we arrived at the abovementioned Tory-land, we pushed on and did not stop till we got quite back to Smith's house. We, particularly myself and the three men who held out all night, were tired enough, having travelled about ninety miles in twenty-four hours, and I had travelled five or six miles further than any of them, in going to, and returning from the spy boats. We were hungry and tired but had nothing to eat. I had six or seven dollars in specie, which one of our corps (an Irishman) had desired me to keep awhile for him, to avoid the importunity of his *friends;* but he was not with us; I however ventured to make use of one dollar that evening and the next morning, in purchasing some bread and cheese, and a little something to wet our whistles with. I afterwards paid the man, and he informed me that that dollar did him more good than all the others. I had, the day before this expedition, put on a pair of new shoes, which, not having got fitted to my feet, caused blisters upon them as large as cents.

The deserters were, all the time we were in pursuit of them, within three miles of the place where they left us. The man whom they forced off with them, made his escape from them soon after and returned; he told me that they saw us on our return; that they were then in Haverstraw mountan, not more than a quarter of a mile from us. Thus I had another useless and fatigueing expedition for nothing.

The next morning we set out after our troops, who had gone on for West point, about eighteen or twenty miles; we found them on the eastern side of the river. Here we got some provisions and a day or two after crossed over to West point, where we encamped and worked some time in repairing the fortifications.

Towards the latter part of the Summer, we went on to Connecticut Island, opposite to West point, and were employed awhile in blasting rocks, for the repair of the works on that side of the river. It was not so dreary at this time as it was when we were there wheeling dirt upon the magazine, in 1780. Our duty was not over hard, but the Engineers kept us busy.

In the month of September, while we lay here and our tents were pitched about promiscuously, by reason of the ruggedness of the ground, our Captain had pitched his marquee in an old gravel pit, at some distance from the tents of the men. One day, two or three of our young hotheads told me that they and some others of the men, whom they mentioned, were about to have some fun with "the old man," as they generally called the Captain. I inquired what their plans were, and they informed me that they had put some powder into a canteen and were going to give him a bit of a hoist. I asked them to let me see their apparatus, before they put their project in execution; accordingly, they soon after showed me a wooden canteen with more, as I judged, than three pounds of gunpowder in it, with a stopper of touchwood for a fuze, affixed to it, all, they said, in prime order. I told them they were crazy, that the powder they had in the canteen would "hoist" him out of time; but they insisted upon proceeding,—it would only frighten him, they said, and that was all they wished to do,—it would make him a little more complaisant. I then told them that if they persisted in their determination and would not promise me on the spot to give up their scheme, I would that instant go to the Captain and lay the whole affair before him. At length, after endeavouring, without effect, to obtain my consent to try a little under his berth, they concluded to give up the affair altogether; and thus, I verily believe, I saved the old man's life; although I do not think that they meant any thing more than to frighten him. But the men hated him, and did not much care what happened to him.

There was the foundation of some barracks, which the British had burnt in their excursion up the North river, in the year 1777, it was composed of stone and lime, perfectly level, and, perhaps, a hundred feet long; the bushes had grown up around it, excepting the side next the river; the place formed a very pretty spot for a contemplative evening's walk. The Captain used frequently, in fine weather, to be seen pacing backward and forward upon this wall, between sunset and dark. The men observed him and itched to discommode him, but, since they had made me privy to their roguery, they dare not play any of their tricks upon him without consulting me, for fear of being discovered. They therefore applied to me for my consent to "cut some caper" with him, as they called it. Their plan now was, to set an old musket, (which they had somewhere obtained,) in the manner that hunters set them to kill wild animals, (charged only with powder.) I consented to let them try this experiment; but, after all, it never took effect; either the Captain discovered it, or it failed by accident, or from some other cause, for I never heard any thing more about it. I did not wish him to receive any personal injury from their roguery; but I cared very little how much they frightened him. I did not consider myself as being under very heavy obligations to him for his civilities to me, and many of the men considered themselves under still less.

One young man, who was the ringleader of this "gunpowder plot," had a particular grudge against the old man, which urged him on to devise mischief against him. I imagine that he considered himself justified by his conscience in doing so, in consequence of several affronts, as he termed them, which he had received from him. I will mention one or two to which I was knowing, that the reader may be able to form some judgment as to the cause he had to be revenged on the poor old Captain.—He once purloined a flour barrel, I think, from the baker, for the purpose of making a washing tub. The pretended owner complained to the Captain, who, apparently, took no notice of it at the time; however, as it appeared, not long afterwards, he did not forget it, for this man, one morning, soon after, went off without leave with some others, (who had permission,) across the mountain to New-Windsor, eight or ten miles distant, and did not return till after evening roll-call, at which time he was reported as absent without leave. The Sergeant-Major (who belonged to our company) chanced that evening to call the roll. He was a sheer sycophant and would, at any time, have a man punished, if he could by so doing ingratiate himself with the officers. He therefore, as might be expected, informed the Captain of the whole affair. The Captain ordered the Sergeant-Major to send the delinquent to him as soon as he returned, which he accordingly did. The Captain used but very little reasoning with him, before he began to use harder arguments than words could convey, urged by the weight of his rattan; after he had satiated his vengeance upon the poor culprit for playing the truant, he told him that the flour barrel was still to settle for, and then paid him for that, principal and interest.

Another affair, in which the Captain and he differed in opinion, happened while we were lying at West point: it was as follows: This man used sometimes to attend on the sergeants' mess, as they were allowed a waiter or cook, he acted as such at the time I mention. One morning after roll-call, we (the sergeants) allowed him, at his own request, to go and work for a farmer in the neighbourhood of the camp; he had done so before, and it was quite agreeable to us all, for he received his wages for his work in milk, butter, &c. which he always brought into the mess. On the day mentioned, he was at work at the farmer's pulling flax; the farmer had an orchard close by where our man was at work; the soldiers, as they passed, used often to pillage some of the good man's apples. To prevent these depredations upon his property, in some measure, he requested our soldier to take an old musket belonging to the house, loaded with powder only, and when any of the plunderers passed by, to pretend that he was a sentinel, and drive them off; not content with going thus far, he must put a small blighted apple into his musket for a ball. It was not long before he had an opportunity to exercise his sentryship, for several soldiers coming by and taking the liberty, as usual, to take some fruit, they were ordered off by our hero, and not obeying so soon as he desired, or expected, he fired his apple amongst them, which did not seem to be very agreeable to their feelings. They knew to what corps he belonged by his uniform; and ours was the first they came to on entering the garrison. As the poor fellow's ill luck would have it, the Sergeant-Major was the first they encountered upon entering. They made bitter complaint against the pretended sentry, and he carried it directly to the Captain, without losing a morsel by the way. The Captain ordered him to send the man to him as soon as he came home. The Captain's marquee had a shade over and round the entrance. I was upon quarters guard at a tent in the rear of the Captain's, when, just after roll-call, I saw poor Pilgarlick repairing to the Captain's tent; I pretty well knew what would be the consequence of his visit; I listened, heard some discourse between them, but the distance was so great that I could hear but little distinctly, but I soon heard the ratan in motion again, very plainly. As soon as the action was over, the man came to me at the guard; I asked him what the Captain and he had been at, as they had, to appearance, been very lively. "I will tell you," said he, "the Sergeant-Major had told the Captain that I had deserted, but when he found I had not, he sent for me to come and see him, and you cannot conceive how glad he was to see me, and nothing would do, but I must dance a jig with him; I told him I had much rather not, as, possibly, it might injure his character to be seen dancing with a private soldier; but it would not signify, a jig we must have at all events, and he got hold of my hand and began to whistle, and I began to dance, and a fine jig I suppose he thought we had.—The plague seize his old carcass, I wish he was *twisted* up fifteen miles above the seven stars, there to remain till every hair of his head was a meteor, and every limb a comet." I could not help laughing at his buffoonery, though I thought if I had been in his place I should not have turned it off so lightly.

After we had ended our stone blasting, we went to building a new range of barracks, and elegant ones too; they were two stories high with wings at each end, brick chimnies, and a gallery in front the whole length of the building, with large flights of steps to ascend to the gallery and the upper room—large enough to accommodate two or three regiments.

Levity and Folly are twin sisters, and are restive jades; when they are yoked together in the same vehicle and have Indiscretion for a driver, they will very often draw a man into wild and ridiculous scrapes, as I know by experience. They run me into one about this time, which I will relate, as I think it an "adventure," and a "suffering," though a foolish one, such an one as I shall not easily forget, if it should not seem of much consequence to any one but myself.

Several of our men, and myself among the rest, by permission of our officers, took a boat one day and went to the western side of the river for the purpose of gathering chessnuts. Two or three miles above West point is a remarkable mountain, jutting quite into the river, called Butter hill, from the colour of the rocks that compose it, which are of a yellowish hue. The end of the mountain next the river is almost perpendicular, and in many places quite so; it runs off gradually to the westward where it is on all sides easy of ascent. Not finding the nuts so plenty as I wished or expected, and being drawn on by the two nags I have mentioned above, I took it into my head to leave my associates and climb this mountain, where I expected to have a prospect of the country around me that would compensate me for all my trouble in climbing the hill, and then by going along on the top I could descend it with ease. My mates tried to dissuade me from the undertaking, but no, I was determined to go, and go I did—a part of the way—I clambered up, sometimes upon my hands and knees, and sometimes pulling myself up by the small bushes that grew in the cliffs of the rocks; passing many places in imminent danger of falling; passing round crags of rocks on the very edges of frightful precipices, not daring to look back; when, after I had ascended perhaps five or six hundred feet, and thought I had nearly obtained my object, I arrived at a spot where I was completely gravelled, and could go no farther one way or the other; I then had to stop of course, and ventured to look back, being forced to do so; I saw the tall trees below me in the valley, reduced in size to whortleberry bushes. I sat down on a crag of the rock, which was hardly broad enough for me to rest upon, and then began to reflect on my folly; to go farther was impossible, to get down again alive seemed equally so, especially when I recollected the many dangerous places I had passed in climbing up; and to call for help was vain, for no one could do aught for me, if they were ever so willing. I thought of my more than madness in attempting such a hazardous, foolish exploit, without any cause for it but my idle curiosity. I recollected the advice of my comrades; and when all these considerations rushing on my mind at once, it almost made me desperate. I had a mind to sit still where I was and starve to death, or, throw myself down the rocks, and put an end to my life and anxiety together. Had the mountain been all solid gold and I the sole possessor of it, I would at that instant, have given every ounce of it to have been in the situation I was but two hours before, but, as the poet says,

"He had slighted good counsel, had reckon'd it cheap;
And now the sad fruit of his folly must reap."

However, after taking breath a little, (for truly I was almost breathless from fatigue, setting aside the danger,) I came to the resolution to make a trial to free myself from the preposterous hobble I had so foolishly poked my unthinking skull into for nothing. I could but die if I fell, and I should die if I staid there. Accordingly, I sat out on my downward passage. Every one knows, that has had the trial, that it is much easier and safer in *as*cending than *de*scending such places. I was sensible of this, and therefore took good care, that, as much as I wished to be at the bottom of the hill, I did not go down faster than was necessary. By much care, more labour, and abundance of danger, for about an hour, undergoing fear and horrour in the extreme, I arrived where I set out from about two hours and a half before. I could hardly stand upon my feet when I reached the foot of the mountain. I looked up the hill with horrour and pleasure; horrour at the sight and thought of the risk I had run for my life, and pleasure to find myself safe once more on level land. I made myself a promise, that nothing but absolute necessity should ever carry me off on such another foolish expedition, so long as I was allowed sense and reason enough to keep myself from running headlong into the fire.

Another scrape of a similar complexion, I got into about this time, when I ran as great or greater risk of losing my life, than I did in the one just related. I have before, in this narrative, informed the reader of my propensity to gunning whenever I could get an opportunity to indulge myself in it. The mountains on the Hudson, called the Highlands, had an abundance of partridges, heath-hens and grey squirrels upon them, especially on the western side of the river. I had one day got over the river and among those hills for an afternoon's hunting. I had not been long there, when, going along by the side of a steep mountain, I saw and shot a squirrel, but only badly wounding it; it fell from the tree just before me, upon a flat part of the rock, which projected from the side of the mountain, and was about twenty feet wide, and perhaps, two or three rods long, as steep as the ordinary roof of a house; the lower edge, or what might be denominated the eves, hung over a frightful precipice, eighty or a hundred feet perpendicular. My game, as I said before, fell upon this rock and was scrambling off across it. I laid down my gun and gave it chase. When I had got about half way across this rock and nearly up with the squirrel, being so intent upon overtaking it that I did not observe the danger I was in, I slipped and fell upon my side and slid directly down the rock, towards the precipice, until my feet were within a foot or two of the brink. There happened, providentially, to be a small savine, or red cedar bush, about the size of a man's wrist at the root, which had grown out of a crevice in the rock, but had fallen down, yet hung by a single root, not larger than a pipe stem; this tree, as it lay, reached almost to the lower edge of the rock. When I had got to the top end of it, and was in full motion directly for the edge of the rock, I instinctively caught hold of the tree, which immediately stopped my way; but when I looked up and saw by what a slender hold I depended, I own that I felt affrighted; however, by using great caution and bearing with as little weight on the tree as possible, I got up to the upper part of the rock, where it was more level. When I had got upon my feet again, I made off, thankful for whole bones, though not with an entire whole skin. I cannot think of the risk I then ran for my hide, without my feet involuntarily moving, even at this late hour of my life.

In the first part of the month of November I was sent down the river, about five miles, with fifteen men to cut wood for our winter's use; our duty was, to cut the wood of proper lengths for the fire and then carry it on our backs to the shore, from whence it was carried to the garrison in batteaux by those who had remained at home. We continued at this business till christmas, when we were ordered to the garrison. I sent off our tents, &c. by the boats, and, on christmas-day, we set off ourselves by land. It was a violently cold, windy, snow-stormy day, and we had to travel eight or ten miles, roundabout, to get home, with the wind directly in our faces. It began to snow before daylight and we started about eight o'clock in the morning; before we reached home the snow had fallen eighteen inches deep, and not a single track but those we made ourselves. I froze my right ear considerably; but otherwise, we all arrived safely at camp, although I was very unwell for several days after. Afflictions always attended the poor soldiers.

As soon as the storm had ceased, we removed into our new barracks; one half of a regiment of Artillerists and a regiment of Invalids, having removed into them before us. And now, having provided our wood for the winter, built our barracks, stowed ourselves away snugly in them, and winter having handsomely set in, it will, of course, bring my seventh campaign to a close.

Chapter IX. Campaign of 1783.

When we see th' end of strife and war—
And gain what we contended for;—
Remember that our thanks are due
To Him whose mercy brings us through.

THE winter set in rather early for that part of the country, and not over gentle. We had a quarters guard and a magazine guard to keep; the magazine was situated on one of the highest hills, or rather ledges, on the island. In a cold northeast snow storm it would make a sentry shake his ears to stand two hours before the magazine. We likewise kept a small guard to protect the slaughter-house, about half the winter, the Invalids kept it the other half. All this made the duty of our little corps (of less than seventy men) rather hard.

I was once upon this slaughter-house guard;—when I went to relieve the sentinel there, who was a room-mate of mine, and a smart, active young man of about twenty-one years of age. As it was an obscure place, we dispensed with the usual ceremonies in relieving sentries; but this young man standing in the door of the house, when I came with the relief, and in his levity endeavouring to cut some odd figure with his musket, by throwing it over and catching it again, not considering where or how he stood, he struck the butt of his piece against the upper part of the door, which knocked it out of his hands and, coming down behind him, the bayonet entered the upper part of the calf of his leg and came out a little above the ankle. I had him conveyed to the barracks, where the wound was dressed by an ignoramus boy of a surgeon, belonging to the regiment of Invalids. A few days after he complained of a pain in his neck and back; I immediately informed the Captain, who had him wrapt up and sent off to the hospital at Newburgh. The men who conveyed him to the hospital, returned in the evening and informed us that he was dead, having been seized with the lockjaw, convulsions, or something else, caused by the wound. Thus a poor fellow, who had braved the hardships and perils of the war, till the very close of it, "died as a fool dieth," causing his own death by his folly. But, perhaps, if another man had been in his stead, he would have acted just as he did. "If I were you I would do so and so," is a very common expression, but a very improper one; if I were in your place, or were you, I should do just as you do.

Here we suffered again for eatables. We, generally speaking, had fared better for a year or two back, than we did in the first three or four years of the war; then all the care of procuring sustenence for the army was entrusted to the commissaries themselves; after our government had obtained loans of money from France and Holland, the money was put into the hands of contractors, who were accountable for the use they made of it, and of course, the contractors made the commissaries responsible for what they received of them. But somehow this winter, between the two stools, the poor soldiers often came to the ground. I lived half the winter upon tripe and cowheels, and the other half upon what I could get. We always had very short carnivals, but lengthy fasts. One evening, in the first part of this winter, there happened the most brilliant and remarkable exhibition of the Aurora Borealis, or northern lights, that I ever witnessed; the wind was in the same quarter and quite fresh.

We passed this winter as contentedly as we could, under the hope that the war was nearly over, and that hope buoyed us up under many difficulties which we should hardly have surmounted without its aid. But we were afraid to be *too* sanguine, for fear of being disappointed.

Some time in the latter part of the month of February, our officers were about to send off some men to Newburgh, ten or twelve miles up the river, to bring down some clothing. As the ice in the river had not broken up, (although it began to be thin and rotten,) several of the non-commissioned officers solicited the job for the sake of a frolic. We readily obtained permission, and seven or eight of us set off in the morning on the ice, with a large hand-sled to bring the clothing upon. About a mile and a half above West point there was a large rent in the ice, quite across the river, in some places not more than a foot or two wide, in others, eight or ten. We crossed this place very easily, and went on, when we met an officer coming down the river, picking his way among the holes in the ice. He asked us, what troops we belonged to. We told him. He bid us be careful, for, said he, "you are too good looking men to be drowned." We thanked him for his compliment, and passed on—arrived safe at Newburgh, got our clothes, and set off on our return. When we came to New-Windsor, about three or four miles below Newburgh, we conceited we were growing thirsty. We concluded, thereupon, to go on shore and get something to make us breathe freer. We could not get any thing but cider, but that was almost as good and as strong as wine. We drank pretty freely of that, and set off again. It was now nearly sun down, and we had about seven miles to travel. Just before we had arrived at the before mentioned rent in the ice, we overtook a sleigh drawn by two horses, and owned by a countryman that I was acquainted with. He had in his sleigh a hogshead of rum, belonging to a suttler on West point. There were two or three other citizens with him, one of whom was, to appearance, sixty or seventy years of age. When we arrived at the chasm in the ice, the teamster untackled his horses in order to jump them over, and we stopped to see the operation performed. He forced them both over at once; and when they struck the ice on the other side, they both went through, breaking the ice for a rod round. The poor man was in a pitiful taking: he cried like a child. Some of our party told him to choke them out. He had but little faith in the plan; we, however, soon got his leading reins, which happened to be strong new cords, and fixed one round each of the horse's necks, with a slip noose. They did not require much pulling before they both sprang out upon the ice together. The owner's tune now turned; he was as joyful as he had been sad before. The next thing was, to get the sleigh and rum over. We got it to a narrow spot in the chasm, and all hands taking hold, we ran it over; but when the hinder ends of the sleigh-runners came near the edge of the ice, they, with their own weight, broke the ice as bad as the horses had done before. The sleigh arrived safe on the other side, but we were, mostly, upon the broken floating ice; but by the aid of Providence, we all survived the accident. The old man that I mentioned, happened to be on the same fragment of ice with me; when I had stepped off, I saw him on the edge of the piece, settling down gradually in the water, without making the least exertion to help himself. I seized him by the shoulder, and at one flirt, flung him upon the solid ice. He appeared as light as a bag of feathers. He was very thankful, and said I had saved his life; and I am not quite sure that I did not. After we had got matters regulated again, we must take a sip of their rum with them. They soon got the bung from the hogshead, the only way they had in their power to get at the good creature. We each took a hearty pull at it, for soldiers are seldom backward in such cases. The rum soon began to associate with the cider, and between them, they contrived to cut some queer capers amongst us; for we had not gone far, before one of our corporals hauled up, or rather upset. We laid him upon the sled, and hauled him to the wharf at West point, where we landed. There was a sentry on the wharf, and as we had to go some distance to deliver the clothing to our commanding officer, we left our disabled corporal in the care of the sentry, with a strict charge not to let him stir from the place, for fear that he might blunder off the wharf and break his neck on the ice. We were gone an hour or more. When we returned we found the poor prisoner in a terrible chafe with the sentinel for detaining him, for the guard had been true to his trust. We then released him from his confinement, and he walked with us as well as he could, across the river, to our barracks, where, during the night, he settled his head. If the reader says there was no "suffering of a Revolutionary Soldier" in this affair; *I say,* perhaps there was not; but there was an "adventure."

The great chain that barred the river at West point had been regularly taken up every autumn, and put down every spring, ever since it had been in use, (that chain which the soldiers used to denominate General Washington's watch chain; every four links of which weighed a ton,) but we heard nothing of its being put down this spring, although some idle fellow would report that it was going to be put down immediately. These simple stories would keep the men in agitation, often for days together, (for the putting down, or the keeping up of the chain, was the criterion by which we were to judge of war or peace,) when they would get some other piece of information by the ears, which would entirely put the boot on the other leg. The political atmosphere was, at this time, as full of reports, as ever the natural was of smoke, and of about as much consequence.

Time thus passed on to the nineteenth of April, when we had general orders read which satisfied the most skeptical, that the war was over, and the prize won for which we had been contending through eight tedious years. But the soldiers said but very little about it, their chief thoughts were more closely fixed upon their situation as it respected the figure they were to exhibit upon their leaving the army and becoming citizens. Starved, ragged and meagre, not a cent to help themselves with, and no means or method in view to remedy or alleviate their condition; this was appaling in the extreme. All that they could do, was to make a virtue of necessity and face the threatening evils with the same resolution and fortitude that they had for so long a time faced the enemy in the field.

At length the eleventh day of June, 1783, arrived. "The old man," our Captain came into our room, with his hands full of papers, and first ordered us to empty all our cartridge boxes upon the floor (this was the last order he ever gave us) and then told us that if we needed them, we might take some of them again; they were all immediately gathered up and returned to our boxes. Government had given us our arms, and we considered the ammunition as belonging to them, and he had neither right nor orders to take them from us. He then handed us our discharges, or rather furloughs, for they were in appearance no other than furloughs, permission to return home, but, to return to the army again, if required. This was policy in government; to discharge us absolutely in our present pitiful forlorn condition, it was feared, might cause some difficulties, which might be too hard for government to get easily over.

The powder in our cartridges was soon burnt. Some saluted the officers with large charges, others only squibbed them, just as each one's mind was affected toward them. Our "old man" had a number of these last mentioned symbols of honour and affection, presented him. Some of the men were not half so liberal in the use of powder as they were when they would have given him a canteen full at once.

I confess, after all, that my anticipation of the happiness I should experience upon such a day as this, was not realized; I can assure the reader that there was as much sorrow as joy transfused on the occasion. We had lived together as a family of brothers for several years (setting aside some little family squabbles, like most other families,) had shared with each other the hardships, dangers and sufferings incident to a soldier's life, had sympathized with each other in trouble and sickness; had assisted in bearing each other's burdens, or strove to make them lighter by council and advice; had endeavoured to conceal each other's faults, or make them appear in as good a light as they would bear. In short, the soldiery, each in his particular circle of acquaintance, were as strict a band of brotherhood as Masons, and, I believe, as faithful to each other. And now we were to be (the greater part of us) parted forever; as unconditionally separated, as though the grave lay between us. This, I say, was the case with the most, I will not say all; there were as many genuine misanthropists among the soldiers, according to numbers, as of any other class of people whatever; and some in our corps of Miners; but we were young men, and had warm hearts. I question if there was a corps in the army that parted with more regret than ours did, the New-Englanders in particular, Ah! it was a serious time.

Some of the soldiers went off for home the same day that their fetters were knocked off; others staid and got their final settlement certificates, which they sold to procure decent clothing and money sufficient to enable them to pass with decency through the country, and to appear something like themselves when they arrived among their friends. I was among those; I went up the river to the Wallkill, and staid some time. When I returned to West point the certificates were not ready, and it was uncertain when they would be. I had waited so long I was loath to leave there without them. I had a friend and acquaintance in one of the Massachusetts regiments, who had five or six months to serve in the three years service, there was also in the same regiment, a man who had about the same space of time to serve, and who wished to hire a man to take his place; my friend persuaded me (although against my inclinations) to take this man's place, telling me that at the expiration of our service, we would go together into the western parts of the State of New-York, where there was a plenty of good land to be had as cheap as the Irishman's potatoes; (for nothing at all, fath, and a little farther on, cheaper nor all that,) and there we would get us farms and live like heroes; the other man offering me sixteen dollars in specie, with several other small articles, I consented; and now I had got hobbled again, though but for a short time. After I had been in this regiment about a month or six weeks, this "friend of mine" told me that he had taken an affront at something, I have forgotten what, and was determined not to stay there any longer, and endeavoured to persuade me to go with him. I told him I had so short a time to serve, and as there was a prospect that I should not have to stay so long as I had engaged to do, I would not go off like a scoundrel, get a bad name, and subject myself to suspicion and danger. I laboured to persuade him to relinquish his foolish resolution, and I thought I had; but he a few days after set off with himself, and I have never heard of him since. I hope he did well, for he was a worthy young man.

Soon after this, an order was issued, that all who had but four months to serve, should, after they had cut two cords of wood near the garrison, for firewood, be discharged; accordingly, I cut my two cords of wood, and obtained an honourable discharge, which the other man might have done if he had not been so hasty in his determination.

I now bid a final farewell to the service. I had obtained my settlement certificates and sold some of them, and purchased some decent clothing, and then set off from West point. I went into the Highlands, where I accidentally came across an old messmate, who had been at work there ever since he had left the army in June last, and, as it appeared, was on a courting expedition. I stopped a few days with him and worked at the farming business; I got acquainted with the people here, who were chiefly Dutch, and as winter was approaching, and my friend recommended me to them, I agreed to teach a school amongst them—A fit person!—I knew but little and they less, if possible. "Like people, like priest." However, I staid and had a school of from twenty to thirty pupils, and probably I gave them satisfaction; if I did not, it was all one; I never heard any thing to the contrary. Any how, they wished me to stay and settle with them.

When the spring opened I bid my Dutch friends adieu, and set my face to the eastward, and made no material halt till I arrived in the, now, State of Maine, in the year 1784, where I have remained ever since, and where I expect to remain so long as I remain in existence, and here at last to rest my warworn weary limbs. And here I would make an end of my tedious narrative, but that I deem it necessary to make a few short observations relative to what I have said; or a sort of recapitulation of some of the things which I have mentioned.

When those who engaged to serve during the war, enlisted, they were promised a hundred acres of land, each, which was to be in their own or the adjoining States. When the country had drained the last drop of service it could screw out of the poor soldiers, they were turned adrift like old worn out horses, and nothing said about land to pasture them upon. Congress did, indeed, appropriate lands under the denomination of "Soldier's lands," in Ohio State, or some State, or a future state; but no care was taken that the soldiers should get them. No agents were appointed to see that the poor fellows ever got possession of their lands; no one ever took the least care about it, except a pack of speculators, who were driving about the country like so many evil spirits, endeavouring to pluck the last feather from the soldiers. The soldiers were ignorant of the ways and means to obtain their bounty lands, and there was no one appointed to inform them. The truth was, none cared for them; the country was served, and faithfully served, and that was all that was deemed necessary. It was, soldiers, look to yourselves, we want no more of you. I hope I shall one day find land enough to lay my bones in. If I chance to die in a civilized country, none will deny me that. A dead body never begs a grave;—thanks for that.

They were likewise promised the following articles of clothing per year. One uniform coat, a woollen and a linen waistcoat, four shirts, four pair of shoes, four pair of stockings, a pair of woollen, and a pair of linen overalls, a hat or a leather cap, a stock for the neck, a hunting shirt, a pair of shoe buckels and a blanket. Ample clothing, says the reader; and ample clothing, say I. But what did we ever realize of all this ample store:—why, perhaps a coat, (we generally did get that,) and one or two shirts, the same of shoes and stockings, and, indeed, the same may be said of every other article of clothing—a few dribbled out in a regiment, two or three times in a year, never getting a whole suit at a time, and all of the poorest quality; and blankets of thin baize, thin enough to have straws shot through without discommoding the threads. How often have I had to lie whole stormy cold nights in a wood, on a field, or a bleak hill, with such blankets and other clothing like them, with nothing but the canopy of the heavens to cover me, me, all this too in the heart of winter, when a New-England farmer, if his cattle had been in my situation, would not have slept a wink from sheer anxiety for them. And if I stepped into a house to warm me, when passing, wet to the skin and almost dead with cold, hunger and fatigue, what scornful looks and hard words have I experienced.

Almost every one has heard of the soldiers of the Revolution being tracked by the blood of their feet on the frozen ground. This is literally true; and the thousandth part of their sufferings has not, nor ever will be told. That the country was young and poor, at that time, I am willing to allow; but young people are generally modest, especially females. Now, I think the country, (although of the feminine gender, for we say, she, and her, of it) showed but little modesty at the time alluded to, for she appeared to think her soldiers had no private parts; for on our march from the Valley forge, through the Jerseys, and at the boasted battle of Monmouth, a fourth part of the troops had not a scrip of any thing but their ragged shirt-flaps to cover their nakedness, and were obliged to remain so long after. I had picked up a few articles of light clothing during the past winter, while among the Pennsylvania farmers, or I should have been in the same predicament. "Rub and go," was always the Revolutionary soldier's motto.

As to provision of victuals, I have said a great deal already; but ten times as much might be said and not get to the end of the chapter. When we engaged in the service we were promised the following articles for a ration.—One pound of good and wholesome fresh or salt beef, or three fourths of a pound of good salt pork, a pound of good flour, soft or hard bread, a quart of salt to every hundred pounds of fresh beef, a quart of vinegar to a hundred rations, a gill of rum, brandy or whiskey per day; some little soap and candles, I have forgot how much, for I had so little of these two articles, that I never knew the quantity. And as to the article of vinegar, I do not recollect of ever having any except a spoonful at the famous rice and vinegar thanksgiving in Pennsylvania, in the year 1777. But we never received what was allowed us. Oftentimes have I gone one, two, three, and even four days without a morsel, unless the fields or forests might chance to afford enough to prevent absolute starvation. Often, when I have picked the last grain from the bones of my scanty morsel, have I eat the very bones, as much of them as possibly could be eaten, and then have had to perform some hard and fatiguing duty, when my stomach has been as craving as it was before I had eaten any thing at all.

If we had got our full allowance regularly, what was it? A bare pound of fresh beef, and a bare pound of bread or flour. The beef, when it had gone through all its divisions and sub-divisions, would not be much over three quarters of a pound, and that nearly or quite half bones. The beef that we got in the army, was, generally, not many degrees above carrion; it was much like the old Negro's rabbit, it had not much fat upon it and but a very little lean. When we drew flour, which was much of the time we were in the field, or on marches, it was of small value, being eaten half cooked, besides a deal of it being unavoidably wasted in the cookery.

When in the field, and often while in winter quarters, our usual mode of drawing our provisions, (when we did draw any,) was as follows:—a return being made out for all the officers and men, for seven days, we drew four days of meat, and the whole seven days of flour. At the expiration of the four days, the other three days allowance of beef. Now, dear reader, pray consider a moment, how were five men in a mess, five hearty, hungry young men to subsist four days on twenty pounds of fresh beef, (and I might say, twelve or fifteen pounds,) without any vegetables or any other kind of sauce to eke it out. In the hottest season of the year it was the same; though there was not much danger of our provisions putrifying, we had none on hand long enough for that, if it did, we were obliged to eat it, or go without any thing. When Gen. Washington told Congress, "the soldiers eat every kind of horse fodder but hay," he might have gone a little farther, and told them that they eat considerable hog's fodder, and not a trifle of dog's,—when they could get it to eat.

We were, also, promised six dollars and two thirds a month, to be paid us monthly; and how did we fare in this particular? Why, as we did in every other. I received the six dollars and two thirds, till (if I remember rightly) the month of August, 1777, when paying ceased. And what was six dollars and sixty-seven cents of this "Continental currency" as it was called, worth? it was scarcely enough to procure a man a dinner. Government was ashamed to tantalize the soldiers any longer with such trash, and wisely gave it up for its own credit. I received one month's pay in specie while on the march to Virginia, in the year 1781, and except that, I never received any pay worth the name while I belonged to the army. Had I been paid as I was promised to be at my engaging in the service, I needed not to have suffered as I did, nor would I have done it; there was enough in the country, and money would have procured it if I had had it. It is provoking to think of it. The country was rigorous in exacting my compliance to *my* engagements to a punctilio, but equally careless in performing her contracts with me; and why so? One reason was, because she had all the power in her own hands, and I had none. Such things ought not to be.

The poor soldiers had hardships enough to endure, without having to starve; the least that could be done was to give them something to eat. "The labourer is worthy of his meat" at least, and he ought to have it for his employer's interest, if nothing more. But, as I said, there were other hardships to grapple with.—How many times have I had to lie down like a dumb animal in the field, and bear "the pelting of the pitiless storm;" cruel enough in warm weather, but how much more so in the heart of winter. Could I have had the benefit of a little fire, it would have been deemed a luxury. But when snow or rain would fall so heavy that it was impossible to keep a spark of fire alive, to have to weather out a long, wet, cold, tedious night in the depth of winter, with scarcely clothes enough to keep one from freezing instantly; how discouraging it must be, I leave to my reader to judge. It is fatiguing, almost beyond belief, to those that never experienced it, to be obliged to march twenty-four or forty-eight hours (as very many times I have had to) and often more, night and day without rest or sleep, wishing and hoping that some wood or village I could see ahead, might prove a short resting place, when, alas, I came to it, almost tired off my legs, it proved no resting place for me. How often have I envied the very swine their happiness, when I have heard them quarrelling in their warm dry styes, when I was wet to the skin, and wished in vain for that indulgence. And even in dry, warm weather, I have often been so beat out with long and tedious marching, that I have fallen asleep while walking the road, and not been sensible of it till I have jostled against some one in the same situation; and when permitted to stop and have the superlative happiness to roll myself in my blanket, and drop down on the ground, in the bushes, briars, thorns or thistles, and get an hour or two's sleep, O! how exhilerating. Fighting the enemy is the great scarecrow to people unacquainted with the duties of an army. To see the fire and smoke, to hear the din of cannon and musketry, and the whistling of shot; they cannot bear the sight or hearing of this. They would like the service in an army tolerably well, but for the fighting part of it. I never was killed in the army; I never was wounded but once; I never was a prisoner with the enemy; but I have seen many that have undergone all these; and I have many times run the risk of all of them myself; but, reader, believe me, for I tell a solemn truth, that I have felt more anxiety, undergone more fatigue and hardships, suffered more every way, in performing one of those tedious marches, than ever I did in fighting the hottest battle was ever engaged in, with the anticipation of all the other calamities I have mentioned added to it.

It has been said by some that ought to have been better employed; that the Revolutionary army was needless; that the Militia were competent for all that the crisis required. That there was then, and now is in the Militia, as brave and as good men as were ever in any army since the creation, I am ready and willing to allow, but there are many among them too, I hope the citizen soldiers will be as ready to allow, who are not so good as regulars; and I affirm that the Militia would not have answered so well as standing troops, for the following reason, among many others. They would not have endured the sufferings the army did; they would have considered themselves (as in reality they were and are) free citizens, not bound by any cords that were not of their own manufacturing and when the hardships of fatigue, starvation, cold and nakedness, which I have just mentioned, begun to seize upon them, in such awful array as they did on us, they would have instantly quitted the service in disgust; and who would blame them? I am sure I could hardly find it in my heart to do it.

That the Militia did good and great service in that war, as well as in the last, on particular occasions, I well know, for I have fought by their side; but still I insist that they would not have answered the end so well as regular soldiers; unless they were very different people from what I believe and know them to be, as well as I wish to know. Upon every exigency they would have been to be collected, and what would the enemy have been doing in the mean time?—The regulars were there, and there obliged to be; we could not go away when we pleased without exposing ourselves to military punishment; and we had trouble enough to undergo without that.

It was likewise said at that time, that the army was idle; did nothing but lounge about from one station to another, eating the country's bread and wearing her clothing without rendering her any essential service, (and I wonder they did not add, spending the country's money, too, it would have been quite as consistent as the other charges.) You ought to drive on, said they, you are competent for the business; rid the country at once of her invaders. Poor simple souls! It was very easy for them to build castles in the air, but they had not felt the difficulty of making them stand there. It was easier, with them, taking whole armies in a warm room, and by a good fire, than enduring the hardships of one cold winter's night upon a bleak hill without clothing or victuals.

If the Revolutionary army was really such an useless appendage to the cause; such a nuisance as it was then, and has since been said to be, why was it not broken up at once; why were we not sent off home and obliged to maintain ourselves? Surely it would have been as well for us soldiers, and according to the reckoning of those wiseacres, it would have been *much* better for the country to have done it, than for us to have been eating so much provisions, and wearing out so much clothing, when our services were worse than useless. We could have made as good Militia men as though we had never seen an army at all. We should, in case we had been discharged from the army, have saved the country a world of expense, as they said; and I say, we should have saved ourselves a world of trouble in having our constitutions broken down, and our joints dislocated by trotting after Belona's car.

But the poor old decripid soldiers, after all that has been said, to discourage them, have found friends in the community, and I trust there are many, very many, that are sensible of the usefulness of that suffering army, although, perhaps, all their voices have not been so loud in its praise as the voice of slander has been against it. President Monroe was the first of all our Presidents, except President Washington, who ever uttered a syllable in the "old soldiers'" favour. President Washington urged the country to do something for them and not to forget their hard services, but President Monroe told them how to act; he had been a soldier himself in the darkest period of the war, that point of it that emphatically "tried men's souls;" was wounded, and knew what soldiers suffered. His good intentions being seconded by some Revolutionary officers, then in Congress, brought about a system by which, aided by our present worthy Vice-Pesident, then Secretary at war, heaven bless him, many of the poor men who had spent their youthful, and consequently, their best days in the hard service of their country, have been enabled to eke out the fag end of their lives a little too high for the grovelling hand of envy or the long arm of poverty to reach.

Many murmur now at the apparent good fortune of the poor soldiers. Many I have myself seen, vile enough to say, that they never deserved such favour from the country. The only wish I would bestow upon such hard-hearted wretches, is, that they might be compelled to go through just such sufferings and privations as that army did; and then if they did not sing a different tune, I should miss my guess.

But I really hope these people will not go beside themselves. Those men whom they wish to die on a dung-hill; men, who, if they had not ventured their lives in battle, and faced poverty, disease and death for their country, to gain and maintain that Independence and liberty, in the sunny beams of which, they like reptiles are basking, they would, many or the most of them, be this moment, in as much need of help and succour, as ever the most indigent soldier was before he experienced his country's beneficence.

The soldiers consider it cruel to be thus vilified, and it is cruel as the grave, to any man, when he knows his own rectitude of conduct; to have his hard services, not only debased and underrated, but scandalized and vilified. But the Revolutionary soldiers are not the only people that endure obloquy, others as meritorious, and perhaps more deserving than they, are forced to submit to ungenerous treatment.

But if the old Revolutionary Pensioners are really an eyesore, a grief of mind, to any man, or set of men, (and I know they are,) let me tell them that if they will exercise a very little patience, a few years longer will put all of them beyond the power of troubling them; for they will soon be "where the wicked cease from troubling, and the weary are at rest."

And now I think it is time to draw to a close, (and so say I, says the reader,) in truth, when I began this narrative, I thought a very few pages would contain it, but as occurrences returned to my memory, and one thing brought another to mind, I could not stop, for as soon as I had let one thought through my mind, another would step up and ask for admittance. And now, dear reader, if any such should be found, I will come to a close and trespass upon your time no longer, time that may, doubtless, be spent to more advantage than reading the "Adventures and Sufferings" of a private soldier. But if you have been really desirous to hear a part, and a part only, of the hardships of some of that army that achieved our Independence, I can say I am sorry you have not had an abler pen than mine to give you the requisite information.

To conclude. Whoever has the patience to follow me to the end of this rhapsody, I will confess that I think he must have almost as great a share of perseverence in reading it as I had to go through the hardships and dangers it records—And now, kind reader, I bid you a cordial and long farewell.

Through much fatigue and many dangers past,
The warworn soldier's braved his way at last.

THE END

CPSIA information can be obtained
at www.ICGtesting.com
Printed in the USA
LVHW031751171220
674449LV00003B/571